THE DYNAMIC CHARACTER OF CHRISTIAN CULTURE

Essays on Dawsonian Themes

Edited by

Peter J. Cataldo

UNIVERSITY
PRESS OF
AMERICA

LANHAM • NEW YORK • LONDON

ACKNOWLEDGEMENTS

Grateful acknowledgement is hereby given to the following for the use of quotations from their copyrighted works:

MRS. CHRISTINA SCOTT
Quotations from the works of Christopher Dawson are reproduced with the permission of Mrs. Christina Scott.

SHERWOOD SUGDEN & COMPANY, PUBLISHERS
Dynamics of World History: Copyright © 1958, Sheed & Ward; Copyright © 1978, Christina Scott. Reprinted with permission of the publisher, Sherwood Sugden & Company, 1117 Eighth Street, LaSalle, IL 61301.

Christianity in East and West: Copyright © 1959, Sheed & Ward, Inc.; copyright © 1981, Christina Scott. Reprinted with permission of the publisher, Sherwood Sugden & Company, 1117 Eighth Street, LaSalle, IL 61301.

OXFORD UNIVERSITY PRESS
The Works of George Herbert. Edited by F. E. Hutchinson, Copyright 1941.

THE CHESTERTON REVIEW
"Christopher Dawson: Recollections from America," by Chauncey Stillman. Copyright 1983.

L'OSSERVATORE ROMANO, English Edition
The Encyclical of Pope John Paul II, Rich in Mercy, Dives in Misericordia. Copyright 1980. Cardinal Casaroli's address to the United Nations on June 11, 1982. Copyright 1982.

CONFRATERNITY OF CHRISTIAN DOCTRINE
Scripture texts used in this work are taken from the NEW AMERICAN BIBLE, copyright © 1970, by the Confraternity of Christian Doctrine, Washington, D.C., are used by permission of copyright owner. All rights reserved.

TABLE OF CONTENTS

v

PREFACE

The papers contained in this volume were originally delivered at the second and third annual con-
ferences (1982-1983) of The Society for Christian
Culture (SCC) held in Saint Louis, Missouri. The
general purpose of the SCC is to promote study of
the thought of Christopher Dawson (1889-1970), who
was widely acknowledged to be the premier Catholic
thinker on the subject of Christian culture, and to
study Western civilization and world history in the
light of Christian culture principles.

The thesis that religion is the vital source of
culture was one of the more significant insights
which Christopher Dawson contributed to our understanding of the nature and development of human
culture. This general principle acquires a definite
form in the context of European culture, which,
simply put, is that the dynamic force behind the
cultural unity of Europe has been Christianity, according to Dawson, and not the rational tradition
inherited from the Hellenic culture, as is so often
assumed today (see <u>Progress</u> <u>and</u> <u>Religion</u> (1960), pp.
185-186).

Gaining an initial grasp of these and other
principles developed by Dawson requires a knowledge
of some of his basal concepts and terms. Two such
items are 'culture' and 'Christian culture'; Dawson's own words provide the best explanation. Concerning the meaning of culture, Dawson writes:

> When I speak of culture I am not think-
> ing of the cultivation of the individ-
> ual mind, which was the usual sense of
> the word in the past, but of a common
> social way of life -- a way of life
> with a tradition behind it, which has

embodied itself in institutions and which involves moral standards and principles. Every historic society has such a culture from the lowest tribe of savages to the most complex forms of civilized life (The Historic Reality of Christian Culture, p. 13).

Dawson tells us what it means for a culture to be called Christian in the following:

> The only true criterion of a Christian culture is the degree in which the social way of life is based on the Christian faith. However barbarous a society may be, however backward in the modern humanitarian sense, if its members possess a genuine Christian faith they will possess a Christian culture -- and the more genuine the faith, the more Christian the culture.
>
> And so when we talk of Christian culture, we ought not to think of some ideal pattern of social perfection which can be used as a sort of model or blueprint by which existing societies can be judged. We should look first and above all at the historic reality of Christianity as a living force which has entered into the lives of men and societies and changed them in proportion to their will and their capacity. (The Historic Reality of Christian Culture, p. 14).

An important qualification must be included in our reading of these definitions. For Dawson, religion and culture are neither mutually reducible nor completely separable from each other. Various aspects of the complex relations holding between Christianity and culture will be explored in the papers of this volume.

There is a threefold unity to the present volume. Considered as a whole, the papers provide a chronological movement in the study of the historical influence of Christian culture, beginning with the first and second papers which treat to a greater or lesser degree some important elements in early Christian culture, moving to the third and fourth which cover intermediate periods in Christian culture, and ending with the fifth and sixth papers on contemporary culture (the seventh being personal recollections). Secondly, each author recognizes the importance of the historical sources of Christian culture for a better understanding of contemporary culture. Lastly, each of these authors draws upon and acknowledges the insights of Dawson in the analysis of his particular topic. What follows are brief summaries of the papers.

Russell Hittinger argues that Christopher Dawson represents the first serious effort of a modern historian to reconsider the significance of the so-called "Dark Ages" in the development of Western culture. Rather than viewing the early centuries of Medieval Christendom (from Constantine through the Gregorian Reforms) as merely decadent classical culture, or simply as an adumbration of the flowering of the "high" Middle Ages, Dawson argues that this period was perhaps the most creative one in Western history. The Christian missions among the barbarians produced a unique synthesis between East and West, Church and State, and in general between transcendent and immanent cultural ideals. Hittinger discusses why Dawson believed that the tensions in this synthesis continue to be the most salient features even in post-Christian or modern culture.

Paul M. Quay, S.J., focuses on Dawson's well-known thesis that culture arises _from_ religion rather than religion being its by-product. Using this thesis as a starting point, Father Quay extrapolates from the "theology of recapitulation" four topic areas within which he examines the "theological groundings for the Church's interest in culture." These topic areas are enumerated in the following quotation from Father Quay's paper: "1) the life and growth of one individual Christian through one lifetime... 2) the relation of the Church to that growth and development of the individual Christian; 3) the growth of societies and cultures on the natural level alone; 4) the Church's development in those societies and cultures in which she has taken root, and their growth as a result of her influence."

Glenn W. Olsen critically evaluates Dawson's schematization of the development of Christian culture, particularly the period which Dawson named "Medieval Christendom" (eleventh to fifteenth centuries). In his evaluation, Olsen clarifies possible misconceptions of Dawson's schematization, and qualifies Dawson's claims about Medieval Christendom in the light of new historiographical data. Another important contribution which Olsen's essay makes is its criticism of modern "social and economic historians" who disregard two of the invaluable historical insights which Dawson's work had embodied: the fundamental links between religion and culture, and the historically creative forces of Christian culture.

R. V. Young assesses Dawson's view of the religious foundation of Baroque culture in the concrete setting of the religious poetry of the 17th century. Contrary to the consensus of art historians at the time, Dawson considered the Baroque period to be not a decadent development of the Renaissance, but as being rich with the religious ideals of medieval Catholicism in alliance with the humanist tradition of the Renaissance.

Young gives evidence of Dawson's view of Baroque culture by examining the poetry of these seventeenth century poets: Sir Philip Sidney, Lope de Vega, John Dunne, George Herbert, Anne Bradstreet, and John Milton. His comparison of their Protestant and Catholic poetry highlights the full Catholic embodiment of the culture of the Baroque.

John J. Mulloy shows why, according to Dawson, both 19th century capitalism and Marxism are distortions of the basic principles of a Christian social order. Such distortions are, for example, found in that demand for unlimited social freedom which promoted the growth of laissez-faire capitalism, and also in Marx's materialistic interpretation of history; an interpretation which, even though couched in purely economic terms, is to an unsuspected degree a secularized offsrping of the Messianic view of history in the Jewish and Christian traditions. Contrary to the emphasis on economic factors in both the Marxist and capitalist views of history, Mulloy points out that, for Christopher Dawson, the basic principle of change in Western civilization is "the dynamic ethos of Western Christianity."

Richard Roach, S.J., makes a critical evaluation of the way in which pacifism is treated by the

Catholic bishops of the United States in their recent pastoral letter, "The Challenge of Peace: God's Promise and Our Response." Father Roach argues against the bishops' assumption that Jesus Christ taught absolute or doctrinal pacifism, and exposes the moral confusion generated by the bishops' failure to distinguish absolute pacifism from relative or practical pacifism. Father Roach finds that the absolute pacifistic interpretation of Christ's teaching is founded upon a misconception of the relation between justice and love in the pattern of the development of moral doctrine in the Church. Father Roach emphasizes that the unity of Christian culture rests in part upon a proper moral theology which makes it clear that Christ does not abrogate the demands of justice in the Old Law, but, leaving those demands intact, fulfills the Old Law by His love and mercy. Finally, another of his main conclusions is that the absolute pacifism "can in some circumstances lead one to sin, at least by omission."

Chauncey Stillman's essay fittingly concludes the work with lively personal recollections of Christopher Dawson and his wife Valery during the years of Dawson's appointment to the Charles Chauncey Stillman Chair of Roman Catholic Studies at Harvard University, 1958-1962.

I would like to acknowledge, with much gratitude, the generosity of Chauncey Stillman in providing the funds for this volume. Special thanks are also due to John J. Mulloy and Russell Hittinger for their invaluable editorial advice and to my wife, Mary, for the support and encouragement she has given me during the work on this volume.

Peter J. Cataldo
Saint Louis, Missouri

THE METAHISTORICAL VISION OF
CHRISTOPHER DAWSON

Russell Hittinger

I. METAHISTORY AND THE STUDY OF CHRISTIAN CULTURE

Those who have had the pleasure to read even a portion of Christopher Dawson's work are well aware that he was a practitioner of something more than ordinary Anglo-American, or what some have called "positivist," historiography. His interest in metahistorical issues regarding the interpretation of causes, patterns, and the meaning of history gave his work an added dimension -- especially in comparison to the limits which are usually observed by scholars devoted to the history of public affairs, as well as those working in ecclesiastical history. It is fair to say that Dawson's interpretive skills and metahistorical orientation were his strongest suit, and indeed these were what his students and readers found most stimulating.

Yet Dawson did not regard himself as practicing what we today would call the "history of ideas." Throughout his career as a scholar and pedagogue he emphasized the need to resist what he considered to be a long-standing tendency toward an overly rationalized approach to culture and to the history of the Christian religion. By this, he meant the tendency to reduce Christianity to a set of ideas, or to a set of "ideational products," which might be adequately understood apart from the social reality in which such ideas have been lived as a way of life. In his Crisis of Western Education, for instance, he stated: "What we need is not an encyclopaedic knowledge of all the products of Christian culture,

1

but a study of the culture-process itself from its spiritual and theological roots, through its organic historical growth to its cultural fruits."[1] In this same vein, criticizing Collingwood's Idealist conception of history, Dawson remarked:

> In reality a culture is neither a purely physical process nor an ideal construction. It is a living whole from its roots in the soil and in the simple instinctive life of the shepherd, the fisherman, and the husbandman, up to its flowering in the highest achievements of the artist and the philosopher; just as the individual combines in the substantial unity of his personality the animal life of nutrition and reproduction with the higher activities of reason and intellect. It is impossible to disregard the importance of a material and non-rational element in history.[2]

Dawson insisted that historical and cultural change -- which is, of course, of principal interest to a metahistorian -- cannot be understood as simply a change of thought, or merely as a spiritual procession of ideas. His admonition in this regard was as frequently aimed at such an emphasis in Scholastic curricula in Catholic schools of the period as it was at Idealist schools of historiography in England or the Continent.[3]

Since in this essay we will investigate some of the main themes in Dawson's understanding of metahistory, it should be said at the very outset that he not only distinguished between an analysis of historical changes and the "history of ideas," but also between metahistory and the "philosophy of history." At least since the ninteenth-century these two have been understood as the same thing. Dawson's refusal to equate metahistory with philosophy of history involves both philosophical and religious reasons. In the first place, he denied the possibility, in principle, of a philosophy of history. Given the contingent, particular, and plural character of the lives of men and cultures, he argued that it is impossible to achieve a scientifically rigorous universal history of man qua man.

In other words, there can be no "history of human-ity" in a strictly philosophical or scientific sense of the term because a universal genus humanum does not exist as a concrete historical subject. His-tory, he argued, "deals with civilizations and cultures rather than civilization," which is another way of saying that history properly deals with men rather than "man."[4] The ideal of a historical science that explicates its material according to a genus humanum has its roots in the Renaissance and Enlightenment. It was inevitable, Dawson contended, that despite its claims to have moved beyond the religious mythos of Christian historical thinking, the new ideal degenerated into mythology -- specifi-cally, into the myth of an ahistorical universal "man." From a religious standpoint, Dawson was profoundly suspicious of a philosophy of history because he viewed the historical incarnations of the ideal as being hostile not only to the historical details of the Christian religion, but also to the authentic Christian conception of history. In the traditional Christian view, the unity and universal meaning of history is to be understood according to a theodicy rather than a science, for the unity of history is not, finally, a work of man.[5] Hence, Dawson critiqued the ideal of a philosophy of his-tory because, on the one hand, it is untenable methodologically, and on the other hand because it represents the distinctively modern surrogate for religious faith.

This is not to say, however, that Dawson denied or belittled the traditional, philosophical effort to provide a universal ontology of human nature and, beyond that, to establish within the framework of cosmology a rigorous account of the generic traits of being, causality, temporality, and so forth. But these constitute the conditions, not the determina-tions, of human actions and histories. One cannot infer histories from an explication of the structure of time. Dawson's rejection of a "history of human-ity" does not mean that he was a cultural or histor-ical relativist, at least not in the contemporary sense of the term. A significant part of his work was devoted to isolating the essential components of cultural excellence, particularly the religious and spiritual facets. Indeed, the main theme of his historical investigations concerns the world-histor-ical importance of the particular historical pattern embodied in Christian cultures. He believed that metahistorical analysis is crucial in terms of what it illuminates and implies about certain causes, patterns, and meanings so long as one resists the temptation to make metahistory bear the burden of a natural theology, metaphysics, or science. Pointing to the work of Tocqueville, Dawson observed that "metahistory is not the enemy of true history but is its guide and friend, provided that it is good metahistory" -- that is to say, a metahistory that acknowledges its limits. In an essay on "The Problem of Metahistory," Dawson concluded: "The experience of the great historians such as Tocqueville and Ranke leads me to believe that a universal metahistorical vision of this kind, partaking more of the nature of religious contemplation than of scientific generalization, lies very close to the sources of their creative power."[6] In fact, Dawson himself can be regarded as the twentieth-century Tocqueville to the subject of Christian culture, but he in no way plays the role of Hegel to the subject.

Two Catholic thinkers from whom Dawson derived both an intellectual and moral sense of how to engage in metahistorical analysis of Christianity are the Church Fathers Irenaeus and Augustine. He particularly admired St. Irenaeus' "spirit of historical realism," his attention to the material media through which, and about which, Christianity understands its theological data.[7] From his study of St. Augustine, Dawson became attuned to the "eschatological and social dualism," to the cross-grained tensions, which constitute the dynamism of human actions and culture in history.[8] In the main, it was to theologians rather than philosophers that he turned for his models.[9] One reason for this is, as we have already pointed out, Dawson's suspicion regarding the logic and the intent of various philosophies of history. Another, though less important, reason had to do with pedagogy: it was Dawson's conviction that Catholic thought and education prior to the Second Vatican Council tended to be preoccupied with the coventions of scholastic philosophy; so far as Dawson was concerned, it needed the enrichment of a sensibility also rooted in history and theology. As we will observe later in this essay, he was very much interested in calling attention to patterns of Christian thought and

4

practice which existed before and after the "high" Middle Ages.

The more direct and important reason behind Dawson's interest in the theological aspects of metahistory is simply that theology is built into the subject matter of the history of Christian culture. It is involved, first of all, in the very project of investigating the relationship between religion and culture in general, and between the Christian religion and culture in particular. Furthermore, the "theology of history" has played a considerable role in the historical formation, and self-understanding, of Christian culture. Finally, and most important, Dawson believed that theology is the most appropriate way of disclosing the meaning of Christianity, and of history itself. In an essay entitled "The Christian View of History," he wrote:

> ...the Christian view of history is not a secondary element derived by philo- sophical reflection from the study of history. It lies at the very heart of Christianity and forms an integral part of the Christian faith. Hence there is no Christian "philosophy of history" in the strict sense of the word. There is, instead, a Christian history and a Christian theology of history, and it is not too much to say that without them there would be no such thing as Christianity.[10]

Perhaps we can draw into sharper focus some of the fundamental issues in a metahistorical treatment of Christianity if we reflect upon Dawson's statement that there is a "Christian history" as well as a "Christian theology of history." The distinction and the relationship of these two is somewhat impor- tant for an appreciation of Dawson's own method.

In the first place, there is what Dawson calls a "Christian history." By this he means that Chris- tianity must remain faithful to the material fac- tors. For instance, at the very outset of his Adversus Haereses, St. Irenaeus maintained that the welter of gnostic sects have at least this much in common: "certain men, rejecting the truth, are introducing among us false stories and vain genealogies."[11] St. Irenaeus accused the gnostics of destroying the "pattern of the gospel" by distorting the material media of the story; their esoteric accounts of cosmic processions, emanations, and dispensations neglect the actual historical events which, viewed in their concrete sequence, constitute the non-negotiable ground for any theological claims 'about' the Redemptive history. In short, the gnostics attempted to divorce the Christian history from the Christian theology of history by setting the interpretive scheme of the latter against the material facts of the former. In this sense, the gnostics represent a fundamental misuse of the metahistorical mode of thinking -- one that will have a long and disturbing career after the specific gnosticisms of late-antiquity. Against this kind of move, Dawson underscores the importance of a "spirit of historical realism" such as that of St. Irenaeus. It is interesting in this regard that although St. Irenaeus' _Adversus Haereses_ represents the first sophisticaed orthodox account of the Christian theology of history, its chief purpose is to emphasize what Dawson calls the "Christian history" in its material detail.

Dawson points out that the traditional understanding of the successive stages of sacred history is not simply a claim about "new truths," nor even simply about the "direction of history."[12] Above all, it entails a view of "certain definite points in time and place," and the "events through which the truths are revealed." Just as the ontological "realism" of St. Thomas involves the intelligibility of "forms" in terms of their composition in matter, so too, assertions about the meaning of God's action in time are derived from concrete historical media. The Christian theology of history is not a doctrine in search of material _exempla_, for the doctrines are inextricably related to historically concrete events.

Because the traditional Christian conception of history posits a very specific relation between the matter and meaning of history, it is extraordinarily vulnerable to having the meaning altered by a neglect or distortion of the matter. Dawson was alert to this problem in terms of modern historiography. "It is quite possible," he notes, "to write of Western history leaving the Christian tradition

6

entirely out of the picture, without the average readers' realizing that anything is missing."[13]

> [This] view which necessarily ignores the achievements and even the existence of Christian culture, was passed on almost unchanged from the Renaissance to the eighteenth-century Enlightenment and from the latter to modern secularist ideologies. And though today every instructed person recognizes that it is based on a completely erroneous view of history and very nearly on a sheer ignorance of history, it still continues to exert an immense influence, both consciously and unconsciously, on modern education and on our attitude toward the past.[14]

Since, to a large extent, the material events crucial to a Christian metahistory also fall within the purview of ordinary historiography, one should expect a tension between what believers and unbelievers have to say about those events. One need not be committed to a notion of Divine Providence in order to treat the emergence of the Constantinian imperium, or to sort through archeological debris in Syria. It is precisely because Christian sacred history is anchored in actual history that there can be an overlap and tension between the interests of sacred and profane historiography. The point of Dawson's concern, however, is the inclination of many schools of secular historiography to either neglect or distort the subject-matter in which Christianity has considerable interests.

It is worth bearing in mind in this regard that, in the case of a historian like Edward Gibbon, the meaning of the Christian history was not directly assaulted in terms of its doctrines; rather, the main thrust of Gibbon's Decline and Fall was delivered against the material nature and role of Christianity. Consigning Christianity and its institutions to the so-called "Dark Ages" -- to a time of decadent classicism and cultural barbarity-- Gibbon, by means both of ommission and demotion of the material facts, called into question the cultural contributions of the Christian religion. In 1776, shortly before his death, David Hume congratulated Gibbon, for he saw the peculiar subtlety and force of Gibbon's critique. Without having to address the theological understanding of what constitutes the meaning of Christianity, and without having to engage in interminable debates over the cosmological implications of miracles (which, thanks in large part to Hume, had transfixed the attention of philosophers and theologians at the time), Gibbon had accomplished in more subtle fasion the apologetical goal simply by rendering Christianity a relatively minor, though unfortunate, chapter in the history and development of Western culture. Voltaire, it seems, had a similar goal in mind when he argued in his Essay on Manners that it is only necessary to treat "the history of the human spirit and not the detail of facts which are usually distorted anyway." The main theme, he went on to say, is the transition of the West from "barbarian rusticity" to the "politeness" of the present age.[15]

Although in the Crisis of Western Education Dawson argued that for any effective renewal of Catholic education "it is essential above all to recover the traditional [Christian] conception of history," he insisted at the same time that this is dependent upon retrieving those "definite points in time and place" which are so crucial to discussion of the "meaning" of Christianity.[16] In his own work, Dawson kept his metahistorical hermeneutic firmly anchored in at least three different material sources: (1) the sociological and cultural function of religion in general; (2) the specific history and institutions of the Christian religion; (3) the history of the relationship between Christianity and various cultures -- both Western and non-Western. Dawson is rightfully recognized as having provided many extraordinarily lucid interpretations of the historical and cultural role of Christianity, but he was first a social scientist who saw a pressing need to re-incorporate the full material scope of the subject. He frequently criticized, for instance, the collapse of what we have called "the Christian history" into the discipline of "ecclesiastical history." It amounts to an isolation of the second area outlined above. As Dawson put it, ecclesiastical history is usually viewed as a "kind of special subject which lies outside the margin of political history."[17] Hence, separated on the one hand from a study of religion and culture, and on the other from the more specific culture and history of the

8

West, the limits imposed by ecclesiastical history make it difficult to interrelate the material data which any judgment about the significance of Christianity must rest. Moreover, having no scientific unity in relation to anything other than itself, the discipline of ecclesiastical history tends to become exclusively identified with the corporate traditions of this or that particular sect. The artificial isolation of ecclesiastical history has been criticized by thinkers other than Dawson. Ernst Troeltsch's The Social Teaching of the Christian Churches (1911), as well as Max Weber's The Sociology of Religion (1922), represent efforts to restore sociological flesh to ecclesiastical history; but what is characteristic of thinkers such as Troeltsch and Weber (and we should add here the work of certain thinkers within the various neo-Marxist schools) is a tendency to emphasize the first and third areas outlined above at the expense of the second -- not to mention the spiritual and theological facets.[18]

The best way through the limitations which modern methods and attitudes place upon the subject of Christian history and culture is, according to Dawson, the adoption of a multi-disciplinary approach. Speaking at Harvard on the theme of the "Formation of Christian Culture," he prefaced his lectures with the following statement on method:

> It is impossible to understand Christianity without studying the history of Christianity. And this, as I see it, involves a good deal more than the study of ecclesiastical history in the traditional sense. It involves the study of two different processes which act simultaneously on mankind in the course of time. On the one hand, there is the process of culture formation and change which is the subject of anthropology, history and the allied disciplines; and on the other there is the process of revelation and the action of divine grace which has created a spiritual society and a sacred history .... In Christian culture these two processes come together in an organic unity, so that its study requires the close co-

operation of Theology and History.[19]

What Dawson meant by a multi-disciplinary approach, then, embraces both the "allied" disciplines of the social sciences which attend to the "Christian history," and theology which attends to the "theology of history."

Before we move on to discuss Dawson's explication of metahistorical themes we should say a few words about the theology of history. Just as the Christian conception of history is vulnerable to a mutilation of its material media, it is likewise vulnerable to narrative revisions of its sacred history. A narrative -- or story -- is the fundamental hermeneutic by which historical action is understood, for it is the principle that gives unity to events. Therefore, the revision of a narrative can give new meaning to material facts, even when all of the facts of the previous narrative are retained. For instance, if one reads the polemical literature of the first three centuries, it is clear that the debate between Christians and Jews did not merely pivot upon the 'facts' of salvation history. Christian theologians included all of the events which the Jews themselves observed in their account of sacred history. The point at issue was a thorough-going revision of the narrative -- one that rendered the Jewish story obsolete, and, according to the Christian position, intelligible only within the framework of the "new" testament. Hence, debates between the rabbinical establishment and Christian apologists proved to be intractable, since the dispute involved the very vantage point from which the data of the Old Testament should be viewed, and indeed whether the Old Testament is "old" in the first place. Christianity began as positing a sacred history that was a narrative revision of its predecessor. It not only has a stake in protecting the material media of this sacred history, but also the hermeneutic by which the material is understood in a unified fashion.[20]

Dawson was keenly aware that the metahistorical ambitions of a considerable part of post-Renaissance historians contained not only a distortion of the material facts of Christianity and its role in Western history, but perhaps more important, there was an effort to introduce a new story that completely changed the meaning of this history. From the Renaissance onward, the re-periodizing of history has been essential to the project of supplanting the traditional theology of history with an immanent eschatology, and of showing the traditional view to be only a superceded moment in the historical progress and self-understanding of Western humanity. As Eric Voeglin has pointed out in several of his studies on this subject, from Joachim of Fiora to the Hegelian and Marxist systems, there is a persistent "process in which Christianity becomes historized and history secularized."[21] Indeed, one might say that modernity required the re-periodizing of history in order to provide a historical drama in which the very category of "modernity" can emerge as a privileged vantage point from which to understand the unity and meaning of history. In this sense, modernity is as much a hermeneutic that establishes itself as a datum, as it is a fact that required subsequent interpretation.

Dawson understood quite clearly that the traditional theology of history stands in direct opposition to the systems which sought to replace it. While the modern ambition to supply a metahistorical framework for the unity of history has, in some cases, been coloured by certain Christian themes (which is to be expected, since the very ideal itself is derived from the traditional theology of history), its introduction of a temporally immanent, and necessarily rational, standpoint is not congruent with Christianity, but is rather a surrogate for it. "This new approach to history," Dawson argued, "was one of the main factors in the secularization of European culture."[22] In contrast to it:

> Christian history is inevitably apocalyptic, and the apocalypse is the Christian substitute for the secular philosophies of history. But this involves a revolutionary reversal and transposition of historical values and judgments. For the real meaning of history is not the apparent meaning that historians have studied and philosophers have attempted to explain. The world-transforming events which changed the whole course of human his-

11

> tory have occured as it were under the
> surface of history unnoticed by the
> historians and philosophers.[23]

Like that of its secular opponents, the Christian
view involves an understanding of the unity and
meaning of history that is co-extensive with time,
and with the whole life of humanity; but the Christian theology of history requires faith and hope in
a transcendent order, for the only authentic vantage
point for the "whole" of history is Christ, and this
is revealed only to faith. A theology of history is
precisely the reliance upon a theo-logic -- the
"whole" story is neither completely caused nor
measured by men; its principal theme, Dawson observes, is "the growth of the seed of eternity in
the womb of time."[24]

Paul Ricoeur, in his essay "Christianity and
History," has likewise stated that the Christian
conception of history posits a "meaning" that is ac-
cessible to man, yet it is one that remains a "hidden meaning."[25] This meaning elicits faith and
hope that, despite the fact that the ebb and flow of
history often resembles "a tale told by an idiot,"
there is a fundamental unity. Ricoeur writes:

> The Christian meaning of history is
> therefore the hope that secular history
> is also a part of that meaning which sa-
> cred history sets forth, that in the end
> there in only one history, that all his-
> tory is ultimately sacred. This meaning
> however remains an object of faith. If
> progress is the rational part of his-
> tory, and if ambiguity represents the
> irrational part, then the meaning of
> history for hope is a surrational mean-
> ing .... The Christian says that this
> meaning is eschatological, meaning
> thereby that his life unfolds in the
> time of progress and ambiguity without
> his seeing this higher meaning, without
> his being able to discern the relation
> between the two histories, the secular
> and the sacred, or, in the words of St.
> Augustine, the relation between the "Two
> Cities." He hopes that the oneness of
> meaning will become clear on the "last

day," that he will understand how everything is "in Christ," how the histories
of empires, of wars and revolutions, of
inventions, of the arts, of moralities
and philosophies -- through greatness
and guilt -- are "recapitulated in
Christ."[26]

Ricoeur goes on to add that because the Christian
has, by faith, a confidence in the hidden meaning,
he is encouraged by hope to attempt to construct a
comprehensive scheme that includes secular history,
culture, and the whole range of human instrumentali-
ties. But because the unity that gives meaning to
such a scheme is not simply "there" for reason, the
Christian must be "on guard" against the "fanati-
cism" of secular and rationalized schemata which
aspire to retain the comprehensive view freed from
the supra-rational orientation of faith and
hope.[27]

As we have already mentioned, the material elements in a metahistorical account of Christianity
are not, for the most part, esoteric. In his Essay,
Newman remarked that since the "doctrines, percepts,
and objects" of Christianity are factually concrete,
at least in the sense of having become for centuries
a part of our history, they can be regarded a kind
of "public property."(28) Nevertheless, the theology of history has an irreducibly esoteric character.[29] It is not derived from philosophical reflection on history. The disciples on the road to
Emmaus were well aware of the factual events which
took place during the public life of Jesus, but they
did not understand the meaning of these events until
it was revealed to them. Dawson points out that "it
is very difficult, perhaps even impossible, to
explain the Christian view of history to a non-
Christian."[30] The hermeneutical and kerygmatic
facets of the story interpenetrate, and the persuasive power of one entails the other. In short, the
hermeneutic is itself revealed. Yet the temptation
to isolate the two has been all the more intensified
by the modern preoccupation with "historical consciousness" and "historical-critical" methodologies.
Thus, there is pressure to re-assemble the Christian
theology of history on non-theological, or at least
extra-theological, grounds for the purpose of polemical or scientific discourse with secular philoso-

phies. The strength and the weakness of the Christian conception of history are two sides of a coin:
while there is a confidence, rooted in faith and
hope, in the ultimate comprehensibility and unity of
history, the Christian does not enjoy a flexibility
with regard to his theology of history comparable to
the notion that secular theorists have of their
working paradigms; these paradigms are regarded not
only as rationally persuasive, but also as dispos-
able in the sense of being open to revision or
replacement by more adequate models. This is not
available to the Christian. Inasmuch as historical
models have come to play a role in contemporary
thought not altogether different than that which
used to be reserved for natural theology, the Christian has to face the fact that the operative paradigm that is built into the theology of history
cannot in principle compete in the market-place of
secular model making. Because "every Christian has
his 'philosophy of history' given in his religion,"
Dawson warns, "he cannot make a new one for himself."[31] The acceptance of a different philosophy
of history is tatamount to changing one's religion.

II. THE "ARCHTYPAL PATTERN" IN THE HISTORY OF CHRISTIAN CULTURE

Now that we are prepared to take a closer look
at the way Dawson thematizes certain patterns in the
history of Christian culture, it is important to
keep in mind the distinction between the theology of
history proper, which is a theological understanding
of the successive ages of divine revelation, and the
more mundane task of periodizing, thematizing, and
interpreting the developmental phases of Christian
culture. While the former pertains to what St.
Augustine called the narratio plena of sacred revelation, the latter deals with this historical evolution of the Church in the world. Dawson, of
course, was interested in both. Yet the periodization of the history of Christian culture does not
directly entail theology as it takes it for granted,
and thus goes on to employ metahistorical categories
which are congruent with what the Church believes
that God has revealed about the nature and destiny
of the Church in the world.

14

Dawson follows the theological tradition of St. Augustine and others in understanding the _articulus temporis_ of sacred history as comprising five ages: (1) The calling of Abraham; (2) The Exodus, and the covenant between God and Israel; (3) The testing of Israel through the prophets; (4) The Incarnation, Redemption, and creation of a new humanity in Christ; (5) The extension of this new dispensation through the life of the Church, which is the ongoing incorporation of the Gentiles into the regenerate community.[32] The theological schema of the five ages is an all-encompassing framework for situating the historical details. In _De Catechizandis Rudi -bus_, for instance, St. Augustine explains: "We should begin our narration, starting out from the fact that 'God made all things very good,' and continuing, as we have said, down to the present period of Church history, in such a way as to account for and explain the causes and reasons of each of the facts and events that we related, and thereby refer them to that end of love from which, in all our actions and words, our eyes should never be turned away." He compares the sacred narrative -- the _narratio plena_ -- to the "gold which holds together in harmonious arrangement the jewels [i.e. the particular facts] of an ornament."[33] So, the sacred history that embraces the beginning and end of all things sets the context in which the narration of Church history should be conducted. This principle of Christian historiography was passed along to Medieval culture, and is readily apparent in the histories of Gregory of Tours and Bede. Thus, in his _History of the Franks_, Gregory of Tours does not immediately narrate the genealogy of the Franks, and the steps by which their culture was Christianized; he begins "In the beginning God made the heaven and the earth in His own Christ, that is in His own Son, who is the origin of all things."[34] To return for a moment to St. Augustine, it is important to see that the sacred history not only orients, but also places limits upon the histories of cultures and the action of particular churches. St. Augustine stressed that from a theological standpoint it is heretical to interpolate new "ages" in the sacred history (such as what the Montanists proposed in terms of their post-pentecostal age of the "paraclete"). We presently live in the final age, and history will be no more eschatological than it already is.[35] Therefore, no

15

local or regional history can lay claim to being the bearer or the manifestation of a new dispensation; the epochs of cultures -- even Christian cultures -- cannot constitute grounds for revising the articulus temporis of the sacred history.

Dawson characterized his work as an explication of the historical development of the Church and culture as they exist within the final age. His schematization of this history is sixfold: (1) Primitive Christianity (from the first to the fourth century), which was marked by the expansion of the Christian religion under the surface of the existing Graeco-Roman civilizations; (2) Patristic Christianity (from the fourth to the sixth century), which saw the establishment primarily in the Eastern part of the Empire of a Christian-Roman or Byzantine culture; (3) The Formation of Western Christendom (from the sixth to the eleventh century), which involved the conversion of Northern Europe, and the emergence of what Dawson calls the "archtypal pattern" of Christian culture; (4) Medieval Christendom (from the eleventh to the fifteenth century), which represented both the full flowering and the gradual erosion of the synthesis between Christianity and culture; (5) Divided Christendom (from the sixteenth to the eighteenth century), which, although it involved a religious and political civil war within Christendom, also saw the expansion of Christianity and its institutions to the New World; (6) Secularized Christendom (from the eighteenth century to the present), during which time the older framework of Christian culture was swept away by revolutionary movements.[36]

In this section we want to outline the main metahistorical theme in Dawson's work, which we have already alluded to in terms of the "archtypal pattern." According to Dawson, this archtypal pattern is not only to be found in the extraordinary flowering of Christian culture associated with the 13th century, or the "high" Middle Ages. It is surprising, perhaps, that the scholar whose name is so closely identified with the history of Christian culture should rather emphasize the significance of the so-called "Dark Ages." Although he believed that the 13th century represented the "culminating point of the Middle Ages -- the crown of the preceding six centuries of development,"[37] the larger

16

portion of Dawson's work was devoted on the one hand to the "Dark Ages," and on the other to the contemporary period of "Secularized Christendom." (And if I can here interject my own opinion, this shift of focus to what preceded and followed the "high" Middle Ages is Dawson's most important contribution as a Catholic metahistorian.) Because he was as interested in culture as he was in ideas, Dawson was more willing than many other scholars to attend to the primitive and incipient stages of creativity. He remarked in his Harvard lectures that: "We now realize the importance of the dynamic creative periods in history when a new start is made from small beginnings, since for an historian the seed time is more important and deserving of study than the time of harvest."[38] Moreover, because it was also his conviction that religion exerts the most creative influence in the development of cultures, Dawson was equally interested in exploring how the dissipation of religious values is related to cultural decay. Whereas in the ancient "Dark Ages" he finds the seed for the pattern of subsequent European history, in the so-called "progress" of modernity he finds a new, and real "dark ages." Though the sixth period in his schema is the least favorable, and in Dawson's estimation, regressive, chapter in the history of Christianity and culture, it nevertheless substantiates many of his themes concerning religion and culture. Indeed, he refers to modernity as "Secularized Christendom" in order to call attention to the fact that the ideological and cultural divisions built into modern societies are even now a civil war within Christendom. For Dawson, modernity has not escaped the ideals of unity inherited from the earlier centuries of Christian culture.

Since Dawson, like most Catholics, had a special appreciation for the "harvest" of Catholic culture in the "high" Middle Ages, it took considerable discipline on his part to refocus attention upon the Church's mission among the barbarians -- both ancient and modern. As a scholar, however, Dawson saw that it was crucial to maintain an organic sense of all the periods of Christian culture, including the 13th century. Many historians and philosophers, he remarked, are "so impressed by the logical completeness of the medieval synthesis, as revealed in the works of St. Thomas and Dante, that

they have failed to realize its dynamic character."[39] This has created a problem on two levels.
In the first place, an exclusive identification of
Christian culture with the "high" Medieval period
tends to lend encouragement to the attitude that
Christian culture is no more than an antiquarian
subject. In the second place, by rendering such an
equation, the "high" Middle Ages themselves are
reduced to an inert and timeless set-piece, neither
caused-by nor causative-of a larger pattern. Dawson
was not alone in highlighting this problem. Étienne
Gilson, whose scholarly interest was more oriented
to intellectual history, persistently argued that
Medieval scholasticism must be understood against
the historical and religious background of the
Patristic age. Furthermore, Gilson's early work on
Descartes helped scholars recover a sense of continuity between Medieval scholasticism and some of the
regulative ideals of the Enlightenment; there was no
"black hole" separating modern science and philosophy from Medieval sources. Dawson, too, wanted to
widen the focus to include within the purview of a
historian of Christian culture something more than
mere "medievalism":

> We cannot leave this to the medieval-
> ists alone, for they are to some extent
> themselves tied to the error by the
> limitations of their specialism.
> Christian culture is not the same thing
> as medieval culture. It existed before
> the Middle Ages began and it continued
> to exist after they had ended. We can-
> not understand Medieval culture unless
> we study its foundations in the age of
> the Fathers.[40]

The archtypal pattern of Christian culture is
both related to, and distinct from, what has been
called the Medieval "synthesis." Expressed in summary form, Dawson's view is that the "synthesis"
that characterized the Christian culture of the
Middle Ages involved an incorporation of two otherwise discordant ideals: the humanistic ideal, drawn
principally from Hellenism, and a transcendent or
eschatological ideal, drawn from Judaism.[41]
Christianity provided the medium for the synthesis,
though Dawson hastened to point out that Christianity is neither the synthesis itself, nor the result

of the synthesis.[42] Seen from this standpoint, Christian culture is a unique sociological and religious expression of humanistic and prophetic ideals. Dawson also insists that the synthesis represents only the super-structure. The more fundamental and important pattern that gave vitality to the synthesis was the recognition of a polarity and tension between Christianity and culture. Because the Church never completely identified itself with the cultural synthesis, it was able to retain a spiritual autonomy from which it continually re-introduced the religious dynamism upon which the culture rested, and from which it was created in the first place.

This historical relationship between the synthetic ideal and the spiritual undercurrents is the metahistorical theme to which Dawson devoted his scholarly career. Virtually all of his books and essays are interrelated according to this theme. To understand the overall shape of Dawson's interpretation, it is helpful to understand his assessment of St. Augustine's role in the development of Christian culture, and the extent to which Dawson himself was imbued with an Augustinian cast of mind. At the outset of his lectures at Harvard, he pointed out that his interpretation of the pattern that evolves through the six periods of Christian culture is based upon the Augustinian hermeneutic of the Two Cities: "My view, however, of the multiplicity of Christian culture does not necessarily involve an evolutionary theory of religious development. The course of this development is rather to be explained as St. Augustine describes it in his thesis of the Two Cities, as due to the continual conflict between the two opposing spiritual and social principles." "Every age," he concluded, "is an age of crisis for the Christian Church."[43]

Beginning in his earlier works, like _Progress and Religion_, and continuing through his later works, such as _The Formation of Christendom_, Dawson explicitly endorsed the Augustinian hermeneutic as the key to his own. In a memo written in 1953, he explained his relationship to St. Augustine very clearly when he remarked that although St. Augustine grasped the theological meaning of history "as clearly as anyone can," he did not enjoy a sufficiently sophisticated "conception of the complexity of the pattern of culture." In this regard, Dawson's work can be accurately described as an effort to conjoin an Augustinian theology of history with the insights and methods of modern social science. The single most important essay written by Dawson on St. Augustine is entitled "St. Augustine and His Age." Originally published in a collection of essays with several other Catholic scholars under the title, A Monument to St. Augustine (1930), Dawson's piece was re-published either in whole or in part in no fewer than four of his subsequent books.[44]

Dawson finds in St. Augustine's City of God the prototype of the synthetic ideal. While the Hellenic world had an ontology for man's social and political nature, it lacked an adequate conception of man's historical nature; and while the Jewish and Christian traditions enjoyed a remarkably well-developed historical sensibility, the social and political ontology required additional explicitation. St. Augustine brought the two together.[45] It is true, of course, that this kind of synthetic work had been undergoing some evolution in pre-Augustinian Christian thought. Yet, Dawson contends that the originality of St. Augustine's project was the extent to which the social, moral, and political were given a full-fledged expression in terms of a theology of history. While in the East the predominant interest in the synthetic ideal tended to focus upon the philosophical and cosmological elements, St. Augustine inherited and developed the peculiarily North African aptitude for personal, moral, and political matters. "He did not base his treatment of the subject on philosophic and metaphysical arguments, as the Greek Fathers had done," Dawson notes, "but on the eschatological and social dualism which ... was the characteristic of the earliest Christian teaching and to which the African tradition, as a whole, had proved so faithful."[46]

(Incidentally, Dawson's appreciation of the African tradition and its role in the formation of Western Christendom is an instructive example of his inclination to find significance in what appears to be primitive. With the exception of the rather sophisticated school of Alexandrian theology -- which was oriented toward the theologically speculative discourse of the East -- the rest of the North African church was much less polished intellectually and culturally. Yet, Dawson argued that it was precisely this segment of the Church that eventually came to have a profound influence upon Western institutions. One of the reasons for this was the fact that North Africa had resisted political and cultural absorption into the Graeco-Roman world; and although this was continually a source of problems for ecclesial unity (in the form of movements such as Montanism and Donatism), Dawson observes that even the heresies of the region tended to exhibit the attraction to moral and political issues. Both in terms of orthodoxy and heterodoxy, the North African tradition proved to be a fertile source for the tension between the humanistic and eschatological elements that Dawson judged to be at the very core of the archtypal pattern of Christian culture.)[47]

The synthetic ideal was not the regulative principle, but rather, the outer frame of the Augustinian view.(48) The drama of the Two Cities guided the synthetic ideal according to an understanding of an essential polarity at work in history. Dawson argues that the key to the synthetic power of Christian culture was the more fundamental eschatological and social dualism that prevented the synthetic ideal from degenerating into a static order, or from being conceived of as a merely intramundane dialectic. In St. Augustine's work, the dualism that Dawson calls attention to is not metaphysical, but moral. History includes two co-existing principles which are expressed in the individual will and in society: the law of Divine Love that restores and transforms human nature, and the centrifugal dynamism of self-love that tends toward division, and ultimately to a desiccation of what, even on a natural level, the motive force of human love is able to accomplish. History bears the tension of both principles ("permixte" says St. Augustine), but it is not a synthesis of the two. Despite the dynamism of the "city of man," it is not self-transformative, and for this reason is not able to sustain progress in the moral and spiritual sense of the term. Dawson prefaced his essay on "St. Augustine and His Age" with the following passage from St. Cyprian of Carthage:

The world itself now bears witness to its approaching end by the evidence of its failing powers. There is not so much rain in the winter for fertilizing the seeds, nor in summer is there so much warmth for ripening them .... Can anything that is old preserve the same powers that it had in the prime and vigour of its youth? It is inevitable that whatever is tending downwards to decay and approaches its end must decrease in strength, like the setting sun and the waning moon, and the dying tree and the failing stream. This is the sentence passed on the world; this is God's law: that all that has risen should fall and that all that has grown should wax old, and that strong things should become weak and great things should become small, and that when they have been weakened and diminished they should come to an end.[49]

In this same vein, it was Dawson's conviction that just as religion is the creative force in human culture, the synthesis distinctive of Christian culture owed it existence to the spiritual power of Christianity -- without this power, the synthesis must follow the law of decay built into the earthly city.

If it is true -- as historians have insisted for quite some time -- that St. Augustine's City of God was the foundational treatise for the Christian Church and culture in the West, it exerted such an influence not so much because he achieved the kind of intellectual and aesthetic synthesis that marked the works of St. Thomas and Dante, but because he anchored the framework for synthetic activity in what Dawson calls the "deeper law of spiritual duality and polarization." For Dawson, this is the point that has to be grasped above all else in order to understand the archtypal pattern. Though it might seem paradoxical, the eschatological and moral dualism emphasized in the Augustinian tradition enabled the Western Church to envisage the "prospect of a Christian age and civilization" precisely because it was not conceived of as a "millennial kingdom but a field of continual effort and conflict."[50] The hermeneutic of the Two Cities gave incentive to the missionary and culture-forming energies of the Christian religion.

22

There are several reasons that can be adduced for this symbiotic relation between Augustinian thought and a vigorous interest in cultural activity.(51) Here, let us mention three. First, the Two Cities scheme encourages a sensitivity to the necessity of ongoing labor in the world, for the world will not, and cannot, transform itself. Indeed, as I once heard this expressed by a Protestant Evangelical who would not otherwise be very sanguine about Christian culture -- "The world doesn't know its just a world." One of the first acts of charity on the part of the Christian Church vis-a-vis culture is a de-mystification of its presumption to autonomy. The Augustinian position, Dawson says, "closes the gate which leads back to the dream of a social utopia and a state of natural perfection."[52] Once the Church is not con-fused with culture, it is free to be available creatively _for_ culture. Second, because in the Augustinian system history and culture are viewed as a field of conflict, the stakes of which involve a moral regeneration of man that transcends history and culture, they are allowed to be open-ended -- and this open-endedness of history and culture dramatically intensifies their importance. In other words, the Christian religion does not confront culture as something that is necessarily closed or unreceptive. If history and culture are made to bear the burden of a millenial kingdom, the Church would have to confront culture as an irremediable foe or, perhaps, as a closed system from which to escape. Third, the Augustinian moral dualism is not first of all a sociological insight, but more radically involves an understanding of the freedom of the human heart. The dynamism of the individual personality is paramount. Hence, cultures are to be created and renewed in the same fashion as the individual -- not through a mere tinkering with sociological structures, but through free spiritual associations and movements that are based upon a charity that is not reducible to politics.

To illustrate his point concerning the importance of the Augustinian framework in the evolution of Christian culture in the West, Dawson contrasts it with the form that the synthetic ideal took in the East, which has a much less vivid sense of the eschatological and social dualism.[53] The Eastern Church was eager to establish a "parallelism" be-

23

tween Christian culture and the millenial kingdom. In his Ecclesiastical History, for instance, Eusebius treats the state in a way that is, for all practical purposes, diametrically opposite to St. Augustine's position. At the end of his narration, Eusebius delivers the following ecominum to the significance of Constantine:

> But the mighty and victorious Constantine, adorned with every virtue of religion, with his most pious son, Crispus Caesar, resembling in all things his father, recovered the east as his own, and thus restored the Roman empire to its ancient state of one united body; extending their peaceful sway around the world, from the rising sun to the opposite regions, to the north and the south, even to the last borders of the declining day. All fear, therefore, of those who had previously afflicted them, was now wholly removed. They celebrated splendid and festive days with joy and hiliarity. All things were filled with light, and all who before were sunk in sorrow, beheld each other with smiling and cheerful faces. With choirs of hymns, in the cities and villages, at the same time they celebrated and extolled first of all God the universal King, because they were thus taught, then they also celebrated the praises of the pious emperor, and with him all his divinely favored children. There was a perfect oblivion of past evils, and past wickedness was buried in forgetfulness.[54]

We see here the synthetic ideal expressed in full plummage: the recovery of ancient Hellas, now irradiated in the transcendent light of Christianity. It is instructive, Dawson thought, that the facts upon which Eusebius rests his exaltation of the imperium will be interpreted by St. Augustine, scarcely one generation later, to indicate that the "yoke is Christ is on the neck of kings."[55] While the Byzantine notion of the synthesis of the Church and polis was used in the East to justify the role of the state in intervening in ecclesial matters,

St. Augustine, Dawson notes, "bases his claim to make use of the secular power against the Donatists, not on the right of the state to intervene in religious matters, but on the right of the Church to make use of the powers of this world which God has subdued to Christ."[56] The City of God, after all, was intended by St. Augustine to warn Christians against identifying the rise and fall of secular kindgoms with the millennium. The central point is a critique of "parallelism," and thus the meaning of the rise of the Catholic Church under Christ's vicar in Rome does not consist in a recovery or transformation of Rome.

"The Byzantines were so conscious of this all-embracing unity," Dawson states, "That they tended to regard the Empire as the embodiment of this universal spiritual society and thus to overlook or minimize the essential duality of Church and State."[57] Dawson, however, did not give short shrift to the Christian culture of Byzantium. Against Gibbon and other historians, he stressed that Byzantium was not simply a decadent classical culture; and against the position of theologians such as Adolph von Harnack, he argued that Byzantium did not involve a Hellenization and corruption of authentic, primitive Christianity. The details of Dawson's thinking on the Christian culture of the east would take us too far afield at this point, but at least in passing let us outline a few of his ideas on the subject. First, he argued that the Byzantine culture was, from an historical and sociological point of view, a unique culture. It affords "almost the only example of the process by which one of the higher civilizations is transformed from within and achieves a completely different form."[58] Whereas the Christian culture of the West was created in the midst of the debris of civilization, the Christian culture of the East occupied, and transformed from within, an already existing higher civilization. Dawson saw this as not only confirming his thesis concerning the role of religion in the process of culture-formation, but also as a testimony to the extraordinary creativity of the Patristic period. Second, he argued that the Byzantine culture was authentically Christian, and indeed was the first Christian culture. "For no society in history," he points out, "has identified itself more closely with the Christian religion than the Byzantine Empire, and for a considerable period (e.g. in the sixth century) the Byzantine State was practically coterminous with Christendom."[59] Furthermore in this regard, the static tendency of the identification of the Church and the polis was counterbalanced by the role of monasticism which, although it was the antithesis of the ancient polis, was an essential organ of Byzantine culture.[60] Monasticism was a principal contribution of the Eastern Church to that of the West; and if the West did not finally accept the "parallelism" of Byzantium, it was fertilized by monasticism, which came to be the main sociological "cell" upon which the Christian culture of the West was built. Finally, Dawson argued that Byzantium involved not only a Hellenization of the Judaic and Christian ideals and practices, but also an orientalization of the Hellenistic-Roman tradition. The Christian culture of the East was a synthesis of Western and Oriental (i.e. what we call today "Near Eastern") sources. Adolph von Harnack regarded the metaphysically-based doctrines of the post-Constantinian period as the intrusion of an alien, Greek Hellenism into authentic Christianity. Harnack's case concerning the Hellenization of doctrine is really only a subspecies of the older Protestant notion of the so-called "Constantinian Settlement" -- a category which, like the "Babylonian Captivity," expresses a range of historical, moral, and spiritual issues having to do with the loss of the integrity of the early Church. (It has been the fundamental metahistorical category for nearly all of the Protestant churches because, as we said earlier in connection with the term "modernity," it entails a dramatic revision of Christian history that is necessary to the Protestant argument, and vantage-point.) Whatever else might be engaged in debate with Harnack, Dawson argues that the features of Byzantium which are frequently taken to be Graeco-Roman (e.g. political hierarchy, liturgy, monasticism, and speculative theology), acutally exhibit an Oriental influence. It was Dawson's judgment that the Protestant Reformation eliminated the Oriental elements: "It abolished asceticism and monasticism. It subordinated contemplation to action, the spiritual to the temporal authority." Ironically, what was thought to be a purification of the Graeco-Roman accretions actually "gave free scope to the development of the Occidental mentality."[61]

To return to the point of Dawson's contrast between the Christian culture of the East and West, the lesson that he wanted drawn is twofold: (1) that the synthetic ideal without an equal dose of something like the Augustinian "tension" tends toward a stasis; and (2) that the spiritual and cultural unity of Byzantium was not, in fact, as easily perpetuated and reformable as the pattern in the West. The Western Church assumed a more independent attitude toward the polis, and Dawson argued that it was of great importance that the West inherited the Augustinian rather than the Eusebian model:

> If we consider the matter, not from the narrow standpoint of the juristic relations of church and state, but as St. Augustine himself did, from the point of view of the relative importance of the spiritual and material element in life, we shall see that his doctrine really made for moral freedom and responsibility. Under the Roman Empire, as in the sacred monarchies of the oriental type, the state was exalted as a superhuman power against which the individual personality had no rights and the individual had no power. In the East, even Christianity proved powerless to change this tradition, and alike in the Byzantine Empire and in Russia the Church consecrated anew the old oriental ideal of an omnipotent sacred state and a passive people. In the West, however, St. Augustine broke decisively with this tradition by depriving the state of its aura of divinity and seeking the principle of social order in the human will. In this way the Augustinian theory, for all its otherworldliness, first made possible the ideal of a social order resting upon the free personality and a common effort towards moral ends. And thus the Western ideals of freedom and progress and social justice owe more than we realise to the profound thought of the great African who was himself indifferent to secular progress and to

the transitory fortunes of the earthly state.[62]

To borrow an expression by Paul Ricoeur, a "hermeneutic of suspicion" is central to the Augustinian perspective. In the subsequent history of the West this suspicion has been absolutized and used as a way to negate the very possibility of a Christian culture; this strategy is evident in Luther, the Anabaptists, Jansenists, and in the "Crisis" theology of the Barthians. Yet it also finds another mode of expression in the peculiarily Anglo-American sobriety concerning the pomp and claims of the state. Distorted and extreme forms of Augustinianism, however, illustrate the basic point. As inheritors of the culture formed by the Western Church, we enjoy a sixth-sense, as it were, of the danger of theocratic pretentions, and of a state that would pretend to be a Church. While the "Secularized Christendom" of the East even today still hankers for a comprehensive synthesis of Church, state, and culture (and, for Dawson, the totalitarian regimes of the East can thus be viewed as a debased and regressive Byzantium in which secular ideology occupies the place of the Church in the synthesis), the "Secularized Christendom" of the West continues to retain, albeit in residual form, a sense of the Augustinian problematic. The tensions and problems of modernity, Dawson argued, take shape according to patterns established in Christian culture centuries ago. Although post-Renaissance historians have been inclined to pass over the Byzantine culture of the East, and the "Dark Ages" of the West, these are crucial for any adequate interpretation of modernity.

In addition to the Augustinian vision, the archtypal pattern of Christian culture as it evolved in the West involved two other components, each of which began to take shape after the fall of Rome, and must be seen in terms of the way that the Christian religion incorporated itself sociologically among the barbarian peoples. The first of these has to do with the cultural situation faced by the Western Church on the eve of its missionary expansion. "In the Roman West," Dawson points out, "in spite of its lower standard of civilization, the conditions were more favourable to the development of an original and creative Christian culture."

"For here," he continued, "the Church did not become incorporated in a social and political order which it was powerless to modify; it found itself abandoned to its own resources in a world of chaos and destruction."[63] In the early middle ages there was no fixed political-cultural center in the West in any way comparable to Constantinople. Beginning with the Celtic missionary enterprise of the early 5th century, and continuing through the successive waves of missions back through the north of Europe, the Western Church did not implant along with the faith a uniform political-cultural structure. If one reads St. Bede's Ecclesiastical History, or Gregory of Tour's History of the Franks, one is struck by the fact that the missionary extension of the so-called "Roman" model was not, strictly speaking, an imposition of Roman culture. Although the Roman Church conveyed important linguistic and juridical structures which were somewhat continuous with the ancient Empire, the principle of unity was more directly drawn from the Church's spiritual understanding of itself, primarily in terms of the ecclesial form of cenobitic monasticism. Dawson writes:

> Hence the new civilization which slowly and painfully began to emerge in the early middle ages was in a very special sense a religious creation, for it was based on an ecclesiastical not a political unity. While in the East, the imperial unity was still all inclusive and the Church was essentially the Church of the Empire, in the West it was the Church that was the universal society and the state was weak, barbarous and divided. The only true citizenship that remained to the common man was his membership of the Church, and it involved a far deepr and wider loyalty than his allegiance to the secular state. It was the fundamental social relation which overrode all distinctions of class and nationality. The Church was a world in itself, with its own culture, its own organization and its own law. Insofar as civilization survived, it was directly dependent on

the Church, whether in the great Carolingian monasteries, such as St. Gall
or Fulda, which were the chief centres
of cultural and economic life, or in
the cities which came to depend on the
bishops and the ecclesiastical element
for the very existence. The state, on
the other hand, had become divorced
from the city and the civic culture and
reverted more and more to the warlike
traditions of a barbarous tribal aris-
tocracy.[64]

In other words, the model of unity that united the
Western peoples was drawn from the rib of the
Church. These peoples were constituted by a spiritual membership in a trans-cultural and trans-politi-
cal society.

Perhaps a believer would read this history as a
matter of Providence, yet in any event it is interesting that the concrete cultural and political situation found in the West was ideally suited to an
application of the Augustinian vision of the relation between the Two Cities. Throughout his writings, Dawson emphasizes that the unity of Western
European culture did not rest upon racial, cultural,
or political homogeneity, but rather upon the religious and spiritual energies of the Church. In
Progress and Religion, he says: "For mediaeval
Europe no longer possessed a homogeneous material
culture, such as we find, for example, in China or
India. It was a loose federation of the most diverse types of race and culture under the hegemony
of a common religious and ecclesiastical tradition.
This explains the contradictions and disunity of
mediaeval culture -- the contrast of its cruelty and
its charity, its beauty and its squalor, its spiritual vitality and its material barbarism. For the
element of higher culture did not spring naturally
from the traditions of the social organism itself,
but came in from outside as a spiritual power which
has to remould and transform the social material in
which it attempted to embody itself."[65] As we
will discuss in more detail later, the cultural
entity of what we today call Europe was created as a
Christian culture, and therefore has continued
throughout the centuries to be dependent for its
unity upon the religion that brought it forth in the

first place. When the religious principle is obscured or eliminated, Europe tends to revert back to its multiple components. Efforts in our own century, for example, to establish a new center of unity on the basis of racial or political homogeneity have proved tragically disasterous.

The other element constitutive of the archtypal pattern has to do with the relationship between religious reform and cultural progress. Underneath the synthetic ideal and its "higher" culture that reached its apex in the 13th century, the sociological and religious currents were continuously in tension with one another. If the Medieval "synthesis" is viewed not only as intellectual and artistic, but also as religious and sociological, then one can appreciate why the culture was as fragile as it was creative. On the other hand, the culture allowed for certain centrigual forces rooted in the heterogenous elements of race, geography, and local traditions. The Medieval Christendom of the West was extraordinarily pluralistic; the modern caricature of the period as a depressingly uniform and static culture is simply an anachronistic reading into the Middle Ages of what is actually more characteristic of the homogenizing pressures of modern culture and politics. On the other hand, the centripetal forces operative in the religious sector were complicated by the fact that although the Church was responsible for the unity of the culture, the Church also had to protect its autonomy against the natural pressures that tended to collapse the Church into the institutions and ambitions of the world. Here, we find the paradox -- or at least the main tension -- of Western culture.[66] The cultural unity of Europe is a result of a religious tradition that cannot remain loyal to itself, or to the culture, if it becomes too identified with the culture. It is a profound historical theme that surpases even the bacchanalian revel of Hegelian dialectics. One needs the Augustinian open-ended dialectic to make sense of it. Intertwined with the synthetic ideal, the history of the Christian culture of the Middle Ages involved an almost continuous tension, and frequently open conflict, between the Church and culture -- with the Church demanding a certain moral and spiritual progress on the part of the culture and, nearly as often, with the culture demanding that the Church recover its own integrity. Whether it was the crisis posed by the Carolingian ambition to create a theocratic monarchy, or the ecclesiastical and political turmoil of the Avignon papacy, the history of the Middle Ages can be written as a story of successive efforts to maintain the equilibrium of the culture as Christian, while trying to retain the Augustinian distinction between the Two Cities. Dawson writes: "The history of the medieval Church consists largely of a series of attempts to remedy this state of affairs and to emancipate the spiritual power from lay control and exploitation by a return to the traditional principles of canonical order."[67]

The point that Dawson makes in this regard is that the fortunes of Western culture in terms of its internal mechanisms of change are deeply tied to patterns and motives of reform which have arisen within the religious sector. In Religion and the Rise of Western Culture, he has this to say:

It is only in Western Europe that the whole pattern of culture is to be found in a continuous succession and alternation of free spiritual movements; so that every century of Western history shows a change in the balance of cultural elements, and the appearance of some new spiritual force which creates new ideas and institutions and produces a further movement of social change. [68]

There is an old Pennsylvania-Dutch proverb that states, "Don't break what you can't make." Applied to the subject at hand, Dawson calls attention to the fact that, since Western European culture was formed on the backs of religious missionairies, there is no other way to re-form it except in that way. Even the reform movements of "Secularized Christendom" -- to the extent that they have proved successful in promoting any kind of internal change -- have relied upon evangelical models which have as their ancestor the monastic movements of the so-called "Dark Ages."

Thus far in this essay we have more than once mentioned that Dawson wanted to correct the tendency to exclusively focus upon the role of ideas in West-

32

ern history. As yet another example of this, he argued that it is quite misleading to conceive of the cultural service of monasticism simply in terms of its preservation of "high" culture through the barbaric ages. Although professional historians of the period are, for the most part, aware that this is a rather simplistic understanding of Medieval monasticism, it has become part and parcel of the popular view. the view is related to the modern myth that the Christian era was a debased classical culture, and that the service of the monk was akin to a kind of ecclesial Gungha Din, transporting the waters of classical learning across the desert of the "Dark Ages" to the Renaissance. The main service of monasticism, and later, of the religious orders and institutes of the Baroque era, consisted, according to Dawson, in their preservation of "the principle of an autonomous Christian order which again and again proved to be the seed of new life for the whole Church."[69] The ideals of "asceticism and otherworldliness and fidelity to the Rule," Dawson argues, "are the important matters, for it was these that gave it its spiritual independence, its powers to resist the pressure of its environment and to initiate movements of religious reform."(70) It is significant that the great reforming Pope, Gregory VII, allied himself with the relatively primitive, though spiritually energetic, Cluniac movement rather than with the more culturally sophisticated monastery of St. Gall; just as, in the 13th century, Pope Honorius III perceived the importance of the Franciscsn Regula Primitiva -- which proved to be a movement of cultural and religious reform that is practically unparalleled since in Western history. While one can point to the importance of the recovery of Peripatetic logic and science in the 12th century, and to the rise of the schools, it is worth recalling that it was the spiritual energy of the rustic friars that enlivened the project of the "high" culture. Sts. Bonaventure and Thomas Aquinas were not the products of new found "ideas," but were rather the embodiment and fruit of an ascetical and religious reform that had as its goal, not "high" culture, but the integrity of the City of God.[71]

Today it has become almost counter-intuitive that a relatively obscure religious order engaged in corporeal works of mercy can be the seed for signi-

ficant cultural change. However cunning the Hegelian "Geist," it was -- at least in the hands of
Hegel -- notoriously elitist in terms of who it
would use as the occasion for its dialectical movements. Dawson, however, insists that the "world-
transforming events which changed the whole course
of human history have occurred as it were under the
surface of history, unnoticed by the historians and
philosophers."[72] The "true makers of history," he
said, "are not to be found on the surface of events
among the successful politicians or the successful
revolutionaries: these are the servants of events.
Their masters are the spiritual men whom the world
knows not, the unregarded agents of the creative
action of the Spirit."[73] Dawson conceded that it
is "often difficult to trace the connection between
this spirit of religious faith and the new movements
of change which often seem to represent a radical
denial of any common spiritual basis;"[74] but he
believed that the archtypal pattern is still the
issue, and continues to be the reality around which
the peculiar problems of modernity are related.

III. THE RELEVANCE OF THE HISTORY OF CHRISTIAN CULTURE

In the previous section we outlined the three
main facets of what Dawson called the "archtypal
pattern" in the history of Christian culture. We
saw that the Augustinian framework, according to
Dawson, played a crucial role in the way that the
Western Church envisaged the moral nature of the
Church's temporal agency in history and culture.
Then, we discussed the importance that Dawson at-
taches to the specific sociological foundations of
Western culture. Its novelty and significance
consisted in the fact that it incorporated a cultural pluralism along with a dynamic principle of
unity that transcended politics, race, and geography; the pluralism valued in Western culture was
nourished and protected precisely because the principle of unity did not depend entirely upon the
hegemony of any one of the parties in the sociological order. Finally, we examined why Dawson contended that the principle of continuity in the
Western tradition has been continuously exhibited in
"free spiritual movements."

We also discussed why Dawson considered a re-examination of the "Dark Ages" to be indispensible to the task of showing the overall importance of the history of Christian culture. It is the "seed time" not only for the "harvest" of the 13th century, but for the more general pattern of European culture itself. As we said earlier, in terms of the volume of Dawson's material, a significant portion of it is devoted to the sixth period in the scheme -- to what he called "secularized christendom." In this section we will sketch-out some of the main lines in his interpretation of the relationship between modernity and the archtypal pattern.

In Understanding Europe, Dawson wrote that the post-Christian era has not altogether shaken the older pattern:

> It is obvious that there is a profound difference between the old dualism of the Christian way of life and unregenerate human nature on the one hand, and the new dualism between the revolutionary ideas of liberalism, nationalism, and socialism and the traditional order of society on the other, but there is a certain relation between the two, so that it is possible to maintain that the whole revolutionary tradition is a post-Christian phenomenon which transposes a pre-existent psychological pattern to a different sociological tradition. But even if that were the case, it would make it all the more important to understand how the archtypal pattern had originated. [75]

Modernity can be interpreted as an ongoing effort to re-align, by transpositions, the three components of the original pattern. Dawson is certainly correct in observing that there continues to be a reliance upon dualistic historical dramas which insert content quite different than that of Augustine, but which are operatively more similar than different. While the Hegelian system is, for reasons too complicated to pursue here, patently opposed to, and different than, the Augustinian position, it is fair to say that the Marxian system is in more than one sense similar. And although it would entail a treatise in its own right to explore this relationship, one can suggest that it is not coincidental that the reason why the Marxian system has proved far more influential is due to its resemblance to the Two Cities theme in the archtypal pattern.[76] The third component of the pattern is clearly evident in the post-Revolutionary reliance upon "movements" as the agents of cultural change. Even the Marxist-Leninist regimes which, after they come to power, tend to shackle what Dawson calls "free spiritual movements," nevertheless depend precisely on such movements to advance their cause. Finally, inasmuch as the ideals of such modern ideologies as liberalism, socialism and capitalism view themselves as worthy of international and universal allegiance, they represent an effort to recover the trans-cultural unity that was so essential to the development of Europe itself. In Dawson's judgment, it is not coincidental that the ideologies which are now world-wide in scope should have emerged from Western European culture.[77]

Dawson wanted to explain the nature and historical development of modernity in terms of transpositions in the archtypal pattern, so that modernity could be understood as a situation (now world-wide) in which the unity of the pattern has dissolved, yet not the constitutive elements. To return to an example discussed earlier, secular metahistorians since the Renaissance have claimed in one way or another that the Medieval pattern has been superceded or nullified. But there is more at work than what the various historical ideologies choose to reveal about themselves. The "Liberal interpretation of history," Dawson observes, "has taken over from the Catholic tradition not only its universalism, its sense of a spiritual purpose which runs through the whole life of humanity, but also its dualism."[78] The Liberal interpretation of history is preoccupied with the image of the Two Cities, though "it is now the Church which is the embodiment of those 'reactionary forces' which are the liberal equivalent of the powers of darkness, while the children of this world have become the children of light."[79]

In this respect, it is interesting to find John Stuart Mill, in On Liberty, basing his critique of

Calvinism in particular, and the reactionary nature of Christianity in general, upon an unacknowledged Augustinian motif:

> It will not be denied by anybody that originality is a valuable element in human affairs .... This cannot be gainsaid by anybody who does not believe that the world has already attained perfection in all its ways and practices. It is true that this benefit is not capable of being rendered by everybody alike; there are but a few persons, in comparison with the whole of mankind, whose experiments, if adopted, by others, would likely be any improvement upon established practice. But these few are the salt of the earth; without them, human life would be a stagnant pool.[80]

Thus, when Mill goes on to state that unless "there were a succession of persons [of] ever recurring originality," society would sink into a torpid "mediocrity," he seems to have transposed the content rather than the form of the original pattern. He differs from St. Cyprian of Carthage and St. Augustine principally in the sense that it is now the liberated bohemian rather than the monk who stands in apposition to the rest of society; and rather than the Church being the "salt" of culture and progress, Mill introduces the ideal of the liberated "genius" whose experiments hold the promise of ongoing reform. Whatever else, pro or con, might be said about Mill's philosophy, it is saturated with the rhetoric and the ideals of the religious and cultural tradition that he calls into question.

The idological nature of these transpositions is determined by the use of historical ideas which suppress both in the philosophical system, as well as in the consciousness of the systematician, the historical, institutional, and organic continuity linking the thinker to the historical issues themselves. All its claims to "historical consciousness" notwithstanding, modernity tends to forget its own historicity. Alasdair MacIntyre once remarked that "Liberalism begins as the myth that humanity has freed itself from all previous historical determinations."[81] We call this "ideological" because it entails a systematic employment of ideas which divorce the thinker from the facts of which he speaks. Dawson argued that this absolutism regarding the status of the present age must be traced back to the literary culture of the Renaissance, "which revived in abstract form the old dualism of Hellenism and barbarism and thus for the first time introduced a cleavage between the facts of social development and the ideals of the educated classes."[82]

The use of history as an instrument to posit ruptures in history itself was perhaps the main factor in the secularization of European culture; it was the Promethean move that preceded, and indeed made possible, the Cartesian philosophical enterprise that begins <u>de novo</u> with regard to the inheritance of Western thought. It is worth recalling that in his <u>Discourse on Method</u> Descartes revealed that before he found the "Archimedian" lever of the <u>cogito</u>, he saw the need to set aside the ancient cultural inheritance, which he describes according to the metaphor of a haphazardly arranged city:

> One of the first of the considerations that occurred to me was that there is very often less perfection in the works composed of several portions, and carried out by the hands of various masters, than in those on which one one individual has worked. Thus we see that buildings planned and carried out by one architect alone are usually more beautiful and better proportioned than those which many have tried to put in order and improve, making use of old walls which were built with other ends in view. In the same way also, those ancient cities which, originally mere villages, have become in the process of time great towns, are usually badly constructed in comparison with those which are regularly laid out on a plain by a surveyor who is free to follow his own ideas.[83]

He concludes that "since we have all been children before being men, and since it has for long fallen to us to be governed by our appetites and our teachers ... it is almost impossible that our judgments should be so excellent or solid as they should have been had we had complete use of our reason since our birth, and had we been guided by its means alone." Thus, Descartes resolved to "reform my own opinion and to build on a foundation which is entirely my own."[84] It is precisely the "cleavage" that Dawson speaks of concerning the facts of social development and the "new" standpoint. To understand modernity it is not enough to simply grapple with Cartesian dualism; the dualism operative in the historical consciousness sets the context and motivation for such thinking.

As Dawson interprets the Renaissance, it involved two different movements within the archtypal pattern of Christian culture. Whereas the southern Renaissance wanted to rid Christendom of the gothic barbarity of the "Dark Ages" -- and thereby to wed together the ideal of Christendom with the cultural ideals of ancient Graeco-Roman civilization -- the northern Renaissance wanted to purify Christianity of what it perceived to be a decadent Hellenism -- and thereby to restore an ecclesiastical relation between the present age and primitive Christianity.[85] While each of these movements posited a historical gap between the present age and the beginning of Christendom (the gap, of course, is nothing other than the Middle Ages), they differed in terms of which component of the "synthesis" embodied in Christian culture required purification. Dawson stresses that underneath the war of ideas, the Renaissance was a cultural civil war within Christendom:

> Men saw the revival of classical learning as the recovery of a lost inheritance. They revolted against the mediaeval culture not on religious grounds but because it was alien and uncivilized. They entered on a crusade to free the Latin world from the yoke of Gothic barbarism. In Northern Europe it is obvious that the movement of national awakening had to find a different form of expression, since there was here no older tradition of higher cul-

ture, and behind the mediaeval period there lay an age of pagan barbarism. Consequently Northern Europe could only assert its cultural independence by re-moulding and transforming the Christian tradition itself in accordance with its national genius. The Renaissance of Northern Europe is the Reformation.[86]

The one posited a Re-Naissance, the other a Re-Formation; what each had in mind was a simplification of the inherited historical pattern; one sought to re-Hellenzie, the other to re-Judaize, Christendom. What was set loose, in Dawson's estimation, was not a complete negation of the pattern of Christian culture, but rather a civil war within it -- one that can be symbolically characterized as a battle between Athens and Jerusalem, or what Dawson calls the humanistic and transcendent components of the culture synthesis.

These movements continued the Augustinian contrast between the regenerate and unregenerate, but as we pointed out in connection with John Stuart Mill's position, the dramatic conflict was rendered according to a linear scheme of historical contrast, and therefore departed from the Augustinian notion of the inherent tension built into history. The Renaissance envisaged an historical cleavage between late-antiquity and the point at which the classical ideal was recovered, while the Reformation viewed the history between Constantine and the recovery of primitive Christianity as a time of "Babylonian Captivity." In each case, narratives were used in order to pre-empt the cultural and spiritual value of the formative period of Christian culture. In short, a merely linear conception of dramatic conflicts produces historical gaps, for the meaning of the conflicts is drawn from the supposition that there exist fundamental discontinuities. Modernity is inagurated in terms of a distorted employment of the theology of history that set the framework for the emergence of the archtypal pattern in the age of St. Augustine. In other words, the unity of the pattern of Christian culture became fragmented precisely at the level that the pattern first began. Dawson points out that the twin movements of the Renaissance and Reformation conceived of themselves as having universal and international significance,

and as sufficient to re-introduce the proper trans-
political spirit of unity that bound the pattern of
European culture together. As we know from hind-
sight, neither proved capable of re-establishing the
cultural and spiritual unity of Europe. This is why
Dawson insisted that it is crucial to study the
nature of the archtypal pattern of Western culture.
For although these movements retained the cultural
aspirations of Christian culture, the unitive force
of the culture never consisted in either the synthesis or its component parts (i.e. the humanistic and
transcendent ideals); these were the cultural fruit
of the spiritual energies of Catholic Christianity.
Therefore, the demotion of the place of Catholicism -- as an organic and historically continuous
reality -- not only collapsed the unity of the
culture, but prompted a series of movements which,
however unconsciously, attempted to play the role of
unifying the various elements of the pattern.

Once historiography was pressed into the service of justifying the absolutism of the present age
against the past, "it was easy," Dawson says, "for
the Enlightenment to take one step further by send-
ing the Protestant churches to join the Church of
Rome outside the pale and by canonizing the apostles
of free thought as the saints of rationalism."[87]
Were time and patience to permit, the Dawsonian
analysis would show the extent to which our contemporary -- some would say "post-modern" -- age continues unabated in the problematic framework of the
culture caused by Christianity. Each successive
contender has not been successful in rendering the
archtypal pattern obsolete, but has only accentuated
the divisions and tensions of Christendom without
the Christian religion. In Understanding Europe,
Dawson maintained that it is quite proper to admit
that modern Europe is no longer a Christian culture,
while at the same time understanding that its secularism continues to draw upon the cultural processes
which preceded it:

> This does not mean that we ought to ig-
> nore or slur over the gap between Chri-
> stian ideals and social realities. On
> the contrary, the existence of this du-
> alism created that state of vital ten-
> sion which is the condition of European

culture .... Where this tension is ab-
sent -- where civilization has become
"autarchic," self-sufficient and self-
satisfied, there the process of Christian culture has been extinguished or
terminated. But even today we can hardly say that this has happened. Indeed
what we have seen during the last century has been something very different
-- an increase in the spiritual tension
which has become almost world wide.[88]

Insofar as the entire civilized world today lives
under ideologies spawned by the effort of Western
European culture to provide a secular equivalent of
Christendom, there is a pressing need to study the
history of Christian culture not so much immediately
for the sake of understanding Christianity, but for
the purpose of understanding modernity itself.[89]

At this point it is appropriate to gather together the various strands of our discussion.
Perhaps it would be helpful to ask, what is the
point of Christopher Dawson's metahistorical analysis? First, it should be said that although his
analysis attempts to provide a broad interpretation
of the pattern of cultural changes from the time of
St. Augustine to our contemporary age, Dawson would
insist that it is not a philosophy of history; and
even though he argues that the cultural pattern of
Western Christendom has acquired world-wide significance, it is nevertheless a particular pattern.
Second, while Dawson's account underscores the
importance of the Christian religion in the formation of Western culture, it was not intended to be a
merely backward-looking defense of Medieval Christianity; nor did he view his metahistorical account
as an apologetical cudgel to be used against
modernity. The main object of his metahistory is
the correction of a deep-seated understanding on the
part of Western European peoples concerning their
own history. Put more positively, Dawson wanted to
call attention to the need to recover the spiritual
tradition at the root of this cultural history.

One of the ways that Dawson went about this
task was his investigations into the relationship
between religion and culture. Here, he hoped to
indicate from the standpoint of cultural anthropol-

ogy the more general material and spiritual laws governing the evolution of cultures. But when we turn to the kind of metahistorical investigation discussed in this paper, we can summarize Dawson's case in terms of two moves: first, his refocusing of attention upon the generally disparaged "Dark Ages"; and second, his argument that the societal and moral tensions of the contemporary would have to be understood against the background of a cultural pattern that stretches back to that disparaged era. The first of these, I believe, is the most radical and important -- and this for at least two reasons: (1) One cannot empirically understand the pattern, much less appreciate its ongoing relevance to history, so long as the period of its formation is dismissed; (2) The ideological use of historical thinking to dismiss the period is precisely what has to be criticized, for this thinking is itself part and parcel of the historical problem. That is to say, the systematic divorce of the facts of social development from the ideal of progress involved a certain view taken of the early period of Christian culture, and has had quite specific consequences, not only in the domain of ideas but in culture as well. The object, therefore, is not simply to discuss the so-called "Dark Ages," but to indicate the extent to which the various metahistorical views of the period are symptomatic of a wider historical issue: namely, whether European history and culture owes its existence and intelligibility to the Christian religion. Dawson was at the very nerve of the problem when he shifted attention away from the 13th century to the preceding centuries, for even the secular understanding of European history concedes the value of the "high" culture represented by Aquinas and Dante (if for no other reason than its value as a museum piece); but the "high" culture can be interpretively assimilated as a passing moment of humanism en route to the full recovery of the scientific ideal, or en route to the emergency of modern nations. The "Dark Ages," however, raise the issue of the foundation of Europe itself, and here the religious problem is impossible to skirt.

In an essay entitled "The Relevance of European History," Dawson observed that in contemporary historiography "the old European view of history is now condemned as provincial or parochial or 'ethnocentric,' and it is generally admitted that if we wish to study world history we must pay as much attention to China and India and Islam, not to mention Indonesia and Africa, as to Europe."[90] As he goes on to note, at first sight this would seem to be an advance in historical method and learning; after all, given the ideal of a "global village," as well as the fact of the interdependence between sectors which were once geographically and culturally remote, an advance beyond a parochial European viewpoint would seem necessary if historical learning is to keep pace with reality. Dawson calls this attitude into question. His reasoning here is directly related to the issue we just discussed concerning the tendency of Europe to misconstrue its own history.

Dawson contends that "it would be a mistake to kick away the ladder of European historiography"[91] (i.e. a view of world history that takes Europe as its axial point) because the ideal of a historic world as an intelligible unity, as well as the specific causes responsible for the political, economic, and ideological movements on the international level, are the result of European culture. "Thus it seems to me impossible," he suggests, "to avoid the conclusion that the new Asia and Africa which are emerging with such revolutionary suddenness do not represent simply the reaction of Asiatic or African culture against the influence of an alien civilization, but rather the extension of Western civilization and Western international society into the extra-European world."[92] The study of the European past is relevant to modern world history because Europe is the source of both the ideals and the problems.

Just as the post-Renaissance histories tended to occlude Europe's self-understanding of its cultural roots, so too the contemporary histories fall into a similar forgetfulness of the relationship between the spiritual energies of European culture and the crises which now embrace the entire world. Thus we find many Western thinkers, after the fashion of a Hegelian or Spenglerian view, who vividly perceive the moral exhaustion and cultural erosion of the West, and conclude that the direction and hope of world history must be withdrawn from the decadent West and re-invested in the "emergent" societies. The West, it is thought, is obliged to perform the role of a midwife to the Zeitgeist being born in the non-Western world. This is yet another example of the "absolutism" that we referred to earlier with regard to the Renaissance. It completely overlooks the material and spiritual continuity between Europe and the world. Dawson, of course, did not have the opportunity to discuss our contemporary "Liberation Theology," but in a book written nearly fifty years ago -- The Modern Dilemma (1932) -- he notes the role of a "religious absolutism" in this historical thinking:

> Religious absolutism rejects any compromise with modern civilization and puts its hope in a purely religious solution that transcends all temporal forms. The religious absolutist is prepared to agree with the secularist that modern civilization has gone too far to turn back, but so much the worse for modern civilization. Europe is under the sentence of death, but Christianity will not perish with it. It will turn to the new peoples and find fresh opportunities for its spiritual mission in the civilizations of the future.[93]

Dawson would be the first to agree that the Christian religion should not be equated with Europe, and that its ongoing task is the "mission among the Gentiles." But whatever one would want to say about the role of Providence, it is an historical fact that European culture was formed by the Christian religion, and that it is this culture that has become international.

In an essay entitled "The Spread of Western Ideologies," Dawson remarked that the "Communist will argue that this is a necessary stage in the evolution of modern culture; that as the feudal Christian order was replaced by the bourgeois humanist order, so the latter must now give place to the new social order of scientific social ideology based on modern science."[94] In other words, Europe has made its contribution, and like John the Baptist, must now give way to the new order. Dawson responds by saying that what Europe has given to the modern world is the archtypal pattern of its own foundation, though distorted and without its religious center of unity. The non-European world has received in the ideological form of mass movements, the ancient European cultural ideal of progressive moral reform; and it has received the scientific and technological results of European humanism, yet in a way that is divorced from the religious and transcendent pole of the original synthesis. In short, Dawson argues that Europe has given the world a broken image of its own Christendom, and the underlying cause of the problem is Europe's historical and spiritual amnesia. The recovery of the West's historical self-understanding is inextricably related to relevance of Christian culture. As Dawson writes: "For Europe is the only cultural area in which all the ideologies meet, and it is the only culture which still maintains a living contact with the deeper spiritual traditions which underlie and transcend the ideologies."[95]

As Europe stood on the brink of suicide in 1935, Edmund Husserl -- a German Jew, and the patriarch of the school of Phenomenology -- presented a lecture to the Vienna Cultural Society on the theme of "Philosophy and the Crises of European Humanity."[96] Husserl asked why it is that "no scientific medicine has ever developed [as] a medicine for nations and supranational communities?" Have the humanistic disciplines so richly developed by European humanity failed to provide in the domain of the spirit what the modern sciences have provided in their sphere? In a vein quite similar to Dawson, Husserl urged that the crisis has to be understood in terms of "an entelechy inborn in our European civilization which holds sway throughout all the changing shapes of Europe and accords to them the sense of a development toward an ideal shape of life and being as an eternal pole." There exists, he said, an inner kinship of spirit among European peoples that transcends national differences -- it is "something unique here that is recognized in us by all other human groups, too, something that, quite apart from all considerations of utility, becomes a motive for them to Europeanize themselves."

For Husserl, the spiritual birthplace of the European telos is the ancient Greek nation in which there arose a "new sort of spiritual structure"

46

called philosophy, or the ideal of a universal science. Philosophy, or science, he said, "is the title for a special class of cultural structures" which even in their variety and changing historical shapes constitute the "style-form of European supranationality." Through the intentional life of individuals, and suffusing that of social units, and finally including the organism of nations bound together as a supranational culture, the infinite goal of "philosophical and scientific humanity" is what distinguishes the shape of European history from all other types of historical development. Thus, Husserl argued that the crisis of Europe is the divorce of scientific activity, with its progressive acquisition of even more sophisticated techniques, from the spiritual and humane telos that gave it birth, and which is essential to its regulation. The de-spiritualization of science represents a fall of European culture (and with it, the rest of humanity) into "barbarity."

We shall cite the conclusion of Husserl's lecture because however close it may be to Dawson's thinking, it illustrates the fundamental misconstrual of European history that Dawson's metahistorical analysis is meant to correct. Let's allow Husserl to speak:

> The "crisis of European existence," talked about so much today and documented in innumerable symptoms of the breakdown of life, is not an obscure fate, an impenetrable destiny; rather, it becomes understandable and transparent against the background of the teleology of European history that can be discovered philosophically. The condition for this understanding, however, is that the phenomenon of "Europe" be grasped in its central essential nucleus. In order to be able to comprehend the disarray of the present "crisis," we had to work out the concep of Europe as the historical teleology of the infinite goals of reason; we had to show how the European "world" was born out of ideas of reason, i.e., out of the spirit of philosophy. The "crisis" could then become

distinguishable as the <u>apparent failure of rationalism</u>. The reason for the failure of a rational culture, however, as we said, lies not in the essence of a rationalism itself but solely in its being rendered superficial, in its entanglement in "naturalism" and "objectivism." (emphasis in the original)[97]

The speech is eloquent, and is rightly understood as a classic expression of the humanistic element in the philosophical community of this century. But is it true that the philosophical spirit of "Athens" is the foundation and telos of European culture, its "entelechy" as Husserl puts it? Or is it not precisely the secular historical vision that owes more to the naivete of the Renaissance than it does to "Athens"? Dawson, of course, argues that a recovery of the philosophical telos cannot deliver the medicine for the sickness of Europe, for European culture was nver built upon humane rationalism, but rather was constituted in a synthesis of humanism and a transcendent-oriented religion. Husserl does not so much as mention the element represented by "Jerusalem," much less the role of the Christian religion.

The issue between Husserl and Dawson is finally a question of the discernment of spirits. Dawson's metahistorical analysis takes as one of its principal themes the insufficiency of the humanisms such as that of Husserl. It is not a demonic spirit, but a worldly one that in failing to accurately name the problem is ultimately helpless before it, and indeed becomes part of the problem itself. Writing in his <u>The Judgment of the Nations</u> in 1942, Dawson stated: "It is therefore impossible to dismiss the claims of Christianity as irrelevant to the problem of international order, for the demonic powers which have entered the empty house of secular civilization are not to be exorcised by the economist or the politician: religion is the only power that can meet the forces of destruction on equal terms and save mankind from its spiritual enemies."[98] The attempt to remain in the myth of post-Renaissance modernity, and therein to exorcise the demons of the present age is not unlike the story told in Scripture:

> When the unclean spirit has gone out of
> a man, he passes through waterless
> places seeking rest, but he finds none.
> Then he says, "I will return to my
> house from which I came." And when he
> comes he finds it empty, swept, and put
> in order. Then he goes and brings with
> him seven other spirits more evil than
> himself, and they enter and dwell
> there; and the last state of that man
> becomes worse than the first. So shall
> it be also with this evil generation.
> (Mat. 12.43-45; RSV).

NOTES

[1]The Crisis of Western Education. (New York: Sheed and Ward, 1961), p. 137.

[2]Dynamics of World History. Edited by John J. Mulloy. (LaSalle: Sherwood Sugden & Co., 1978), p.387f.

[3]Ibid., p. 262. Of course, the fundamental issue behind his The Crisis of Western Education is the need to balance the Scholastic curriculum with the study of Christian culture. He was not very successful in convincing the Catholic educators of the time. As James Hitchcock has remarked in a recent article entitled "Postmortem on a Rebirth - The Catholic Intellectual Renaissance": "it was customary for Neo-Scholastics to speak rather patronizingly of Dawson's work, since he was doing mere history, where generalizations were of a lower order of significance than those supplied by metaphysics .... [He] was held in suspicion by some Catholics because of his refusal to make Neo-Scholasticism, or indeed any philosophy, the center of the Catholic intellectual enterprise." (The American Scholar, v. 49, n. 2, Spring 1980). In April of 1960, Dawson delivered a lecture at St. Mary's College, Notre Dame, defending the idea that there do exist distinctively Christian materials to be studied in a program of liberal arts; it was subsequently published in Thought (v. 35, n. 139, Winter 1960). For an exchange of opinions on Dawson's lecture, see the articles by John J. Mulloy and J. George Lawler in the Harvard Educational Review (Spring 1962). Now that the Scholastic philosophy has been swept away in the wake of Vatican II, one can appreciate Dawson's point, for the attitude that now justifies the abolition of Scholastic philosophy as an obsolescent science is not unrelated to the view taken by many of its former proponents — i.e., that as a system of ideas, it stands on its own, without

the need of theology, history, literature, or culture in order to carry its weight in the market-place of ideas. Many of the same Catholic educators who, before the Council, looked upon Dawson's program as dangerously innovative, regarded him afterward as a conservative.

[4]Dynamics of World History, p. 273; cf. p. 244.

[5]Ibid., p. 272.

[6]Ibid., p. 293.

[7]The Formation of Christendom. (New York: Sheed and Ward, 1967), p. 108.

[8]Enquiries into Religion and Culture. (New York: Sheed and Ward, 1933), p. 238.

[9]In a memorandum written by Dawson on August 22, 1953 in reply to certain questions raised by John J. Mulloy, he said: "In my view and dominating my whole life work, the key problem is that of Theology and History."

[10]Dynamics of World History, p. 234.

[11]Adversus Haereses, I.1. Trans. E. R. Hardy, in Early Christian Fathers, Edit. Cyril C. Richardson (New York: Macmillan Co., 1970), p. 358.

[12]Dynamics of World History, p. 235f.

[13]Understanding Europe. (New York: Doubleday-Image, 1960), p. 221.

[14]The Crisis of Western Education, p. 131.

[15]Remarques de l'Essai -- II, Oeuvres, 21; as cited in Eric Voegelin, From Enlightenment to Revolution (Durham: Duke Univ. Press, 1975), p. 9.

[16]The Crisis of Western Education, p. 163.

[17]The Formation of Christendom, p. 18f.

[18]Ibid., p. 19.

[19]Ibid., p. 18.

[20]As an example of the power of the narrative method, we might consider the influence of Mathias Francowitz's (alias Flaccius Illyricus) Centuries of Magedeburg upon the debates of the Reformation period. Published serially between 1559 and 1574, the object of the work was to rewrite history in order to show that the Lutheran Church is the Church of the Apostles. It was regarded by Protestants and Catholics alike as the single most effective tract of the period. The Pope commissioned the German Province of the Society of Jesus to refute the Centuries; but Peter Canisius, writing to Francis Borgia (Superior General of the Jesuits), replied: "Hardly a man among us is even moderately versed in ecclesiastical history." Baronius, whose Annals really appeared too late to do the job, admitted in the preface that "nothing had hitherto been so much neglected in the Church as genuine, sure, and exact study of ecclesiastical history, and its adequate narration in books." In his biography of Bellarmine, James Brodrick notes that the incident of the Centuries alerted the young Bellarmine to the fact that "not by syllogisms only was the Lord to save His people." See, James Brodrick, Robert Bellarmine: Saint and Scholar (Westminster: The Newman Press, 1961), pp. 43ff.

[21]Voegelin, op. cit., p. 18.

[22]Dynamics of World History, p. 245.

[23]Ibid., p. 237.

[24]Ibid., p. 249.

[25]Paul Ricoeur, Truth and History (Evanston: Northwestern Univ. Press, 1965), p. 94.

[26]Ibid., p. 94. Cf Dawson's essay entitled "Christianity and Contradiction in History," Dynamics of World History, p. 262, where Dawson emphasizes that the fundamental Christian insight into history is its essential duality.

[27]Ibid., p. 95.

[28]John Henry Newman, Essay on the Development of Christian Doctrine, Introduction (Middlesex: Penquin, 1974), p. 69.

[29]Understanding Europe, p. 222.

[30]Dynamics of World History, p. 235.

[31]Memo, op. cit., to John J. Mulloy.

[32]Ibid.

[33]De Catechizandis Rudibus, Vl.10. Trans. by J. P Christopher; The Catholic Univ. of America Patristic Studies v. VIII (Washington D.C.: Catholic Univ. of American, 1926) p. 35. It is interesting that whereas Dawson begins the sacred history with the calling of Abraham, St. Augustine designated the first age as the period between Adam and Noah (cf. De Cat., XXII.29). I am not sure how to explain Dawson's position, except to say that he perhaps wanted to underscore the relation between the sacred history and culture, and thus Abraham stands as the Father of the sacred community.

[34]Gregory of Tours, The History of the Franks, I.1 Trans. Lewis Thorpe (Middlesex: Penquin, 1974), p. 69.

[35]City of God, XXII.30.

[36]The Crisis of Western Education, p. 140f; The Formation of Christendom, p. 14f.

[37]The Formation of Christendom, p. 240.

[38]Ibid., p. 173.

[39]Ibid., p. 271.

[40]The Crisis of Western Education, p. 131.

[41]The Formation of Christendom, p. 14; Cf. Dyanmics of World History, p. 184f; Progress and Religion (New York: Doubleday-Image, 1960), chapter VII.

[42]The Formation of Christendom, p. 99.

[43]Ibid., p. 15.

[44]Cf. Enquiries into Religion and Culture, Religion and World History, Dynamics of World History, and Medieval Essays. In this paper we shall cite the essay as it appears in Enquiries into Religion and Culture.

[45]Enquiries into Religion and Culture, p. 224.

[46]Ibid., p. 238.

[47]Ibid., pp. 232ff; The Formation of Christendom, pp. 111ff. Also, see his essay "Cultural Polarity and Religious Causes of Schism" (Dynamics of World History, pp. 80ff).

Here, Dawson suggests that: "heresy as a rule is not the cause of schism but an excuse for it, or rather a rationalization of it. Behind every heresy lies some kind of social conflict, and it is only by the resolution of this conflict that unity can be restored .... But, whatever view we may take of the causes of any particular schism and the social significance of particular religious movements, there can, I think, be no question but that in the history of Christendom from the Patristic period down to the modern times, heresy and schism have derived their main impulse from sociological causes, so that a statesman who found a way to satisfy the national aspirations of the Czechs in the fifteenth-century, or those of the Egyptians in the fifth, would have done more to reduce the centrifugal force of the Hussite or the Monophysite movements than a theologian who made the most brilliant and convincing defense of Communion in One Kind or of the doctrine of the two natures of Christ. Whereas it is very doubtful if the converse is true for even if the Egyptians had accepted the doctrine of Chalcedon, they would have found some other ground of division so long as the sociological motive for division remained unaltered" (Dynamics of World History, p. 81, 86.).

What Dawson has in mind from a social perspective is similar to a distinction made by Ronald Knox in his work Enthusiasm. Knox distinguished between "mystical" and "evangelical" types of enthusiasm: the former tending to emphasize spiritual immediacy (e.g., Quietism), and the latter tending to stress the eschatological and moral struggle (e.g., Jansenism). Knox points out that while the "mystical" type often develops a heterodoxy with regard to speculative doctrines, the "evangelical" mode tends to cultivate an "excess of charity: regarding the practical, moral, and political sphere. Augustinianism, he said, has provided in the West the "dogmatic background of revivalism."

[48]Enquiries into Religion and Culture, pp.198ff, ad passim.

[49]Ad Demetrianum, c. iii. Cited in Enquiries into Religion and Culture, p. 198.

[50]Dynamics of World History, p. 239.

[51]Progress and Religion, p. 132f; Enquiries into Religion and Culture, p. 258.

[52]Dynamics of World History, p. 109.

Russell Hittinger

[53]<u>Enquiries</u> <u>into</u> <u>Religion</u> and <u>Culture</u>, p. 231f.

[54]Eusebius, <u>The</u> <u>Ecclesiastical</u> <u>History</u>, X.9.   C.F. Cruse (Grand Rapids: Baker Book House, 1974), p. 438f.

[55]<u>Enquiries</u> <u>into</u> <u>Religion</u>, p. 255.

[56]Ibid., p. 255f.

[57]<u>The</u> <u>Formation</u> <u>of</u> <u>Christendom</u>, pp. 129ff.

[58]Ibid., p. 152.

[59]<u>Medieval</u> <u>Essays</u> (New York: Doubleday-Image, 1959), p. 19.

[60]Ibid., p. 23ff; <u>The</u> <u>Formation</u> <u>of</u> <u>Christendom</u>, pp. 132ff.

[61]<u>Christianity</u> <u>in</u> <u>East</u> <u>and</u> <u>West</u> (LaSalle: Sherwood Sugden & Co., 1981), p. 61.

[62]<u>Enquiries</u> <u>into</u> <u>Religion</u> and <u>Culture</u>, p. 62.

[63]<u>Progress</u> and <u>Religion</u>, p. 132.

[64]Ibid., p. 134f.

[65]Ibid., p. 135.

[66]<u>Religion</u> <u>and</u> <u>the</u> <u>Rise</u> <u>of</u> <u>Western</u> <u>Culture</u> (New York: Doubleday-Image, 1958), p. 23.

[67]<u>Medieval</u> <u>Essays</u>, p. 73.

[68]<u>Religion</u> <u>and</u> <u>the</u> <u>Rise</u> <u>of</u> <u>Western</u> <u>Culture</u>, p. 21.

[69]<u>Medieval</u> <u>Essays</u>, p. 64f.

[70]Ibid.

[71]Christopher Dawson wrote that: "When the Christian way of life, which is the center of Christian culture, is reduced to its simplest elements and organized on the basis of first principles, it is practically indestructible and can preserve its institutional form indefinitely. This has proved to be the case with the Benedictine way of life, and it is thus perhaps the most remarkable instance of the indestructible element in Christian culture" (<u>The</u> <u>Formation</u> <u>of</u> <u>Christendom</u>,

p. 177); cf. The Formation of Christendom, p. 213.

[72]Dynamics of World History, p. 237.

[73]Ibid., p. 364f.

[74]Religion and the Rise of Western Culture, p. 23.

[75]Understanding Europe, p. 28f.

[76]Dynamics of World History, pp. 354ff.

[77]Christianity in East and West, pp. 104ff.

[78]Dynamics of World History, p. 355.

[79]Ibid.

[80]John Stuart Mill, On Liberty (Indianapolis: Hackett, 1978), p. 61.

[81]"Perspective Series," University of Notre Dame, February, 1975.

[82]Progress and Religion, p. 18.

[83]Descartes, Discourse on Method, Part-II. Trans. Haldane & Ross (Cambridge: Cambridge Univ. Press, 1931), p. 87f.

[84]Ibid., p. 90.

[85]Christianity in East and West, pp. 49ff.

[86]Progress and Religion, p. 143f.

[87]Dynamics of World History, p. 355.

[88]Understanding Europe, p. 28.

[89]The Judgment of the Nations (New York: Sheed and Ward, 1942). Essays in Order. By Jacques Maritain, Peter Wust, Christopher Dawson; with a General Intro. by Dawson. Essay written by Dawson entitled, "Christianity and the New Age." (New York: Macmillan Co., 1931).

[90]Christianity in East and West, p. 29.

[91]Ibid., p. 32.

[92]Ibid., p. 43.

[93]Medieval Essays, p. 31f.

[94]Christianity in East and West, p. 112.

[95]Ibid., p. 114.

[96]Husserl, The Crisis of European Sciences and Transcendental Phenomenology, Appendix-I. Trans. David Carr (Evanston: Northwestern Univ. Press, 1970), pp. 269ff.

[97]Ibid., p. 299.

[98]The Judgment of the Nations, p. 220.

THE THEOLOGY OF RECAPITULATION:
UNDERSTANDING THE DEVELOPMENT OF
INDIVIDUALS AND CULTURES

Paul M. Quay, S.J.

1
INTRODUCTION

For some 400 years now, Western intellectuals
have been fascinated, first with the diversity, then
with the internal structure and the history of particular cultures, and most recently with the laws
governing the rise and fall of any culture whatever.
The new disciplines that resulted, especially philosophy of history and cultural anthropology, grew
vigorously and came gradually to take to themselves
the task of adequately explaining man to himself, of
saying what can be said about the meaning of human
existence, a task formerly reserved to divine revelation.

This is no accident. The passion to develop a
philosophy of history, to weigh and balance cultures,
and to understand the causes at work in their development -- a passion that is itself a highly specific
and characteristic trait of our modern Western
culture -- seems to have arisen from the efforts of
the academic establishment (the Renaissance universities) to remediate, transcend, and eventually to
relativize the claims of the Church and the torn-off
members of the Body of Christ. It was to escape
from an understanding of the world rooted in divine
revelation that philosophy of history began during
the Enlightenment,[1] as a sort of substitute for
the Christian view, which finds no definitive solution in time for man's woes and no intelligibility

to his history that remains solely within this world. But if one would cut away the supramundane and yet would not regard the life of the entire race as a tale told by an idiot, full indeed of sound and fury but signifying nothing, then the intelligibility must be extracted somehow from man himself and his world.

Despite the best efforts of novelists and philosophers, however, it has been hard to convince people that meaning and intelligibility of an exclusively intramundane sort can be drawn from the lives of single individuals. "The life of quiet desperation" lived by the Jewish bourgeoisie of turn-of-the-century Vienna has by now become the life of Western man generally.

Hence, at least part of the drive towards the study of the history of cultures comes from the size of the unit, from the hope that what seems random and happenstance at the level of the individual may show some true pattern as one takes the average over an entire culture. But even this does not suffice. Since, as Dawson so persuasively demonstrated, a culture arises from a religion, not the religion as some sort of by-product of the culture, to gain the intelligibility sought one must turn to the comparison of many cultures and many religions, standing above or apart from them all in order to grasp the overall intelligibility of their rise and fall in time.

The great explanatory systems that resulted were not exercises of idle speculation. "Knowledge is power", the slogan runs. Understanding was sought in order to control, direct, and improve human cultures. These explanatory systems were gnostic responses to the Christian faith, each a _gnosis_ that would bring salvation. Now, despite the fact that these efforts contributed much to our understanding of ourselves through the detailed investigations of human cultures carried out by anthropologists, yet the promise of all the great explanatory systems seems always to have withered before fruition.

If one takes into account that what some rejoice in as progress others abominate as degeneracy, one can see that the major thinkers in this domain are in agreement that Western culture is in serious decline. From Hegel and Marx through Spengler to Toynbee, Jaspers, and Dawson, almost all attest to the virulence of the disease that ravages the traditional Christian culture of the West. A reasonable consensus has been reached even as to the causes, or many of them, for this state of affairs though, again, limned sadly by some as decadence, with exultant defiance by others as progress. Toynbee gives little more ground for optimism than Spengler, despite his difference of manner; and Spengler is not really more grim than Hegel. Thus, the faith of the secular humanist in an ineluctable progress has come to resemble nothing so much as Faustus' petulant reliance on the word of Mephistopheles; and the underlying despair is the same in each.

Christopher Dawson seemed no less gloomy in his assessment of the current state of Western culture. "The events of the last few years," he remarks in 1947,

> portend either the end of human history or a turning point in it. They have warned us in letters of fire that our civilization has been tried in the balance and found wanting -- that there is an absolute limit to the progress that can be achieved by the perfectionment of scientific techniques detached from spiritual aims and moral values.[2]

Probing the matter further, he says,

> We are faced with a spiritual conflict of the most acute kind, a sort of social schizophrenia which divides the soul of society between a non-moral will to power served by inhuman techniques and a religious faith and a moral idealism which have no power to influence human life.[3]

This comment about "a religious faith and a moral idealism which have no power to influence human life" points, I think, to the root of the bleakness on all sides. The great practical works of charity of our own day, such as the Pro-Life movement, the Catholic Worker, the original Cana

59

Paul M. Quay, S.J.

Conference, the work for those dying in destitution begun by Mother Theresa of Calcutta for the mentally and physically handicapped by Jean Vanier, and many others, while finding some small resonances among those academics who have been disappointed by the gnostic emasculation of our culture, seem all to have in common that they have grown up in independence of, even defiance of, the academic and regnant cultural world. Any religion, even Catholicism, that allows itself to be bound by the chains that a gnostic academicism would impose on it, even if it were to retain intact its faith and worship, is certain to have no chance of influencing positively the life of any group of men. Faith itself is given for hope; and both, for charity -- the love that grows from faith and gains its courage from hope, and that dies if it is not freely active.

Yet, as Dawson was intensely aware, the Church has had from her earliest days to wrestle with these problems: What is the proper relation of the newly converted gentiles to those rooted in Israel according to the flesh? And how much allowance should be made for Jewish culture, as distinct from Jewish religion and true faith? (For, the problem of circumcision can be looked at from this aspect as well as its strictly religious one.) How is the Church (the new Israel) to be related to the State (pagan and emperor-worshipping Rome)? How are the various and profoundly different cultures of the ancient Mediterranean and Near-Eastern worlds all to be one in the one Church? How can the Christian understand the rise and fall of the Roman empire theologically, despite the would-be Gibbons of Augustine's day? What can, in brief, human cultures contribute, if anything, to salvation?

The Fathers of the Church worked out a theory of all this, though not in terms of the categories we are accustomed to using. I should like to introduce what I think to be their thought, while extrapolating, generalizing, and extending it, and putting it into the language and thought patterns that we use, trying to remain faithful to the basic thrust of their thought.

The topic falls naturally into four sections: 1) the life and growth of one individual Christian through one lifetime (the case of primary interest

60

to the Fathers); 2) the relation of the Church to that growth and development of the individual Christian; 3) the growth of societies and cultures on the natural level alone; 4) the Church's development in those societies and cultures in which she has taken root, and their growth as a result of her influence.

2
RECAPITULATION BY THE INDIVIDUAL

2.1 SUMMARY

Patristic teaching concerning the psychological and spiritual growth of the Christian is rooted in the insight that all things, human and divine, "things in heaven and things on earth", are summed up in Christ. He is that Image of the invisible God according to which we have been created, as natures no less than as graced. Our natural being and our supernatural are both created in Christ and for Christ. Anything that revelation has to say about us on either level tells us something about Christ. On the other hand, if we live in Christ, we must live in Him in accordance with His own mode of life. His life, then, serves as a pattern for ours. And anything revelation has to say about the Son of Man must state something about Man, whose son He is; about us, to the extent that we really do live in Christ.

Now, starting with St. Irenaeus, there is a clear teaching that Christ's own life had a pattern,[4] that which is determined for Him by His being the Christ of the Lord, the fulfillment of the promises of God to Israel. This pattern Irenaeus speaks of as <u>recapitulation</u>:[5] Christ in His earthly life re-did all that Adam did. The Second Adam summed up in action, "recapitulated," all that the First Adam had done, before the Fall and after, doing well what the former Adam did ill, doing perfectly what he did only stumblingly. Origen gave the doctrine a larger development, emphasizing that Christ recapitulated not only Adam's life but the history of God's people from Adam to Christ, and that all who live in Christ must do the same. By the time of his great Cappadocian successors, e.g., St. Gregory of Nyssa, the notion of recapitulation seems to have become sufficiently common property of

61

the entire Church that its use no longer called for explanation or even comment.[6]

In its strongest form, "recapitulation" names a principle intended to shape the entire life of the Christian: By that grace which is our life in Christ, each Christian is meant to recapitulate in one lifetime all that God led His people through from the fall of Adam to the death of Christ and then, in the same lifetime, to live in the freedom of the Spirit through the time from Christ's harrowing of hell and resurrection till His Second Coming.

The transition from the life of recapitulation of the Law and Prophets to the life of the apostles and those saints of the New Law shown in Acts, a life that is freely directed by the Spirit, corresponds to Jesus' passage out of this world by His death on the cross to His taking His seat at the right hand of the Father and pouring out His Spirit upon His disciples. It is a transition from the life characterized by active prayer and growth in the moral virtues to that which is characterized by the passive prayer of infused contemplation and the total domination of charity. That process of spiritual, and also psychological, growth which, without this outpouring into our hearts of the love of God, would take as long as the time from Abraham to Jesus (indeed, far longer: from Adam to Christ) can be compressed from 2000 years into the short span of an ordinary Christian's life. A development of this seemingly simple notion in enough detail to show its power for the spiritual life of the Christian will lead directly to its application to the growth or decay of cultures and, in an analogous way, to development or decline within the Church.

This means that the individual Christian is meant to relive -- not as the Jews did, however, but in Christ -- the whole pattern of the Old Testament, as the first portion of his spiritual journey in the Lord. This pattern is normative for us. Only if we accept it and live through it, shall we arrive at that fullness of charity and conscious love of God and our neighbor that is our restoration, even on this earth. Nor, without it, will we ever find the response to Dawson's problem of a religion that has no influence on its culture.

THE THEOLOGY OF RECAPITULATION

2.2 TYPOLOGY

One could speak at this point, as I may not do if I am to keep this paper within reasonable bounds, of the theological framework for this principle of recapitulation. Those who have done some reading in the earlier Fathers know that their basic mode of theological understanding was what is known as typology. They saw Old Testament people and events as "types" of New Testament ones, that is, as having a meaning given them by God (not by the human author of the book), which meaning is found in Christ and His mysteries and manifested through the New Testament.

St. Paul has a number of passages where he is quite explicit about this, e.g., the passage in 1 Cor.10:1-11, where he speaks of the rock that followed the people through the desert as a type of Christ, or the slaughter of the Israelites in the desert as 'typical', that is, serving as an exemplary warning for us. A good number of other New Testament passages expressly designate one or other Old Testament text as typological.

The majority of recent exegetes have regarded this mode of understanding as of little use for contemporary theology. Promising as it looked, for example, in the hands of Fathers de Lubac, Daniélou, and others, it seemed in last analysis to involve an inescapable arbitrariness of interpretation. Much of what is called typology in the Fathers seems to be only extravagant allegory, hardly a basis for a doctrinal understanding of God's word. Further, if only God knows directly the spiritual meaning of any Old Testament figure or incident and if He has given us in the Scriptures only a few such meanings, how can we presume to ascertain others on our own?

The exegetes who set aside the work of de Lubac et al. have missed, I think, two things: a) an understanding of our recapitulation in Christ, by our sharing of His life, as the dynamic principle underlying typology; b) in consequence, the insight that the whole of the Old Testament, without exception, is the type for the New Testament.[7] It is not simply that this figure serves as a type for this other. But the entirety of all Old Testament persons and events are types of Christ and His

63

Church.

This relationship that we call typological, which grounds the insight that real people, real happenings, historical events, all have a meaning, given to them by God, over and above the meaning they have in themselves as grasped by ordinary, human understanding, is the very specific relationship called by the New Testament their "fulfilment" in and by Christ.

Fulfilment is not the same thing as simple similarity -- which would make typology into the sort of extended metaphor or allegory that many have thought it. Consider a simple case. Christ is set forth quite explicitly in the New Testament as the New Moses, leading the new people of God out of the Egypt that is slavery to sin and Satan. How, then, is Moses the type of Christ? For, Moses does many things that Christ never does: killing the Egyptian, fleeing to Madian, marrying two wives, casting his rod before Pharao and his magicians, and many other things which our Lord is never reported or thought to have done, even in some analogous way. But everything that Moses does fits into a pattern which is found in its perfection only in Christ, as the pattern of a plant is found somehow in the seed from which it grew. Everything that the old people of Israel did, therefore, forms a pattern found in its fulfilment in the new people. This fulfilment is a relationship of growth, of development; therefore, of similarity but also of dissimilarity. The plant looks very different when it flowers than when seen only in its germ.

Typology was for the Christians of the New Testament period their mode of explaining to their Jewish brethren who Jesus was and is. Invented, apparently, as a theological method only a hundred years before among certain Jewish groups, it was developed to the point that they realized that the Christ of the Lord would be the fulfilment of all that had been done in Israel.

So, when Jewish Christians spoke, as we see in Acts of the Apostles or in St. Paul, of Jesus as the Christ -- remember how Saul, newly converted spent his time in the synagogues showing and proving "that Jesus is the Christ" -- it was in typological terms:

THE THEOLOGY OF RECAPITULATION

All the promises of the Old Testament find their Yes in this Jesus, whom you crucified. He is the fulfilment. Those who live in Christ, therefore, are those who will live the same life that Christ lived, a life in which all that had been promised, all that had been accomplished by God in Israel and indeed, before Israel, to the whole race, from the Fall until our Lord came, is relived perfectly in Him. In other words, the relationship of fulfilment-in-Christ, which is the distinctive characteristic of typology, can only be adequately understood when it is seen to imply the process of recapitulation. It is by this life-of-Christ, relived in Christ by each Christian, that the meaning of the Old Testament figures and events in their entirety is finally made manifest.

2.3 RUDIMENTS OF RECAPITULATION

Here let me leave the abstract level and sketch out in some detail the simplest form of this notion of recapitulation. Though doubtless there will be more unanswered questions at the end than at the beginning, it will at least provide a sort of image or picture of what I am talking about.

A child is born in Adam, fallen. The life it then begins to live is one that accords with the life of the beginnings of our race as described in the Scriptures.

Cain and Abel: You say, "I've never seen an infant offer sacrifices that were rejected or induce another infant to accompany it into the fields in order to kill it there from envy." But remember that passage in the _Confessions_ of Saint Augustine (1.7) in which he recalls having seen a baby being nursed at the breast and another baby who had been at that same breast livid with envy. He then remarks that, "'Innocence' is the weakness of infant limbs, not the spiritual attitude of infants."

What else is shown us there, in those early days, as belonging to the infancy of our race, that any small child, that all of us have ourselves long ago lived through? There is the child's sense of living forever. The child indeed knows of death, learning of it very early through the squashing of

Paul M. Quay, S.J.

insects, the dying of flowers, the killing of animals or birds for food. So, he does not issue an absolute denial of death or think that life goes on infinitely long in any literal sense. But in a practical sense he sees things much as did the author of the fifth chapter of Genesis, a world where no one dies till after centuries and centuries and one dies young if, like Henoch, he dies after only 365 years. People live on equivalently forever; life will go on like this indefinitely; it has been like this forever. Whatever the child finds about it as it grows up seems to it the way the world has been from the beginning.

Noah: a very good picture of a small child's view of utter wickedness and true virtue. There are only good people and bad ones. When the Lord tires of the wicked ones, He simply wipes them out. The just survive -- note, all of them members of the one family. There is no sadness; there is no hint that Noah missed or regretted the loss of àll his fellows or that he was lonely with none save his small family. The small child, hearing the story of Noah, never questions whether he was sorry for all those peoole who were drowned. They were wicked and were wiped out; one doesn't feel any more sorrow for them than for goblins or witches or other wicked people.

The tower of Babel: The small child has no sense of impossibility. Anything is possible. Anything can be done. There is no sense in a small child's world that there are physical, psychological, or other limits placed on human accomplishment. So, if they wish to build a tower up to the sky, to scale heaven, to impose their will on parents or on God, they set about to do it.

If the child is baptized, it grows for a long time very much as a pagan child would, so far as human vision can see, even though capable of spiritual recapitulation, on the condition that these major traits of the pre-patriarchal period are positively dealt with by its family: that sibling enmity be controlled under pain of an exile like Cain's; that the family has the deep stability that generates the sense of "foreverness"; that the child senses its family to be good, however bad the neighbors may be; and that the child learn to submit its will to God's, especially as expressed in the limits

66

imposed upon it by the reality of the world around it.

The child has now reached a level corresponding to that of Abraham at the beginning of the patriarchal period. Abraham was one whose morals were far from what we would regard as adequate for a Christian. Most Christians, in fact, when they first read about him are a little scandalized. And yet, he was a man who believed, and who believed at whatever cost, whatever the Lord said to him. And that faith -- simple faith in the Lord and simple acceptance of His promise -- was accounted to Abraham as righteousness. The Scripture here simply bypasses any question as to the quality of his morals; it does not concern itself with whether he was a moral man for his day or whether he was better or worse than his contemporaries. Yet the implication is clear (and Paul will later make it wholly explicit) that only because of his faith did he have anything that could be accounted to him as righteousness. The Lord's call for his faith was about all he could understand and respond to. It was, in any event, the only thing the Lord was concerned about. Given that, He could lead him further. Without that, he could go nowhere.

This faith of Abraham was a childlike, unquestioning faith. He met Melchizedech, the priest and king of Salem, specified as the (pagan) priest of El Elyon, one of a myriad deities then worshipped in Palestine. This god of the Canaanites he takes as the one God who had called him forth, El Shaddai. God, whatever His local name, is simply God for Abraham. There is no question posed by Abraham, or for that matter by Melchizedech, as to these being two different gods. Abraham is not a polytheist; but, like the small child, simply assumes that all men worship the God whom he knows, to whom he is devoted.

When God asks him for the great sacrifice, the death of his only son at his own hands, he sets about to offer it. The Lord spares him the actual execution but he must carry it out all the way to the raising of the knife. And this too is typical of a small child's real religion. It is simplistic, if you wish, but it is very deep and capable of enormous sacrifice -- or enormous repudiation and rejection. A small child, when called upon for such a sacrifice, say by the death of a father or mother or of a little brother or sister, someone deeply loved, can rebel against God fiercely, with a rebellion that may, apparently, last a lifetime.

The child that has been baptized will begin to live spiritually much as did Abraham, chiefly in the way it receives God's approaches with an inchoate freedom that may well be capable of moral choice long before the age of reason.[8]

After Abraham, corresponding to the later patriarchs, the child continues to grow in its consciousness of the Lord. Boys (quite characteristically, it seems, much more often than girls) make vows and promises to God, "If You will do this for me, I will do that for You." They do as Jacob, who when starting out on the long journey to get himself a wife, pours oil on a stone he sets up as a stele, the rock he'd used to support his head as he slept the night before, and says, "If You will protect me and bring me back safely to this place, then You will be my God." There is, of course, a veiled threat: "If You don't bring me back this way as asked, then I won't take You as my God." But the Lord seems not to take this transaction amiss, or the similar vows of children.

Later, Jacob and his family go down into Egypt. The subsequent generations fit unobtrusively into their surroundings -- so much so, that the Scriptures tell us exactly nothing of the entire period (in this and many ways analogous to the latency period of later childhood) or of any of those who lived in it. Yet Israel remained separate in fact from the Egyptians, since acting as shepherds for them, who regarded this occupation as unclean. The Israelites, however, seem to have had no horror of Egyptian idolatry or manner of life so long as they did not have to take part in it themselves; and their separateness seems to have been protected chiefly by their employment. So, the child before adolescence, the young Catholic -- or the young Jew for the matter -- learns his religious identity from more or less accidental social differences, but makes no radical distinctions in terms of his inner life, his own relation to God.

THE THEOLOGY OF RECAPITULATION

The going forth from Egypt on the night of the Passover marks the point at which one leaves childhood spiritually and becomes a young adult, i.e., the true coming to full use of one's "reason" (as in "the age of reason") so that one is now capable of marriage, solemn vows of religion, and mortal sin -- to follow St. Thomas (e.g., S.T., II-II, 189.5.c and ad 1). Hence, the passage through the Red Sea is, as has been constantly maintained since St. Paul at least, the type of our baptism into Christ and our being taken into His people, the Church. If so, then the period between Abraham and Moses corresponds to a stage in which the Christian child will differ in a very few but important ways from the non-Christian child, though remaining very like him in most, even religiously. Before Abraham, one could argue that baptism makes no appreciable psychological difference to the child, i.e., the infusion of the supernatural powers of the life of grace in Christ, remaining untouched by any personal activity (i.e., without even inchoate freedom), does not manifest itself in the growth of the child.

Till Abraham, whether the child is Christian or not will make relatively little difference to its recapitulation; it will grow up much the same in any culture in which the conditions for this period are met, as discussed above.[9] But from Abraham to Moses, the Athenian child, say, would begin to differ appreciably from the Jewish child, being readied for a culture that will over-intellectualize and will set too high a priority on the fine arts, rather than being trained towards a freedom in the Lord that is already sacrificial in content. But only at Moses' level does either reach a freedom of choice that is known to be always at hand, for which one is responsible at all waking moments.

With adolescence, the youngster becomes acutely and passionately conscious of its self, as well as often miserably self-conscious, like Moses making his excuses while looking unhappily at the ground in front of the burning bush and worrying about his lack of speaking skills. But, perhaps in compensation, he does as the Jews did, who went out from Egypt as a motley group of tribes under Moses' leadership to receive a new law[10] which was to constitute them a people. As with the adolescent, the Law comes down in fire and thunder and threats:

69

Paul M. Quay, S.J.

"Anyone that touches the mountain will die, even an animal." No explanation is given as to why Israel should do these things save that the Lord so wants it. Do it, or else...! So, the youngster is told God's law also and the penalties for breaking it.

He, too, belongs to a people, and is, say, an Irish catholic democrat, even as the ancient Jew had his religion, his politics -- there wasn't much, but what of it there was (e.g., the intrigues of Aaron and Miriam, or the revolts of Dathan and Abiron and Korah) -- his laws, his culture, and all else, all given him simply by being one of this people. The varied aspects we carefully distinguish were all there squashed into one. There was no purely secular activity in Jewish life then, and very little that was exclusively sacred (remember how many sacrifices ended with a sacred banquet for all participants); they tended to fuse together. If you wanted a sheep to eat, there in the desert, you had to have it slaughtered by the priests and its blood poured out on the altar in sacrifice. The priests would then take their prescribed portion from the victim and give you back the rest of the sheep to eat. All actions, except the offering of incense and holocausts, were what most modern society would call both secular and sacred. As the believing child quickly learns at adolescence, all of his life, waking and sleeping, down to its least details, falls under the gaze and judgment of God and is to be governed by His commands.

Something else is very typical of the slightly later state described in Judges. The people are greatly devoted to the Lord under a certain judge. He dies and they fall away into the worship of the false gods of their neighbors. They are punished, and call upon the Lord, who sends them another judge to save them in His name. But after him, they fall away again, again are punished, again repent, and so on, a perpetual seesawing, back and forth. The whole book of Judges is constructed so as to underline this instability. So, adolescents go limping, as Elijah was to say of Israel much later on, unable from day to day to make up their minds which way they're going to go, whether it be a matter of chastity or of faith or of use of their newly discovered reason or of their relations with their families or of almost anything else in their lives.

70

THE THEOLOGY OF RECAPITULATION

A bit later, we come to David. David is, if
anybody, the young man on the make, who has sized up
his culture and estimated his opportunities for
getting ahead. He is not above demanding protection-money so that his men in the desert may not be
turned loose to raid or destroy the property of
others. Yet, he is just, according to his lights.
If you pay the protection-money, not a sheep is
stolen; his men keep their hands off your property.
And though he is "a man of blood", he will not kill
to satisfy private vindictiveness nor lay hands on
the Lord's anointed, even to avoid risk to his own
life. Yet he knows how to take full advantage of
every situation. But he consciously does these
things before the Lord (and in simple conformity
with the culture of his people), at least until his
adultery with Bathsheba and the murder of her husband.

With Solomon, we find a man somewhat older. He
has now got it made. He has money, women, power,
all that it takes. But he is already weak in his
faith, not as to belief apparently; but he isn't
much concerned about its practical consequences.
With three hundred wives and six hundred concubines,
Scripture asks us to consider him the wisest of
men -- few mysteries of the faith seem harder to
accept at first glance. But wisdom among the Jews
of his day was a practical virtue, not an Augustinian enlightenment; and in context, so great a harem
was pretty clearly not principally a matter of
sexual satisfaction but of prestige and power. Who
but a great monarch with endless wealth could support such a ménage? And if he was as virile as the
size of his harem suggests, one might think him a
potent warrior against anyone who crossed him.

Solomon wasn't much concerned about the prohibition on mixed marriages, like many a Catholic
since (so long as it all gets blessed by the Church
or, in his case, not publicly disapproved by the
priests). Even his marriages to all those pagan
wives, simply of themselves, he could probably have
gotten by with. The harem was not his sin. His sin
was that he allowed these women to worship their
false gods on Jewish territory, in the very shadow
of the Lord's own Temple, which Solomon himself had
built. He introduced idolatry among God's people,
not as their practice but as something that could be

tolerated in others who were living among the people of the Lord -- what is now called "pluralism" in religion. Then, as since, settling down and enjoying all the good things of human life, especially in a position of power, leads one easily to an early stage of religious indifferentism. He may personally retain the truths of faith but considers them pretty much a private matter, certainly not important enough to let them cause any civic or familial disturbance, even among those for whom one has responsibility, who are under one's authority.

This same tendency to subordinate the practice of religion, if not one's faith itself, to the utility of the state or merely the convenience of the individual continues to grow under the later monarchy. Things come to the point where kings are against human sacrifice (of infants offered to Moloch) "in principle"; most of them would "never do it themselves". But they do not wish to make an issue of it. And though they do nothing to prevent people from going out to the valley of Hinnom to burn their babies alive to placate Moloch -- or, worse perversion yet, the Lord -- they still find no problem in going up regularly to the Temple to worship the Lord. Whether they think the foreign gods really exist is not clear. In any event, they wish to play it safe, just in case. The kings and people are too weak in faith to act on their belief that the Lord alone governs the world -- if they really do believe it at all. They are too addicted to their way of life to let it be carelessly threatened by not taking the same precautions as their pagan neighbors, culturally so far their superiors.

In the meantime, the prophets have been doing something very different. They have begun to understand the Law from within. Seeing it more and more clearly as a direct expression of the Lord's will and coming to love Him more and more, they no longer see the Law as simply an imposition, no matter how legitimate, from without. What David did without reflex understanding in interiorizing the Law, -- for, without being able to explain it to himself or others, he had a true instinct for its weightier demands, for "justice and mercy and faith", while yet walking in great freedom without fears or constraints, thus startling, even astounding his contemporaries -- these prophets were able not only to live but to understand and express. They could say why God had given the Law.

A high point in this interiorization is reached when Jeremiah denounces, in the Temple itself and speaking in the name of the Lord of the Temple, the worship his countrymen are offering in the Temple, because he knows so well what the Temple is for. He has understood what the worship of the Lord in the Temple according to all the ritual prescriptions of the Law and custom is meant to signify and imply about the Lord and one's own life. He sees that a sacrifice is worthless unless the offerer is at least seeking to live what is signified by his sacrificial act. Of course, they don't want to hear his message, they set upon him, and will seek eventually to kill him.

We too, if we live reasonably well, as we grow more mature, find this same transition taking place in ourselves. The young adolescent's carrying out of the Law under threat and out of fear or, even at times, of terror, is gradually transformed, as he lives in obedience to the Law. He gradually learns how to act with less of fear and more of an inner understanding growing out of his experience of right and wrong actions. He sees that the Law is indeed good. He understands it as we Catholics have tended to understand the natural law, the law of our nature. God commands these things, not as a despot or because He wishes to force our wills by arbitrary commands, but because He made us so that only in this way can we live and function well and fully.

The Exile is, of course, the great interruption. If one has been living badly, this is the great punishment that God uses in His mercy to bring him back. But even those who had lived well, like the prophets, and who understood the Law rightly did not, save in their descendants, survive the seventy years. These descendants came back to Jerusalem, however, a people chastened, thoroughly freed from idolatry themselves, though still it seems tending to compromise a bit on intermarriage with pagans. At long last, Jews were firm and convinced monotheists -- no other gods were real to them, whatever their personal lives might be. Above all else, the cult and worship of the Lord in His Temple, newly rebuilt, was now the center of their lives.

73

The same is characteristic of those who have grown sufficiently in the Christian life, who have lived long years, often years of exile, their own or their share in others', and then begin to recapitulate this long four hundred years when there was only silence from God. There was no prophet from Haggai till John the Baptist; no word came from the Lord for four long centuries. The people had to live on the memory of the Lord's great deeds, by faith. They were being tested by time itself, day after day after day -- intermixed with persecution for those who held firm. There was not only the persecution from the pagan world outside. Their national life and their religion were mined from within. They were betrayed to the pagans even by their own high priests. Yet a faithful remnant, led by the Maccabees for a time till their line too was corrupted, held on against everything, in faith, centered on that worship of God in Jerusalem, no matter how corrupted by the high-priestly party of the Sadducees, no matter that often they could take no direct part in that worship, either because the pagans had seized Jerusalem and the Temple or because they themselves were scattered far and wide in the Diaspora. Their great virtue was fidelity; they continued simply to hang on in spite of everything.

Notice how I & II Chronicles, compiled in this period, tell much the same story as the two books of Kings yet very largely reinterpret their materials in terms of cult and the Law, very much as a Catholic adult who looks back over his childhood and all his earlier life, seeing it new, facing it all with the same simple honesty that the Deuteronomist and the Chronicler display in recounting their sins and those of their fathers, about which wickedness they no longer have any illusions. They have offended the Lord; they can fully acknowledge their sins and accept their punishment; and yet, in all this, they recognize His continual mercy. They have repeatedly deserted Him; He has never, they now see, deserted them. So, they love the Lord; and His Law is now seen as the greatest of the marks of His love for Israel. Even Ben Sirach, crochety old fellow that he was, found the Law the very embodiment of God's mercy and presence among men.

This was, it would seem, the great theoretical problem of the Pharisees with our Lord. When He came, <u>He</u> claimed to be the mercy of God incarnate, the Law <u>and</u> the Lawgiver literally embodied. He found, on His arrival, a people well prepared, as Gabriel had said. A people with a strong culture, nurtured on solid knowledge of the true God, refined and purified for so many centuries, they were ready for His coming. But His coming was to be a fulfilment, to require yet further growth, not to be a mere projection from the past.

Too many among them were unwilling to empty their hands sufficiently to recieve this new and greatest gift of God to His people, by which they should become His own flesh and blood. They did not wish to relax their grip on all the good gifts God had given them in the past in order to receive this one that summed up all that had gone before and brought all gifts to completion. Those who refused Him, it is worth noting, did so by rejecting what they could not understand even though warranted by miracles and purity of doctrine and consistency with the best of their own past -- a rejection quite unlike the rejection by prophets and faithful of the deceivers and betrayers of earlier days or, more recently, by devout Catholics of teachers of false doctrine. The Pharisees sensed Christ's newness as a threat, not truly to the Law and the Temple but to their possession of the Law and the Temple. Closing upon themselves and excluding ever more rigorously the claims that charity makes even with regard to false teachers, they shut out that which would have led them to a life of fulfilment of the Law and the Prophets, the new life given by the Holy Spirit, in the Christ of the Lord.

It is this life of intense charity, in which no obstacles to its dominance in either personal or communal life are allowed to stand, in which the true mystical life of infused contemplation begins, that was the life of those early Christians who seemed so unsurprised when the Lord would appear to them or speak directly to them. Their Lord, long ago dead on the Cross but now risen and glorious, constantly directs them, encourages them, tells them where they are to go, how long they are to stay, what places they should by-pass on the apostolic journeys.

But this freedom in the Spirit, by whom the love of God is poured out in our hearts, cannot be had by those who block out His love, who refuse this great and difficult step in their growth, by which they would come truly to love their "enemies", as they first perceived our Lord and His followers, to do good to those who, they thought, might hate them, to pray for those who could provoke, at least, the Romans to "persecute" them by coming to take away their city and their holy place.

This is the step that St. Theresa of Avila speaks of as the one between the third mansion and the fourth, one which, she opines, most Christians do eventually take, though many of them only towards the end of their lives, having waited much too long. Yet, I think it is not possible for us to hurry the process. It is a process through which we must grow, by the activity of the life we live in the Lord. Yet, if we cannot hurry it, surely if we understand it better, we might by God's goodness do less to impede it.

3
RECAPITULATION WITHIN THE CHURCH

We have seen that each individual Christian who is alive in Christ necessarily recapitulates in Christ all that He recapitulated. This we are enabled to do through the Church, His Bride and our Mother, the Mother of every Christian. It is she in whose womb we are implanted, once conceived by the power of the Holy Spirit, and in whom we grow until she brings us to birth into the glory of heaven (Gal.4:24,26,31).

But we have already been reborn into newness of life by baptism. Hence, it is also the Church -- her mystery now seen from another vantage point -- who provides the connatural context within which all this complex process of growth in Christ can take place.

For, the Church is the Body of Christ. If Christ grew to maturity by recapitulating the whole of human history till His day, doing this as no one else can do, perfectly, flawlessly, without fault, and therefore most rapidly, so must His Body do, albeit imperfectly and often reluctantly and slowly. For, the Church is part of Him, one with Him; He the Head, the Church His members, together the Whole Christ, living with but a single life, the life of that love of charity that His Spirit pours out in our hearts because we are cells in His Body whom the Spirit anointed with the fulness of that Love. Since, then, Christ's life is typified by the Old Testament, so is that of His Body; so, also, through membership in that Body, is the life of each individual Christian.

The Church, then, is called to present herself to every Catholic in such a way that he can find in her that which he needs at his current stage of individual development if he is to develop further. So, the Church must always be at once pre-patriarchal, patriarchal, Mosaic, monarchic, prophetic, exiled, rebuilding the ruined Church on earth, and waiting through seemingly endless time for the coming of her Lord, strong in her law, devout in her worship, as well as filled with the charisms of the Holy Spirit. Otherwise, she fails to provide an adequate bodily site and organic support for the Christian's growth, and he is seriously hampered in his efforts to grow through all the stages of his recapitulation.

Obviously, too, the Church must be present to all her children at all these levels in a way that is distinctively and integrally Christian; for otherwise, the time-scale is that of millenia, not decades.[11] One need think only of the Roundheads. Refusing patristic tradition, they sought to live according to the Old Testament pattern not, however, by recapitulation in Christ through the sacraments and the Church but as the Old Testament people did. So, despite their intentions, they thus became, spiritually speaking, like Jews of Moses' or Joshua's days and ceased in some essential ways to be Christian at all.

But if the Church is the Body within which each Christian grows, it is through the mediation of the various organs of that Body that this "cell" is nourished and supported. His natural family is meant to represent the Church to him when young, to be that part of the Church most completely and

77

Paul M. Quay, S.J.

importantly present to him in his early growth. Other social organs such as schools, parishes, clubs, or whatever others a given culture affords, each is meant to play a proportionate role in helping the youngster develop in the likeness of Christ.

All this has many implications for the Christian way to raise a child. For example, in early adolescence what is needed is not permissiveness but law, surrounded with a certain amount of inaccessibility and thunder and lightning. For, the adolescent needs someone to push against, to measure himself against, if he is to gain his proper self-identity with respect to his parents. Only if lines are strictly drawn, fair sanctions prescribed and accepted, not, however, with terror but in love, can the young person really grow. Obviously, he may resist, even rebel, break away completely. But only so can he begin to face the mystery of his own will and accept the responsibility for his own actions. Should he push against his parents (or the Church in her representatives) and find only a timid and yielding jelly, the harder he pushes, the less he finds himself distinct. He remains, helpless and hopeless, till he can somehow force a separation that will then, all too often, be tragic.

It is, I think, for this reason that the Church must always have some sort of law, whether codified as canon law or with some other culturally determined structure. But law there must be, understood in its strictest sense: commands that obligate, imposed by legitimate authority with reason, who can punish and instill a just fear, injunctions that restrict freedom not only of the individual but of the community. Without such, the individual will never, without miracle, recapitulate beyond the level of Moses. Without the Law, he can never learn how to transcend the Law through charity, but will waste much of his life in never-resolved, adolescent resentments or rebellions against those in authority.

Yet the Law is only a pedagogue to Christ, an old slave to supervise our behavior while we slowly learn the lessons God has set for us. And we shall learn with reasonable speed only if we are taught the Law in love and, from the start, live the Law in Christ as we grow in knowledge of Him.

THE THEOLOGY OF RECAPITULATION

There are some things that cannot be typified directly of Christ but which are truly typified of us: the fall, sin, guilt, punishment. Hence, we can look to the Old Testament to see what God thinks of our sins and to see the ways He prefers to punish us at the different levels of our growth. For, the punishments He exacted from Israel changed their character in the course of time. The manifestation of what is far and away the most severe punishment was reserved for the New Testament. Hell is first described here, apart from the indefinite account given only fifty years earlier in Wisdom.

Because of his sins, the Christian can die to the life of Christ, fall from grace, be lost. Yet even though filled with sin, he can still be a member -- corrupt and corrupting -- of the Body of Christ. The Church, unlike her Lord, is a refuge even for unrepentant sinners. This, too, God typified in Israel -- from the idolatries under the Judges, the sins of disobedience of Saul, the religious "pluralism" of Solomon, the social injustices of Ahab and Jezebel, the slaughter of infants for Moloch leading to the Exile and beyond -- God's people were actively sinful, deliberately malicious. Thus, even when dead to Christ, the Christian can -- in His Church -- recapitulate, but now the negative side of the Old Testament types.

4
CULTURAL SUMMATION

Most discussions of the history of cultures, Dawson's included, make abundant use of analogies between the cultures considered and living organisms: cultures are said to grow and develop, show vigor, reach their prime, wither, decay, and die. Using the principle of recapitulation, we wish to convert these simple analogies into something stronger, into an analytical tool, a means not only of understanding but of assessing, though not in a quantifiable way, the degree of development of a culture.

I should like to make a sort of technical term out of the phrase, "the psychological (or spiritual) level of maturity" of a culture. If speaking of a psychological level, we are referring less directly to the average level of psychological development that the people of this culture have reached than to the level of maturity that this culture fosters or that it assists the younger members of the community to reach with comparative ease. If we speak of the level of spiritual maturity, then we are speaking of that level of spiritual recapitulation which is characteristic of the adult culture, as mediated to the child chiefly by his family, and which the youngster, from his own vantage point, senses rather than sees. In brief, it is the level towards which he can grow with relative ease, with the support and understanding of his family and people.[12] To spell this out a bit, when one examines any particular culture, he finds that it is very easy for a normal youngster in that society to grow up to a certain level. Any of the Kwakiutls, so much discussed by anthropologists, of the Pacific Northwest, grew up easily enough till very early adolescence -- according to the calendar, one might say. They were marked by an astonishing lavishness in giving, pouring out upon others blankets, food-stuffs, precious metal plates, whatever was prized in the way of possessions. This was the way one showed one's self a man (warfare was practically unknown among them, at least in part due to their physical isolation from hostile groups). The great man was the one who gave endlessly and abundantly, who could show himself as among the most generous and liberal of all. Of course, the one to whom you had given would seek to show himself an even better man than you by giving away even more. The ultimate in this not very well disguised contest was so to bankrupt yourself by giving that those to whom you gave would be forced, if they were to save face, to give more than they could afford and be irrecoverably ruined, while you recouped all your losses.

Most youngsters of "gang"-age in our culture would have little trouble understanding and even sympathizing with what was going on there. But a young adult is likely to find very little resonance in himself with such boisterous squandering. He has outgrown it.

If you were a Kwakiutl, while your culture would bring you very quickly to that stage, more or less on schedule, beyond that there would be very negligible development. And if you began to grow a little beyond this level, you would meet opposition, the opposition of your entire culture. This means opposition from within your own self as well as opposition from others. They do not understand where you are going or why you are acting so; neither do you. All you recognize is that something within is stirring or moving you towards something not yet provided for by the culture.[13]

Even without further thought, one can see that growth to human maturity necessarily will involve suffering -- a suffering that, for the Christian, can be made part of one's share in Christ's cross -- for we are called to grow in Him beyond any limits of culture whatever; and every culture, having so many who are still children or very immature, must, if its people are not all beyond child-bearing years, perforce have an average age that is lower than that of its saints. The following of Christ must lead to opposition by the less mature spiritually towards those more mature, for as less mature, they have no way to understand from within themselves what these others are really about. If they themselves are humble enough, even at a lower age, they can let the more mature be, with relatively little opposition; but recall that even Aaron and Miriam came into opposition with Moses; and Sarah laughed in the tent because her faith was not that of Abraham, great though it was in fact (Heb.11:11-12).

Notice the implication here. There is a sense in which any culture has what might be called a naturally recapitulative aspect. A particular development may have taken thousands of years for the culture as a whole to reach, say, to know how to kindle fire and tame it for cooking and the hearth, to come up with the idea and practical know-how for pottery utensils, to go from stone to bronze, or to go from hunting to agriculture. For pottery, say, a certain degree of sedentary life is called for, hunting and gathering being replaced by an incipient agrarian life. There is also a change in religion in this transition from hunter-gatherer to farmer: one tends increasingly to enter into the processes and movements of nature itself, on their own terms, rather than to continue simply to overpower nature, to pluck or uproot it, or to trap or spear it and drag it off to one's cave.

In all this long, slow growth of technology, there develops, in dynamic interaction with it and in some ways conditioned by it, the cultural, the interior, the spiritual aspects that define the culture. Yet any child of a pottery-making culture will be making little pots in mud almost from infancy. The idea will be part of him, even if he never gains the least technical know-how. By the time he has reached adulthood, he has recapitulated in a natural sense or, as I should prefer to say of this natural process, <u>summed</u> <u>up</u> in himself that culture, which took thousands or even millions of years to develop to this point. He can be, at twenty, more sophisticated about pots and their decorations than his aged grandparents.

Yet, at least in a purely oral culture, he will usually do very little if anything to change the culture further, for to live by the tradition and continue it is of vastly greater importance than to invent novelties. He is unlikely in the extreme to go much beyond the level of his culture, either in these technical matters or in the moral and religious outlooks which gave rise to them and which, in turn, will have been, little or much, modified by them.[14]

A culture which has never received any revelation from God that is meant to direct and govern the people of this culture as a group[15] is a priori very unlikely to have a level of spiritual maturity that is very high in comparison with one in which the Church has been active for some time. For, the progressive summing up of a culture has no other life-principle at work within it than the sin-damaged one of human nature in society. Hence, the growth encouraged will be in many ways corrupt and perverse, to say nothing of the simple limitations of what we have called its age or level of maturity.

Note too that the growth we are speaking of is manifest only in certain aspects of the personality, in particular skills and cultural traits. The unity of the person guarantees, I think that no such growth is without link to the rest of the personality; yet it can leave many aspects at a seemingly much more primitive level.

82

THE THEOLOGY OF RECAPITULATION

As with the individual, each culture has its own seasons, known only to God. And, at any given time, each culture is different in the level it has reached, in its openness or closedness, in its readiness -- in God's plan, not ours -- to hear the Good News. This pattern is already visible in Israel considered in relationship to the nations. From the first, Israel leads all its neighbors not, clearly, in the cultural goods of this world -- where was Israel with respect to Egypt in art, or poetry, or even in the sort of wisdom that was eventually to become a mark of the Israelite sage? -- but in that sober sort of maturity, that facing of the reality of the world and of man in it, all in relation to the Lord, which we find in the earliest parts of the Bible. Even when Israel was very primitive by our standards, he was ahead of his neighbors in spiritual and, one might argue also, psychological maturity. Yet, also characteristic is the fact that, save for a few brief periods, he was constantly tempted to regress and fall behind them.[16]

5
RECAPITULATION BY THE CHURCH

5.1 THE BRIDE OF CHRIST AND MOTHER OF THE NATIONS

We looked briefly at the recapitulation which takes place within the Church, by her power to share with each of her members the life through which her Lord brought each mystery of the Old Testament to its fulfillment by His living of it perfectly. This recapitulation within the Church, however, need not be looked at merely as a particular process within each individual Christian. We should consider also the net effect of all such processes.

For, as II Vatican strongly stressed in Lumen Gentium, the Church is also the new people of God, the new Israel, indeed, the only Israel that is in full continuity of life with the Jewish people of the earlier Covenant. Here, then, the type serves to designate the Church directly, with Christ, the new Moses, at her head, leading her into the Promised Land.[17] And all that is said of Israel in the Old Testament serves to typify the Church, Israel's antitype, who must grow as did her type, though in Christ. This she does by the aggregate effect of the recapitulations of all her members. Indeed, whole peoples and cultures can be influenced by the Church through even a few of her members' growth and influence upon those around them.[18]

Yet, the aggregate effect of the growth of Christians among a people is not explicable solely as a sum of individual recapitulations nor merely as a new kind of internal influence upon the culture. Rather, there exists for the Church, as for ancient Israel, a mode of recapitulation by the entire Church, whether as one universal society or, more easily discerned by human minds, as she grows in each people or cultural region. For, as the Lord espoused Israel, when once she had reached "the age for love" (cf. Ezech. 16.) but required of her continued growth as His bride, so the new Israel is the Bride of Christ. Hence, she too must grow to maturity if she is to be worthy of her Spouse. This growth, when first beginning among a new people, may take place in the long, slow manner of the outcast, wild girl; but its proper mode is that of a life in union with her Spouse, yearning for the eschaton when their union will finally be consummated. Individual recapitulation comes about rapidly, by the power of the grace of Christ, within a single lifetime. The recapitulative growth of the Church takes place far more slowly, at more or less the same rate as the old Israel's, I would suppose.[19]

As Christ's Bride, then, the Church is the Mother not only of each individual Christian but of each entire people, society, and culture. When she reaches a people for the first time, she begins to raise their cultural "ceiling", lifting them above their natural summing up of their own prior cultural development. This she does, not directly but by bringing them into a genuine recapitulation. They must come to live by an inner principle of life that is, in truth, no longer "their own" in the sense of being an independent generator of the specificity of their manner of life, though it is most intimately "their own" since Christ's life has become truly theirs. In principle, there is no upper limit to this raising of their spiritual and cultural level short of the full maturity of the manhood of Christ.

Now, the Church, simply as such, apart from any

embodiment and enfleshment in a people and a culture, is not possible save as a theological abstrac-
tion. Since no body is immaterial or exempt from
space and time, the Church, as Christ's Bride, made
one flesh with Him (Eph. 5) must always be with Him
incarnate, in a particular people and in a determi-
nate culture and through a certain span of historical time.

Thus, as the Church spreads from one people or
culture to another through the centuries, in each
she takes root (Ecclus. 36). She enters a culture
and begins to grow from infancy (recapitulatively
speaking) toward adulthood, though an adulthood always deferred until "the fullness of the gentiles
comes in". Individuals within her usually grow far
more rapidly, especially her saints. These form, by
their union, organs within the culture not only to
aid and foster the growth of other individuals but
to invigorate the whole Body.

The process of individual recapitulation is,
then, a process by which the Catholic, having absorbed his culture into himself from birth, winnows
it, selects from it, ignores much of it, both psych-
ologically and spiritually. This cultural absorption and transformation is not optional; it is an
essential part of the Christian life.

Traditionally treated under the rubric of a-
voiding worldliness, this selectivity in the taking
on of one's culture must be a sort of unconscious
use of the cultural elements a person is familiar
with, not borrowings from an alien culture. The
Jews were often tempted to such borrowings in their
worship of the Lord, (the high places, the sacred
pillars, the golden calves, etc.). But it was their
unconscious borrowings that pleased Him, of what
seemed merely the obvious things of their life and
ways of thinking in order to give the Lord the best
of what they had, in order thereby to praise Him the
better. This selective absorption from one's culture is initiated and carried through principally by
the grace of God, working in the world according to
the times and seasons that He alone knows; it all
goes rotten if men seek on their own to modify their
practice of religion by deliberate adoption of
traits from the mentality of the surrounding
"gentiles" or by deliberate borrowing of their

5.2   THE PARABLES OF GROWTH

The Lord Himself has set before us something of
the nature of the growth of the Kingdom of God in
His many parables of growth. The kingdom of God is
like a mustard seed, like wheat sown in a field,
like good seed among which cockle has been scattered, like a vine, etc. Consider what all these parables really say about the Church. Too often we take
the plant being described as referring to ourselves
or to the growth of God's grace within our soul and,
so, miss the chief point of the parable, which is to
tell us about the Kingdom of God on earth, the
Church in her growth.[20]

Now, in each such case, growth takes place that
is rightly described as the growth of the mustard
plant, of the stalk of wheat, of the vine. But
whence comes this highly specific growth? It is the
principle of life hidden in the seed that brings a-
bout the growth charactistic of the species and
without which there would be no growth at all. Yet
the plant looks nothing like the seed. It has become what it is by sinking its rootlets into the
well manured and dark soil, whence it has selectively absorbed most of the material needed for its
structure. All that additional substance was drawn
from the air and the soil, activated by the light of
the sun (which has always symbolized the grace of
Christ for the Christian) all, however, from outside
itself, by the power of the life it has within it.
It does not take in everything that the soil has;
most of the soil remains there, inert and unchanged.
It can happen, too, that what the plant does absorb
from a poisoned or unhealthy ground will destroy it.
And both earth and air conceal active agents of
destruction, cut-worms and blights, fumes and flying
pests.

So it is with the Church as she enters into a
people and their culture. She takes in from them
all the natural elements of her being, absorbing
from the midst of every sort of rottenness and decay
almost everything that she will visibly be, but
growing steadily and strongly in her own way because
animated by the one principle of life which is the

Spirit of Christ. All things human are mixed together on earth in a mucky soil far darker and more
ill-smelling than any compost-heap. But the Church
draws out of this soil all that she needs for growth
except for the hidden principle of her own life and
for the human agents, martyrs and missionaries, who
scatter the seeds. The Church takes from the culture its arts, its crafts, its styles of thought and
patterns of action, all that this people have been
accomplishing by natural summation through all the
long millenia in which the Lord has left them "to
walk in their own ways," without His revelation, yet
not leaving Himself without witness (Acts. 14:16-
17). During all this season, He lets their natural
culture grow as it will, wildly, twistedly, often
terribly, but overlooking the sins of men, not holding them against them (Acts. 17:30 and Rom. 3:25).
But when He chooses at last to let the warmth of His
Spirit, like the spring winds, under the radiance of
His Son cause the seeds there planted to germinate,
then that life pushes out and the newly sprung
Church takes from that dark soil those things that
are compatible with her life and that she can transform by Christ's life into her own substance. She
absorbs these things spontaneously, easily, simply,
because they suit the current exegencies of her
life, providing what she needs for continued growth.

The Church is not a hunter, to track down and
kill animals to feast on. That was what Esau did;
and he lost to Israel his inheritance and the Promise. She does not go out consciously hunting things
in her surroundings with which to improve her own
status, as do those who envy the pagans their satori
and their mystical experiences of insight or emptiness. Her nourishment is of a different sort and
she has no need of meats from "gentile" sources to
enrich what the Lord has given her.

Whenever the Jews "went hunting", they fell into sin and were punished. But what they took in
spontaneously, without even knowing that they were
borrowing, simply because they wished to give the
Lord the best they had and because this seemed to
them not attractive elements from their neighbors'
religion but the best portions from their own (already acculturated) life -- all this He accepted
gladly.

Paul M. Quay, S.J.

For example, after the Exile, when they set about to restore the Temple and their public worship of the Lord, they took in without realizing it all sorts of elements from Persia and Mesopotamia. Judiasm in the strict sense begins with this return from the Exile, a culture quite drastically distinct in its human traits from the culture of their grand-fathers some seventy years before, precisely because they had absorbed into their ordinary lives, from the pagans among them whom they had been scattered, so many ways of thinking and acting. Even as they lamented that they could not sing the song of the Lord in a strange land, by the mere fact of living or, for most, being raised among alien peoples, they were absorbing all sorts of new elements from that culture, which they carried back with them to Palestine quite unconsciously and which they built into the House of the Lord and their worship of the King of Heaven (a Persian title for Him that they had taken over).

So, each of you here, not a whit less than the most avant-garde of the new theologians or philosophers, are all twentieth-century Catholics. The major difference between you and so many of those whose faith seems to have been blighted by today's choking cloud of secularism is that you live from your roots. You and those like you are taking many of the characteristic elements of American culture, quite without realizing you are doing so, and are putting them to work, humbly and quietly, in the service of Christ. You are aware that you are root-ed in a largely unhealthy soil and that the Church in this country draws in that which weakens her as well as that which can give her strength. But in any case, in the Lord's own time and according to His unknown decrees governing the seasons for the nations, the Church here is growing, we may hope, branches, leaves, flowers, and fruit. Perhaps even, as seems to have happened in the England of St. Thomas More's day, all is to be turned under before flowering or fruiting in order to make the soil better yet (another way, I think, to describe the Exile).

Or we might use St. Paul's image of the domestic olive tree of Israel into which we gentile branches have been grafted. But it is peoples, not cultures, that are grafted in; the cultures must be at

88

least as much transformed by Christ as Old Testament Jewish culture ever was.

And, indeed, if any claimant to the title today looked anything much like the "early Church", so beloved by reformers of every age, the one thing we would know instantly about her would be that she is not the Church of Christ. It is the Lord Himself who pointed out how little the mustard plant, in whose branches all the birds of the air build their nests, looks like the least of all the seeds. It is precisely her infinitely varied inculturations that make the Catholic Church visibly and manifestly a candidate, at least, for being that Church which is animated by the same life-principle as the primitive Christian community.

In brief, the Church herself grows, inculturated, recapitulating within her own history the history of God's earlier people, whose spiritual descendants we are, who are the true Jews even if according to the flesh but gentiles.

One can catch glimpses of this recapitulation in the early Church. The Gospel, as first preached by Paul to the pagans, without other reference to the Law than to attack the iniquity of those setting it against his preaching of Christ, was misconstrued and misapplied precisely because his new Christians were not developed enough culturally to grasp what had been presented to the "people well prepared". So, he is forced to go back, as at Corinth, to teach things already known at the patriarchal level, for example, that it is not tolerable that a man sleep with his father's wife (remember how far back it was that Ruben's similar incest had drawn on him a blessing from Jacob not better than a curse).

So, a bit later, he lays much of the ceremonial burden of Judaism upon the shoulders of his stronger Christians in Rome because of the need for charity for the weak, who still feel themselves bound by these regulations. While the diverse "ages" (as measured by the degree of their recapitulation) of those within the Roman Church caused tension and grief and trouble, yet the truly mature, like Paul himself, still more like his Master, knew how to act: they put up with and were willing even to die for the immature, even for those who had chosen

Paul M. Quay, S.J.

sinfully and freely to be such. So the Church grew gradually among the Greeks and the other cultural groupings of the ancient world, and among many more since.

In every new culture she reaches, the same process of recapitulation must take place. No steps may be skipped -- for, no matter what one pretends, they will not be; a "skipping" is merely a concealment of an immaturity not being faced and, therefore, not being grown beyond. Perhaps the major fault of much modern psychiatry and clinical psychology, especially as practiced within religious communities, is that it seeks to force adulthood or to make people reach it without the pain and long effort of inner and truly recapitulative growth.

Christian apostolate, therefore, cannot be defined solely in terms of preaching the Good News so as to bring about the conversion of individuals to Christ and their incorporations into His Church. Also needed is the development, mostly through these converts, of their culture so that it becomes the suitable and effective medium for raising up new generations in a still easier approach to the Lord. This does not mean that anyone's salvation is determined by his culture or lack of it; but, as creatures of flesh, we find that even the externals of our lives are means of grace or of temptation, the so-called external graces and the external objects we call snares or temptations or occasions of sin.[21]

All of this suggests that the Church exists, in a sense, to rectify cultures and to bring them to their natural fulfillment, which can only be had through their supernatural fulfillment in her, to transform the process of cultural summation into true recapitulation. Any truly Catholic culture serves as paradigm of what every culture is meant to be. A culture that is not integrally and totally Catholic -- and, of course, none ever has been or will be such this side of the eschaton -- is as warped and impoverished as is any human individual who suffers an analogous degree of lack of likeness to Christ. Yet it is as Church that the growth takes place in the Lord, and as culture that it will have all sorts of human and even sinful and destructive components. Hence, the cultural mission of the

90

Church, if rightly conceived in Dawson's sense of culture and not in one of the restricted senses so often given it (e.g., the particularities of our own culture or of one or other leading class or group within it or of but one or other aspect of the culture as a whole, such as, say, the fine arts) is paramount and indispensable in her ministry. It is by the formation of Christian culture that her ministry is carried out.

6
CONCLUSIONS

It seems to me, in view of the Church's task of bringing all things into subjection to Christ (II Cor. 10:3-6) by leading all men to recapitulate in Christ all that happened from Adam till Christ's death and to live the life characteristic of the Spirit thereafter, that the growth of human culture is an essential element of her primary function. The Church's bond with culture springs directly from a culture's relation to recapitulation by individuals and from the essentially social nature of man and of his salvation.

Such growth is not secondary to her life, for she is Bride and Body of Him who is to fill all things. If this view is correct, the Church cannot avoid, if she is to be truly Christ's Body in this world, being passionately interested in the healthy growth of human culture. It is an essential part of her apostolate. Yet it is not one that she can well go about consciously and expressly working at. The process takes place spontaneously, beginning with her roots hidden in the darkness of the soil, drawing the nourishment she needs for her earthly structures under the power of the Sun of justice, slowly maturing till able to produce a fruit worthy of her Lord. Yet biologically identical strains of vine in different plots of a single small vineyard in Burgundy may produce fine wines in each, yet in only one do soil and sun combine to produce "Le Chambertin".

Let us return briefly to Dawson's concern over religion impotent to affect human life. One can now see, I think, that such religion is highly characteristic of certain stages of recapitulation, though for different reasons in each. But what should be clear is that the power of the Gospel resides, humanly speaking, in the outpouring of charity that is characteristic of the life of the Spirit. But this does not come early in anyone's life; and all too often, very late or never. Now, if the Academy has been the major power in the growth of the modern world and if its greatest occupational hazard is gnosticism, a living in and by the mind of man rather than by the charity that the Spirit gives, it is not hard to see why Christian academics may have had, on the one hand, so little influence for good on the culture as a whole and why, on the other, when they have reached a certain Christian maturity, they have been generally rebuffed by their spiritually less mature non-Christian fellows and excluded from direct participation in the formation of younger academics.

The response is clear. Since charity is the love that grows from faith and that gains its courage from hope, the Christian academic must live a life so governed by the full truth of Faith and so invigorated by hope in the Lord, in whose rebuffs and repudiations he gladly shares, that his recapitulation is accomplished in relatively few years, so that he may begin the life of infused contemplation and all-consuming charity before retirement. Then indeed, his religion will have influence on the world, not perhaps as he would have desired but as the Lord desires.

NOTES

[1]Gerhart Niemeyer, _Imprimis_ 6, no. 10, Hillsdale (MI): Hillsdale College (October, 1977).

[2]_Religion and Culture_, New York: Shead and Ward (1948),.

[3]_Ibid._, p. 217.

[4]Though this teaching dominates the theological thought of the New Testament, it is not made explicit there.

[5]This is the consecreted, though somewhat cumbersome, term that St. Irenaeus borrowed from Ephesians to designate this vastly complex concept, which served as the key to his refutation of the Gnostic heresies of his day.

[6]This last fact would seem to be part of the explanation of the subsequent history of recapitulative theology. For, most of those who read the Fathers have concentrated on the later Fathers, who explain their method least. Hence, over the centuries, recapitulation came to be seen as no more than an elaborate form of allegory.

[7]Raymond E. Brown, for example, is aware of St. Hilary's enuntiation of the latter insight, but sets it aside as lacking exegetical sobriety; cf. his "Hermeneutics", Jerome Biblical Commentary, Englewood Cliffs (NJ):Prentice-Hall (1968), 612. The entire section 611-619 offers a useful survey of recent schools of thought that are pertinent.

[8]We often think of "sufficient knowledge and reflection" as meaning a realistic grasp of a whole situation and its consequences. But freedom relates rather to the knowledge of oneself as capable of orienting oneself in one manner or some other. A small child clearly is rarely free in this way. Nor does it have any responsibility as yet to make itself fully free. It has no abstract, conceptual notion of freedom which it could apply to all its actions or any definable subset of them. But all this does not imply that it could never, concretely, be aware of its ability to choose and of its obligation to choose well.

[9]This does not mean that all cultures are alike at this level; they are not. Our own is a prime example of one that has regressed back to a level at which the child is very likely to grow in a stunted or seriously traumatized way. But the culture as such seems the dominant factor here, not the baptism; the life in Christ itself does not seem directly to affect the child's growth.

[10]It is well to remember that the Decalogue was something wholly new and original in the ancient Near-East.

[11]The manner in which this is achieved, through sacraments and the Mass, the Scriptures and the Tradition, the saints and movements of popular devotion, and the dynamics of this entire process must be dealt with elsewhere.

[12]This, perhaps, explains why the children of saints, e.g., Thérèse of Lisieux and her sisters, or the great Cappadocians (Basil the Great, Macrina, Peter, and Gregory of Nyssa) seem so often to have a headstart on holiness, yet why many holy people have had children who have gone far astray. Free will is not removed; but sanctity of a high level is an enormous aid to holiness.

[13]Thus, an individual's growth may be envisioned as a sigmoid curve whose pitch is the steeper the lower its upper asymptote. This asymptote or upper bound or "ceiling" represents a strong limitation beyond which it is exceedingly difficult, though obviously not impossible, to grow even a little.

[14]I would agree with Dawson that a culture grows out of a religion, rather than the contrary. Yet there can be no doubt either that the culture, if it undergoes sufficient change in its basic skills and arts, will react back vigorously upon the religion, even if not always upon those who are its official representatives.

[15]I am not excluding the possibility or even the likelihood of God's having spoken to individuals in all sorts of cultures, albeit privately, i.e., not using His revelation to constitute a people for Himself.

[16]When speaking of regression, I am not assuming a simple backsliding, a sort of passing through all the stages in reverse order. What seems more likely, in fact, is that regression represents a new road, though in an opposite sense, getting back to an analogous stage, but not, save for the impact on children, the same age. For, a culture, say, that has once been late adolescent but has regressed to early childhood, there has been a degeneration from something higher, which is a new experience altogether. For, this adult was once truly this child's age. We in the West today may well wonder if we are not, as a people, much like the Jews during the very last years of the Monarchy, the majority in some dim way seeking to have the Lord as their God, but led by rulers who, for the most part, Josiah excepted, had no such concerns at all but were willing to lead Israel and Judah in their offering of their children as human sacrifices to the gods of their neighbors for the sake of greater concord and getting along with those neighbors and in order to make sure that those other gods looked kindly upon these Jews as well.

[17]The whole Gospel According to Matthew emphasizes this Mosaic typology; cf. also, Heb. 3.

THE THEOLOGY OF RECAPITULATION

[18]Sometimes the Church's influence has been seen as coming simply from without, as an influence infiltrating, forcing its way in, or being imposed by Catholic peoples by military force or by economic, scientific, or other modes of cultural imperialism. This point of view misconceives the way in which cultural interactions, even hostile ones, take place. The Church is made present by her members, whether these are good seed or bad, and their impact on the culture is internal to that culture, even when entirely destructive, so long as the people themselves are not simply wiped out.

[19]A theological grounding for this opinion (or any other on this point) remains to be worked out.

[20]Since "The Kingdom of God is within you", as some translate it, a long tradition exists legitimating interpretation of this personal sort. But this fact does not permit one to push out of its place the primary meaning. Nor should these parables of the Kingdom be confused with the parable of the Sower who casts abroad the good seed which is the announcement of the Kingdom and its mysteries.

[21]This point is often overlooked. Protestantism, in its often iconoclastic zeal for naked faith and a gospel pure of human supports, has always been hostile to any notion of "external grace." Others, chiefly theologians and philosophers infected by Kantian attitudes, would argue that, since the weakness is entirely our own, we should never speak of anything in the world as a snare or a temptation. This latter point is not wholly mistaken; but it does ignore the embodied and enfleshed nature of humankind.

THE MATURITY OF CHRISTIAN CULTURE: SOME REFLECTIONS ON THE VIEWS OF CHRISTOPHER DAWSON

Glenn W. Olsen

Christopher Dawson defined and presented the history of Christian Culture within the conceptual framework of a succession of periods. This division of a vast subject matter was in large part due to the usual reasons which compel historians to speak of ages, periods, and other divisions of time: without sufficient delimitation of related materials, no story appears to be told, and intelligibility disappears under the weight of a mountain of facts, all with some claim on the scholar's and the student's attention. But beyond this practical concern, Dawson used the framework of a succession of periods to articulate an inner pattern and logic in the Christian historical experience. This was not the logic of an interior necessity in events, but the logic of an organic growth in which a multitude of material conditions continuously interacted with Christian teaching to produce cultural forms of life which like a yeast entered into and slowly transformed the history of, above all, the West:[1]

A Christian civilization is certainly not a perfect civilization, but it is a civilization that accepts the Christian way of life as normal and frames its institutions as the organs of a Christian order. Such a civilization actually existed for a thousand years more or less. It was a living and growing organism -- a great <u>tree</u> <u>of</u> <u>culture</u> which bore rich fruit in its season. As I say, it was by no means a perfect

Glenn W. Olsen

civilization. In its origins, it was a
civilization of converted barbarians
and it retained certain barbaric elements which reasserted themselves again
and again in the course of its history.

Dawson believed, and rightly so, that the patterns he found were not simply the work of his own
imagination. Rather, the historical materials he
examined, although being capable of examination from
many perspectives, could not be simply rearranged at
will. They were part of a natural order with its
own causal relations and integrity. Yet, Dawson did
see the history of Christendom deepening the understanding and assimilation of Christianity itself, so
that one could speak of periods of historical matur-
ation and of decline of the faith. His stance
assuredly was determined here by his own Catholicism, and he wrote both as historian and as a committed man of faith. To hold that certain periods
were more mature than others implied a normative
notion of what Christianity was, and this his Catholic faith provided him. The reflections of the
present essay are an attempt to bring to the surface
the presuppositions and implications of Dawson's
approach to his subject.

We begin with a brief definition of what Dawson
understood Christian culture to be. Dawson had
learned much from the sociology and anthropology of
his day, and again and again he lamented the narrow-
ness of his predecessors' study of the history of
Christianity.[2] Most commonly, this had been
conceived as the history of doctrine, a history
written with precious little reference to anything
but the inner history of ideas. Certainly reference
to external events, to popes, councils, and missionary enterprises, had been found too in this older
history, but rarely had the mutual influence of
Christianity on either the material culture or the
thought world of its day been examined in a way that
made clear the constraints each laid on the others.
Historians had paid little attention to the material
embodiment of Christianity, or indeed of any other
religion, in forms of culture, whether artistic,
literary, legal, or other. They tended to overlook
what some of the cultural anthropologists had come
to see as central in the study of culture, the manner in which human values shape life. As the dean

98

THE MATURITY OF CHRISTIAN CULTURE

of American anthropologists, Alfred Kroeber, argued
the case in 1952:[3]

> ...in apprehending cultures the most
> essential thing to apprehend is their
> values, because without these he will
> not know either toward what the cul-
> tures are slanted or around what they
> are organized....if we refuse to deal
> with values, we are refusing to deal
> with what has most meaning in partic-
> ular cultures as well as in human
> culture seen as a whole.

That even Christian historians would more have
assumed than described the cultural forms that
Christianity gave rise to was a special irony, for
Christianity was the religion of incarnation, of the
material embodiment of the Transcendant. Especially
here, one would have thought, Christian historians
should have been sensitive to the tendency of the
ideas of theology and revelation to permeate both
the world view and the material culture of a people,
their habitual ways of understanding and reacting to
the world. But too frequently the history of Christianity had been written as if it were the history
merely of theological development, rather than of
the leavening of the patterns of life in whole
societies under the impact of Christian belief, or,
conversely, the refashioning of Christian ideas in
the light of cultural expectations.

Against all this, Dawson saw himself as an
historian of culture, which he defined as the worldview of a people with a shared historical experience. The gap found between moral ideals and actual
behavior in every culture is if anything wider in
Christian culture than elsewhere, for Christianity
asks very much of man:[4]

> Nevertheless this does not mean that
> moral and spiritual values are socially
> negligible. They influence culture in
> all sorts of ways -- through institu-
> tions and symbols and literature and
> art, as well as through personal be-
> havior.

99

It was to the tracing of this relation between moral and spiritual ideals, on the one hand, and institutional and personal behavior, on the other, that Dawson dedicated the great portion of his scholarly life.

For the presentation of the vast subject he had undertaken to study, Dawson divided the history of Christian culture into six ages. An entire chapter, "The Six Ages of the Church," was devoted to this schema in The Historic Reality of Christian Culture, and the following year (1961) Dawson restated this schema more briefly in The Crisis of Western Education.[5] Ancient Christian Culture was divided into two ages, Primitive Christianity (to about 300), and Patristic Christianity (fourth to sixth centuries). Medieval Christian Culture was divided into two more ages, the Formation of Western Christendom (sixth to eleventh centuries), and Medieval Christendom (eleventh to fifteenth centuries). Finally, Modern Christian Culture was again divided into Divided Christendom (sixteenth to eighteenth centuries) and Secularized Christendom (eighteenth century to the present).

The very structure of this schema suggested that the story of Christendom was one of rise and decline, and Dawson's brief definition of Medieval Christendom, his fourth age, in The Crisis of Western Education, leaves no doubt that this was what he intended:[6]

> This is the age in which Western Christian culture attained full development and cultural consciousness and created new social institutions and new forms of artistic and literary expression.

It is this idea that from the eleventh to the fifteenth century "Western Christian culture attained full development" that I have repeated in the title of the present essay on "The Maturity of Christian Culture." Our task is to discover what Dawson did and did not intend by such a schematization, and to reflect on the possibilities and limitations of his analysis.

Needless to say, although Dawson was a great admirer of much in the Middle Ages, the kind of un-critical enthusiasm caught in the title of James J. Walsh's The Thirteenth, Greatest of Centuries, was far from his mind.[7] He knew that there was much in the Middle Ages that belied cultural unity, and much of which no Christian could be proud. Further, he understood that in, for instance, the later age of Divided Christendom, in spite of strife, the ex-pansion of Christianity continued. Yet he also could see that in our own age of Secularized Chris-tendom, "Western culture...ceased to be Chris-tian...".[8] Thus, in spite of all the nuance pre-sent in his treatment of the Middle Ages, the quali-fications that must enter if one is to speak of this as a period of "full development," the fact remained that he believed that in a purely descriptive sense that could be verified by anyone, enough of the his-tory of Christianity had been lived so that one could look back and clearly perceive a parabola of rise and decline.

There was more to his schematization than this, however, and this becomes clear in The Historic Reality of Christian Culture. Here, having stated that each of the six ages possessed "its own dis-tinctive character," and went through "a somewhat similar course," Dawson -- again using the organic metaphor of growth and decay -- wrote that all these ages, "except perhaps the first, pass through three phases of growth and decay."[9]

> First there is a period of intense spiritual activity when the Church is faced with a new historical situation and begins a new apostolate. Secondly there is a period of achievement when the Church seems to have conquered the world and is able to create a new Christian culture and new forms of life and art and thought. Thirdly there is a period of retreat when the Church is attacked by new enemies from within or without, and the achievements of the second phase are lost or depreciated.

If we put this together with Dawson's idea that Med-ieval Christendom represented the full development of Western Christendom, it seems fair to say that he saw the history of Christianity as a series of ages, each with its pattern of growth and decay, in which the age in which Christianity most expressed itself in mature cultural form was the period from the eleventh to the fifteenth centuries.

Dawson denied that the pattern of growth and decay expressed "some sociological law which limits...[Christianity's] spiritual freedom...".[10] Rather, "the life of the Church on earth is a continual warfare and...it cannot rely on any prospect of temporal and terrestrial success...as soon as one enemy has been conquered a new one appears to take its place."[11] Dawson illustrated this pattern by sketching the main developments of each of his ages, and from this we gain a clearer idea of what he was and was not claiming for the fullness of the medieval development. Thus he noted for the third age, the Formation of Western Christendom from the sixth to the eleventh centuries, that:[12]

> In this age, more than ever before or since, the Church was the sole representative of the higher culture and possessed a monopoly of all forms of literary education, so that the relation between religion and culture was closer than in any other period.

We may conclude that the later Medieval Christendom was not Western Christendom's most mature expression, in his mind, because of the Church's control over or permeation of high culture, or indeed because of the intimacy of the relation between religion and culture: all these had been closer, Dawson believed, in the early Middle Ages.

Indeed, in coming to his description of the fourth age of the Church, Dawson explicitly noted, in regard to the powerful currents set off by the Gregorian Reform:[13]

> ...the movement of reform was never completely successful. The medieval Church was so deeply involved in the territorial economy of feudal society that it was not enough to free the Church from secular control so long as

102

it retained its own temporal power and
privileges.

The medieval reformers were of course aware of this,
and hence the waves of asceticism which threw themselves up against these compromises with the world.
These culminated, by a kind of internal logic, in
the life of St. Francis, who by renouncing corporate
property for Dawson founded not so much a new order
as a new way of life. Further than this, Dawson was
surprisingly reticent about defining exactly what it
was about the fourth age that manifested the full
development of Western Christian culture.[14]   He
mentioned the developments of which we are all a-
ware, the revival of learning and philosophy, the
role of the universities and the papacy, but we must
conclude that in tracing the history of Christianity
his eyes were above all on that hard-to-define
entity, Christendom itself.   Thus he wrote that the
greatness of the medieval papacy was its ability to
recognize and come to terms with St. Francis, and
incorporate his mission into its own.   This created
"an organ for the evangelization of the masses and
an instrument of its international mission."[15]
Implicitly, we are to conclude that the fullness of
Christian development was expressed by two movements, one vertical and one horizontal.   The culture
of the early Middle Ages that the Church had especially influenced was high culture, the culture of
those who these days are called the elites, above
all the monks.[16]   In the high Middle Ages the
Church, although not so dominating high culture as
in the eary Middle Ages, penetrated the other ranks
of society much more completely, and, taken on
balance, Dawson seems to see this as continuing the
historical dynamic of Christianity.   We may call
this the vertical dimension of Christian maturity.
The horizontal dimension of Christian maturity seems
expressed by the quasi-political but more essentially social and religious structure of Christendom
itself, symbolized as to unity by the papacy.   Thus
Dawson immediately followed his observation of the
force that the life of Francis gave to the missionary enterprise -- above all a horizontal enterprise -- by dating the beginning of the time of decay within this age to the troubles of the papacy at
the end of the thirteenth century.   The decay was
found in the disintegration of the international
unity of Western Christendom, the breakdown of the

alliance between the papacy and the reform movements, and in the growing separatism of the national monarchies.

We are to conclude that Dawson was faithful to his initial vision, which had insisted that the history of Christianity should be written as the history of the interaction between Christianity and culture. The fullness of the Christian development was seen not to lie in the great achievements of the scholastics, or ecclesiastical victories such as the Fourth Lateran Council, as much as in the creation of a world view sufficiently common to sustain an entity which was expressed publically more in a common way of looking at the world, and a common set of allegiances, than in a visible political institution. Christendom was more than the Church, and more than any lay political structure: it was the affirmation of a public way of life and shared values. This above all the Gregorian papacy had brought to maturity, and the national monarchies, the Great Schism, and movements like the Wycliffites had brought to disrepute. The progress and regress of this Christendom, this tendency of Christianity to embody itself in a way of life, was the basis for all of Dawson's division of the ages.

This last point is made firm by Dawson's treatment of the post-medieval world. As we have already noted, he saw the age of Divided Christendom as still, in spite of all its religious division, a time of expansion. Here the expansion he had in mind seems primarily horizontal, the missions to both the East and to the new world, the latter of which was spectacularly successful in terms of horizontal growth. But he saw too a deepening penetration of some aspects of the society by Christianity. Thus in The Judgment of the Nations in tracing the ultimate sources of liberalism he argued on a grand scale that "freedom and not equality... has been the inspiration of Western culture and the whole history of Western man has been a long quest for freedom."[17] In this quest, "It was in England in the seventeenth century that the Christian ideal of spiritual freedom and the medieval tradition of political liberties came together to produce the new liberal ideology which was the main inspiration of Western civilization for more than two centuries...".[18] Now although Dawson made this statement in a chapter titled "The Failure of Liberalism," in which he noted "the failure of the liberal parties to give adequate expression to this ideology and to the still deeper social tradition that lies behind it,"[19] our point here is that on specific points he clearly saw Christian ideas reaching their fullest expression and influence at some time after the middle ages. This is perhaps even clearer some pages earlier in the same book where he saw certain developments of the modern period as the fruition of medieval developments:[20]

> It was not, in fact, until after the end of the Middle Ages when the unity of medieval Christendom had been lost that the full effects of this revolutionary spiritual change were felt. Thus the rise of Western democracy like that of Western humanism was not really the creation of a new secular culture but were the results of centuries which had ploughed the virgin soil of the West and scattered the new seed broadcast over the face of the earth. No doubt the seed was often mixed with cockle, or choked with briars, or sown on barren soil where it withered, nevertheless the harvest was good and the world still lives upon it.

Dawson could say of the Renaissance itself, "It was from the accumulated resources of their Christian past that they acquired the energy to conquer the material world and to create the new secular culture."[21] And finally he could speak of the great might-have-beens, as in the case of his introduction to Mission to Asia, where he remarked, "If there had been more men of similar courage and faith to carry on this work in the same spirit, the whole history of the world, and especially of the realtions between Europe and the Far East, might have been changed."[22] The logic of such a remark is that although the middle ages marked the most mature expression of Western Christendom in fact, it could have been otherwise: indeed Western Christendom could have become World Christendom.

We are not to be led from the main point by such qualifications. Dawson's considered judgment

Glenn W. Olsen

was that the eleventh through fifteenth centuries had marked the high point of Western Christian development. Since history is a seamless cloth, it is not surprising that on this or that point what was nurtured at one time bore fruit at another. What was at issue was whether, taken as wholes, this or that age embodied more fully a Christian view of life. The historian is forever an amateur psychologist and a speculator on the ideas and forces that control men's thought. If I may indulge in a speculation on Dawson, it seems to me that the appearance of Protestantism was decisive in his association of the middle ages with Christian maturity. His very name for the age that followed was Divided Christendom, and this suggests that, at least as far as periodization went, his eyes were fixed on the most visible and political expression of Christian culture, Christendom, more than on the other manifold expressions of culture Christianity had generated. This is perhaps illustrated by his treatment of sixteenth century learning in his The Crisis of Western Education. Here his point was to note how similar education remained across the great divide of Protestant and Catholic. The Catholic colleges and Protestant academies had much in common.[23] This observation could be extended to many other areas, and more recent scholars have indeed noted how many basic insights were shared even by Catholic and Protestant theology in the sixteenth century.[24] Both sides built their anthropology and their soteriology on a view of the world much less placid and much more tormented than that of Aquinas. Both spoke of the drama of salvation, the struggle between the forces of light and darkness, the absolute dependence of the human soul on God's grace for redemption. Both radically adjusted Christianity to the new world by turning in large measure from spiritualities of contemplation to those of meditation. The Spiritual Exercises of St. Ignatius Loyola, with their emphasis on a virile image-forming meditation and a life based on the sacraments in order to fortify oneself for struggle in the world, have more in common with Calvin, perhaps even with Bunyan and Wesley, than they do with the confidently integrated cosmos of Aquinas.[25] Dawson knew most of this, but for purposes of periodization he chose to dwell on the breakdown of medieval unity. I thus speculate that when he spoke of Christian culture he first and foremost had in mind the most institu-

106

tionalized expressions of that culture, which may loosely be termed Christendom.

We must now be clear about what Dawson was and was not claiming through the use of his schematization. First, he was not claiming that he was writing the definitive history of Christendom or of Christianity itself. Although a man of unusual breadth of knowledge, who knew much about many cultures, he carefully specified that his schema applied only to Western Christendom. We have already noted his study of the Mongol Mission, and he also took up at a number of points in his writings the history of Byzantine and other historical expressions of Christianity. These forms of Christianity knew their own historical rhythms and development, and these were often only peripherally tied to that of Western Christendom. The fate of Christianity in any particular part of the world was not necessarily the fate of Christianity in general. This fact had a bearing on his portrayal of Western Christendom itself, for even here, although the evidence of historical decline might have been taken to point irrefutably to the end of Christian culture in the West (see above no. 8), Dawson never saw this as conclusive. On the contrary, to refer to the title of one of his books again, he pointed to The Historic Reality of Christian Culture as A Way to the Renewal of Human Life.[26] He was not a Spenglerian, and hoped that Christianity could experience one of its periodic recoveries by return to roots which would signal a new age.

Second, Dawson understood the difference between intellectual history and cultural history, and he did not claim that the greatest Christian intellectual achievements had been medieval. He knew that the life of the mind could develop at a very different pace than that of more general cultural achievements, and perhaps he would not have quarrelled with the idea that the life of the mind can be cumulative in a sense that culture rarely is. Bede had shown, tucked away in a gloomy corner of the world, that the accumulated intellectual achievement of the Latin world, preserved in a library of a few hundred books, could nurture intellectual growth in the most inauspicious circumstances.[27] What if he and his brothers were surrounded by boors who jeered at them, and who needed to have their

Glenn W. Olsen

Christianity delivered to them in the form of jin-
gles sung by wandering preachers from the middle of
bridges?[28]   Here there was a striking disjunction
between the general culture, and the achievement of
the individual person.   That Dawson saw Christianity
exerting its greatest cultural influence in the high
middle ages did not mean that he was in any way un-
appreciative of the sometimes perhaps greater spiritual or intellectual achievements of individuals
living in other periods.

Third, to turn to what Dawson positively was
claiming, it seems to me that Dawson always retained
part of the Romantic and Hegelian approach to history.   He indeed had seen the real contribution
Romanticism had made to historical studies in its
desire to understand other cultures and periods for
their own sake, or as he put it "to re-create the
past, and to enter with imaginative sympathy into
the life and thought of past ages and of different
peoples."[29]   He also saw some of the limitations
of Romanticism, and in the opening chapter of Medieval Essays criticized the sometimes uncritical
treatment of the middle ages by the writers of the
early nineteenth century Catholic revival.   Although
these writers had given great impetus to the study
of the middle ages, too often the beneficiary of
this study had been the cult of nationalism.[30]
None of this is what I have in mind here, however.
What I have in mind, rather, is the manner in which
for Dawson, every age had its distinctive spirit.
He could anthropomorphize a culture so that he would
speak of its soul in a way that bears some resemblance to the Hegelian Zeitgeist:[31]

> ...every culture develops its own types
> of man, and norms of existence and con-
> duct, and we can trace the curve of the
> growth and decline of cultural life by
> the vitality of these characteristic
> types and institutions as well as the
> art and literature in which the soul of
> the culture finds expression.

Thus, no matter how much elsewhere he laid emphasis
for instance on the "violent conflict and revolutionary change" found in the middle ages, in summing
up his subject he did have a propensity to stress
the unitary aspects of medieval culture in a degree

with which many contemporary historians are uncom-
fortable.[32] To give Dawson his due here, we
should note that he saw medieval culture as full of
tensions and thus ever-dynamic. The role of Christianity was to provide syntheses of these tensions.
Thus for him Christianity was at the center of medieval culture not in the sense of having provided a
single and static synthesis of cultural tension, but
as providing an ongoing series of syntheses or su-
per-structures for the shifting subcultures found
within Christendom. Nevertheless, and this is our
point here, the synthesis itself could be seen as
"the soul of the culture" finding expression. Few
would fault Dawson's portrayal of the richness of
medieval cultural diversity, but some would hold
that in his moments of summation he spoke in the ac-
cents of Romanticism: in spite of the cultural
diversity so plainly made clear, one could speak of
the "soul," "spirit," or "life-purpose" of the
culture.

Fourth, Dawson's understanding of Christianity
was specifically Catholic. Near the beginning of
this paper, I observed that Dawson's idea of when
Christianity had received its fullest cultural expression implied a Catholic definition of the faith.
This can easily be illustrated by returning to his
description of the third age of Western Christendom.
We recall that Dawson refused to see the period from
the sixth to the eleventh centuries as the period of
greatest maturity, in spite of his belief that at
this time the relation between religion and culture
was closer than it has been before or since. What
was lacking in this period that disqualified it from
being seen as the high point of Western Christian
culture? Precisely those things that were still un-
developed from a Catholic point of view, namely the
full vertical and horizontal elements already mentioned. But now I want to give these dimensions
different names, and thereby show that as a Catholic
Dawson assumed that religion is both to permeate
every aspect of life, and to express itself publicly. On the first point, the early middle ages was
disqualified because although the bond between religion and high culture was closer than it has ever
been, religion had not yet penetrated through the
many layers of more popular culture. Dawson's Catholic understanding of man involved not simply the
saving of souls, but what Paul Quay has called the

raising of the cultural "ceiling" of the society in general.[33] This latter was done more thoroughly in the high middle ages, and hence this should be seen as the more mature period. The vertical or, to give it its new name, the incarnational dimension of Christianity, the permeation of every aspect of life and class of society by Christianity, was more fully developed in the high middle ages. If Dawson had had a more Protestant understanding of Christianity, for instance an understanding that saw Christianity ordered more single-mindedly around the invididual and his or her salvation, he might reasonably have fastened on one of the post-Reformation centuries as the most mature period of Western Christian history. The second point is not unrelated to the first. We may call this horizontal dimension of Christianity its public dimension. We have already noted that central to Dawson's periodization was his charting of the history of that quasi-political expression, Western <u>Christendom</u>. Again, that he should have kept his eye on this public dimension of Christianity can most easily be traced to his Catholicism. In its permeation of all of life, a natural term of Catholicism is its reordering of public life. A separation of what nowadays are called Church and state has become instinctive to a Protestant view of history -- although the origins of Calvinism are sufficient witness to the fact that this was not always so -- but in Catholicism, except where it has been deeply influenced by Protestantism, the natural term of Christianity is a publicly Christian society in which lay and ecclesiastical offices are differentiated but not separated in a Jeffersonian sense. Dawson had to see in the high middle ages the maturity of Western Christian culture, because after that period the public life of the West was fractured. In a certain sense, for him if Catholicism is not allowed to complete its work, to reorder all of life, as it by definition cannot in a religiously pluralistic society, it cannot attain its maturity. I note in passing that it was precisely this Catholic element in his thought, which saw religion at the core of culture, that made Dawson such an astute observer of the so-called natural religions, which also of course saw religion as forming the whole of life, rather than as one compartment within life.

Undoubtedly our list of what Dawson was and was not claiming could be lengthened, but it is time to

pass to more direct criticism of his views. Before
passing to more substantive matters I must confess
that sometimes I find Dawson writing not very convincing Christian apologetics. We may take as an
example the claim, quoted above, that Western democracy and humanism are the fruit of medieval seed.
Here it is not the claim itself that I would question, as the principle of selectivity. Dawson says
of humanism and democracy "the harvest was good and
the world still lives upon it." Now if one happens
to admire both of these things, none of this will
seem very striking. But what if, for instance, one
does not admire democracy? Then what is to be said?
Certainly it is as easy to trace modern fascism to
the middle ages, as modern democracy. In fact,
there are precious few things which cannot be traced
to the middle ages. Thus a preliminary observation
is that such claims are in danger of meaning little
more than that the future comes from the past. Now
Dawson's desire to defend Christian culture against
its learned despisers by showing medieval Christendom's great achievements and their continuing influence is most understandable. Dawson, however, in
our present example selectively took things he
approved in the present and by linking them to
medieval Christendom denied that they were "really
the creation of a new secular culture" while affirm-
ing that they were the fruition of medieval Christendom. This seems to me an instance of a careless
Christian apologetic. Such complicated phenomena as
democracy have more sources than we will probably
ever understand, and some of the most important of
these lie after the middle ages. To stress their
medieval sources is certainly pedagogically useful
against the despisers of Christian culture, but to
phrase the contrast between Christian and secular
sources in Dawson's manner is arbitrary. I would
add as a note that I have nothing against the use of
history for apologetic purposes: however, when one
does this one is usually playing with loaded dice,
and this seems to me the case sometimes with Dawson's arguments.

To turn to the substance of my criticism of
Dawson, let me take up one of his most arresting im-
ages, that of religion as a river, and apply it to
Western Christian culture itself. Dawson wrote:
"The great world religions are, as it were, great
rivers of sacred tradition which flow down through

111

the ages and through changing historical landscapes which they irrigate and fertilize."[34]   Like all images this image has its usefulness and its limitations.   Christianity in history may be visualized as a small stream which became a great river, and the historical landscape, the cultures, through which it flowed may be seen as irrigated and fertilized by it.   These cultures may be seen as the banks of a river, as channels which also directed Christianity in specific directions.   But in some degree Christianity was such a torrent that it profoundly modified the landscape through which it flowed, ripped out banks, and like a flood made some of the cultures into which it flowed part of itself.   Now it seems to me that the impact of the last generation of research, particularly the impact of the annales school of study and of the new social history, has been to show how many disparate layers of culture are in any society, and specifically how many flows and eddies, how many cross and back currents, there were in the stream of medieval culture.   As we have said, Dawson tended to think of cultures as having their specific "souls" or "spirits."   It seems now that in spite of his accurate portrayal of many of the tensions in medieval culture, he sometimes presented the worldview of some of the top layers of society as somehow speaking for the whole.   We are now more conscious of how impervious to "high-culture" sometimes lower cultural strata are.   Even in the case of the elites, we sometimes see so much incompatibility of views that we despair of presenting any unified picture.   For the middle ages, Dawson certainly could see the tension between, say, the cult of adultery or the various heresies of the high middle ages and the views of the Church, but this never led him to speak of "another middle age," that is of a culture too at odds to be spoken of as possessing a single soul.   In other contexts, for instance in the history of Spain after the middle ages, the lack of sympathy between the various groups composing the upper levels of a culture have now forced some scholars to speak of the "two Spains," that is of traditional and inward-seeking Spain, and liberal and European Spain.[35]   Similarly, in the middle ages, even among its most articulate spokesmen, we now seem to find many Europes. Friedrich Heer, for instance, has spoken of the world of the three rings, a series of partially overlapping cultural spheres between Islam, Judaism,

and Christianity in the high middle ages.[36] But
the more we study each of these phenomena, the more
we see a world of rings within rings.

A recent review of a work on the last century
has made a point that in some degree, in spite of
Dawson's masterful study of such lower class works
as Piers Plowman, could be directed against Dawson.
This review of a book on the decline of the industrial spirit criticizes its author not so much for
the conviction that "ideas are...'real' and have
consequences," as for focusing on middle- and up-
per-class values and then arguing that "the values
of the directing strata...tend to permeate society
as a whole and to take on the color of national
values."[37] It seems to me that, in spite of Dawson's incisive contrast of such things as the war
and the peace culture in the middle ages, the cultures of the North and of the South of Europe, and
of the heretical sub- or anti-cultures, when he came
to summarizing his subject he fell back too often on
his notion of Christendom, of a shared cultural
experience.

Make no mistake. It is not my intention to
dissolve Dawson's framework. Some notions were very
widely shared. In describing early medieval society
in Feudal Society, Marc Bloch wrote:[38]

> 'Ages of faith,' we say glibly, to des-
> cribe the religious attitude of feudal
> Europe. If by that phrase we mean that
> any conception of the world from which
> the supernatural was excluded was pro-
> foundly alien to the minds of that age,
> that in fact the picture which they
> formed of the destinies of man and the
> universe was in almost every case a
> projection of the pattern traced by a
> Westernized Christian theology and es-
> chatology, nothing could be more true.

If we are talking at this level of generality, it
was still true of the high middle ages that the
overriding framework of thought for most people was
Christian: God had created the world, Adam and Eve
through their descendants had populated it, Christ
had saved it and would return to judge it. It is
when we come down to more specific questions that we

find disagreement common. Is work -- or slavery --
a punishment for sin or a part of the order of nature? Does time remove us from God or return us to
God? Is time money, or leisure golden? Are men
noble by birth or by merit? I repeat, my desire is
not to dissolve Dawson's framework, but to suggest
that, here as elsewhere, the more we know about this
period, the more we have to qualify the extent to
which we can speak of culture-wide shared values.

Patterns which once seemed so general and characteristic, no longer do so. For instance, it is
central to Dawson's periodization of the high middle
ages that the fifteenth century in the North of
Europe be seen as a period of decay. But what are
we then to make of new scholarship which suggests
more cross-grained patterns of development? I think
of Colin Platt's book on The Parish Churches of Medieval England.[39] This admirable book contains a
chapter called "A Crisis of Faith," which for the
most part gives us the accepted view of fifteenth
century society, with its low clerical standards,
deep pessimism, etc. Although one reviewer has suggested that Platt may have overdrawn his picture, it
is certainly not one unfamiliar in the historical
literature, or in Dawson's books.[40] But the general direction of Platt's book is to draw a picture
at odds with this somber picture. At the least he
has caught sight of a very strong back current that
needs to find its place alongside the traditional
view. In a period which still does seem to remain
one of pauperization at the parish level, evidenced
by the continuation of such long-standing abuses as
pluralism and absenteeism, we find increasing evidence of Hamilton Thompson's observation that "there
is no period at which money was lavished so freely
on English parish churches as in the fifteenth century."[41] Churches were rebuilt, stained glass
windows were added in profusion, and all kinds of
sculpture and decoration were lavished on the parish
church. Thus we have what seems to be evidence of
the "intensely personal commitment of so many pari-
shoners of the later Middle Ages to their local
church," which is not "easy to reconcile with the
copious administrative evidence for 'spiritual rusticity' and near-scandalous neglect of so many medieval parishes."[42] Platt tries to account for
this in a chapter titled "The Community of the Parish." A reading of this chapter leads our reviewer

to conclude of the parish churches:[43]

> ...when all is said and done their most
> remarkable characteristic seems to have
> been their ability to contain and pro-
> mote, rather than to thwart and deny,
> the most powerful religious and social
> impluses of their age.

> Quite how one accounts for such relig-
> ious success against the economic odds
> no doubt emerges as the single most my-
> sterious question raised by Dr. Platt's
> new book. Part of the answer presum-
> ably lies in supposing that communal
> and private acts of worship within the
> parish churches...were of much greater
> spiritual and psychological significan-
> ce than the historian will ever be able
> to prove.

I cannot possibly show all the interesting ways
in which new research would add to, and present puz-
zles to, Dawson's view of the middle ages. I doubt
that any new research will undermine Dawson's main
reason for periodizing the high middle ages the way
he did, the obvious difficulties of especially the
symbolic focus of Christendom, the papacy, in the
late middle ages. If with him we concentrate our
view on the horizontal dimension of Western Christendom, then there is good reason for dating the
break-up of medieval civilization to the rise of
Divided Christendom. Even if one wants to stress
that the Counter Reformation missions to the new
world added, simply at the level of geography and
numbers, more to the Church than had been lost to
Protestantism, there is an obvious sense in which
Europe from the early sixteenth century was divided
about the matters at the center of the old world
view symbolized by the old papacy. But I have chosen this particular example of Platt's work on the
fifteenth century to show that, if one rather is interested in the vertical dimension of Christianity,
the degree to which it formed society at every
level, one could discover perspectives rather different from those Dawson found.

Let me merely sketch an alternative view, intended more as an impressionistic proposal for fur-

ther research and interpretation than as some new
well-grounded reading of the whole. If we begin
with the early middle ages, I think we must be
struck by the fragmentation of life, by the isolation of social groups and strata from one another.
When we can glimpse the life of the lowest classes,
as in the pages of Martin of Braga or Bede, it often
seems very remote from the life lived by the few
learned men of the time, but also from Christianity
itself. We do of course find thoroughly Christianized laity from time to time, as Einhard or Dhuoda
in the ninth century, but these are almost always
people of the higher ranks of society. Caedmon is
an exception. My point is, as Dawson knew, high
culture and Christianity itself in any more than a
schematic sense was, to judge by the fragmentary
evidence, commonly the possession of small elites.
Thus the wise decision of writers like Jonas of
Orléans to present Christianity to the layman as
above all a code of moral practice built on the Ten
Commandments. One could hardly hope for the development of the higher reaches of spirituality if
basic moral discipline was lacking.

The situation began to change from the time of
the struggle for ecclesiastical freedom in the later
eleventh century. Now we begin to meet, as in the
Patarenes, groups of serious and well-informed
Christian laymen. We begin by the early twelfth
century to find the occasional layman who has so
internalized both the new learning and Christianity
as no longer to accept without question his or her
place in society. Thus in the History of My Mis-
fortunes, Abelard tells us that his father had ob-
tained a little learning before he became a knight,
and then afterwards took up learning with a passion.
Both of Abelard's parents, like some of the earlier
medieval kings, ended their lives by entering monasteries. Seriousness of religion, in a way of
which we still have a record, was descending the
social scale.[44]

In such great works of the next century as
Wolfram von Eschenbach's Parzival, the central character has so internalized Christianity that, in addition to resting easy in a monogamous marriage, he
has come to doubt the value of the life of the
knight. Certainly a century earlier Roland and
Oliver had stood firm in their Christianity, again a

Christianity of the upper classes, but nevertheless
a religion without much internalization. But Parzival is tormented about his duties as a Christian
in a way which is remarkably new -- and not just new
for Western Christendom. Without looking down at
the earlier more external and formal expressions of
Christianity, we must note here a real advance in
the appropriation of Christianity, an advance found
also in the apostolic movements of the twelfth century and in all three orders of the mendicants in
the thirteenth century. Here we find in certain
segments of society a plumbing of the meaning of
Christianity which, added to the common self-con-
sciousness of membership in Christendom, justifies
Dawson's clear preference for this period in comparison to the early middle ages as a time of coming of
age.

Yet when we survey the canons of the Fourth
Lateran Council of 1215, we are certainly taken back
by how little all of this seems to have touched vast
segments of society. We conclude that the perspective which should be adopted is one which sees early
medieval Christianity as primarily the religion of a
monastic and princely elite, and the twelfth and
thirteenth centuries as a period in which this religion of the elites, through the lives of men like
St. Francis, was beginning to reorder the lives of
advanced groups of laymen. Much remained to be
done, from the viewpoint of the permeation of the
culture by religion. This permeation seems, obviously by no clear advance which we can precisely
measure, to have continued apace not just through
the remainder of the middle ages, but past Trent. I
take it that one of the points of Johan Huizinga's
The Waning of the Middle Ages is that, if we remain
at the level of description and do not express our
disdain for the late medieval cults of the saints or
of death, these developments, sometimes supersti-
tious and morbid, reflect a meditation on Christianity, and a penetration of its themes into all levels
of society, with which nothing earlier can compare.
In other words, just as Platt had noted for the
English fifteenth century parish Church, the decline
of Christendom as a horizontal expression did not
necessarily correspond to a lessening of Christianity's influence on ordinary life. I would not hold
that one can conclude from this that in the long run
you can have one without the other, because it does

seem to me that, as Dawson noted, sometimes a culture which has lost its public unity can continue to live for a long time from its accumulated cultural heritage.

It is most misleading to see the fourteenth and fifteenth centuries as a time of paganism. Even in Italy, if we do not confuse the culture of the learned with that of the mass of men, public and private life were permeated by Christianity. In fact, recent study has tended to see even the literati as not so deChristianized as earlier generations had, and when we turn to such things as public and civic ritual we note a great ordering of life by Christian ideas.[45] Worldliness there was, and a kind of shift in the very social meaning of religion so as to adjust to new urban forms of life, but if we remain at the descriptive level it seems to me that fifteenth century society was more formed by Christianity than ever had any earlier period.

If this was true of the fifteenth century, what can we say of the sixteenth or early seventeenth centuries but that this advance of Christianity into the fabric of society continued? Whatever else they did, the struggles between Catholic and Protestant made religion a matter of passion and commitment for far greater numbers of people than ever before. Very few were untouched. If eventually John Donne could argue "All Coherence Gone," this was the harmony of the medieval cosmos that had disappeared. The world was now a stage, on which most men saw, as in the vision of Ignatius Loyola, the forces of good and evil set against one another. The battle for the good was the same as in the middle ages, but the connection of the stage of the world to providence more problematic, as Shakespeare would articulate, and the place of man in the cosmos less clear, because of the discoveries of the scientists and explorers. But for the average man caught up in Protestantism or Catholicism, life remained a struggle in which, in a much more radically psychological way than in the middle ages, one's success depended on faith and grace. Here the religious psychologies of the Catholic and Protestant Reformers share a common ground, which finally found full articulation not in theology but in the Baroque. This, as Martin Larrey has argued, is the quintessential expression of what it means to be a Western European Christ-

ian.[46] All earlier cultural expressions, the Romanesque or Gothic for instance, although expressing
incidentally some Christian ideas, for instance in
their use of triads or in the subject matter of
their windows and decoration, expressed religious
ideas not uncommon in the other religions. The
Romanesque was a kind of fortress architecture, the
Gothic a praying architecture. But the Baroque expresses a view of reality found nowhere else in the
world. It has been the only distinctively European
art form, both in the sense that it appealed across
religious boundaries to men of all rank and thus was
the last popular art form the West has known, and in
the sense that it captured a very widely held view
of life that came as close as anything to defining a
shared European experience. Life was dynamic and
active, about matters of great import, and the only
rest found here below was that fleeting one in which
great forces were captured in a moment of balance or
anticipation.

I have passed beyond the period of history in
which I hold any historical expertise merely to suggest that if we pursue the vertical dimension of
Dawson's notions of periodization, there is much to
be said for seeing the period roughly between Charles V and Westphalia as the time when Christianity
most influenced Western Christian life. If at one
level all this has been merely a quibble about words
and labels, at another it seems to me to involve
serious questions of perspective which could be extended beyond the bounds of this paper.

I close by reiterating our debt to Dawson. He
it was who introduced us to the basic definitions
which have proven so fruitful in discussion down to
the present. More importantly, without falling into
any radical romanticism, he it was who taught us an
appreciation of the role of religion in culture.
Some schools of historical writing could learn much
from the sensitive, respectful, and generous way in
which he treated the matter of religion. One example must suffice. In spite of the real advances of
the annales historians, their points of view often
seem to me a real regression from that of Dawson. I
will note only of one of the books from this school,
Georges Duby's The Early Growth of the European
Economy.[47] This book, illuminating on many matters, nevertheless offers some points of view which

seem to me almost grotesque: I can only speculate that they result from a certain insensitivity to the role of religion -- and here I mean the role of religion for the good -- in society. Duby writes as an economic historian who rather frequently passes moral and technological judgments from a point of view outside of and hostile to the cultures he describes. Thus:[48]

> Worship of trees and forests had erected powerful taboos, holding back the activities of settlers and hindering food-production on margins of clearings, and Christianity was an unconscionable time in rooting them out.

Here Duby pauses as little to ask why the Germanic peoples believed as they did, and what role this belief played in ordering their culture, as he does to ask how easy it is to separate peoples from such beliefs. Would he have been happier if St. Boniface had cut down every tree in Europe? There is involved here the kind of simple-minded reading of human nature one so often finds with the economic historians, in which everyone in the past is condemned for not acting according to twentieth century standards of rationality and efficiency. Virtually no attempt is made to see the internal logic of the culture as its members perceived it. This historian of the left, it might also be noted, gives Christianity the go-ahead for the destruction of other cultures when this advances their technological development: one wonders if this permission extends to other matters. And what must he think of the French equivalent of the Sierra Club?

Two pages later Duby says of the earlier medieval monks in general: "They produced nothing. They lived off subventions on the toil of others." Now, according to time and place, there is some truth in this, but as a generalization it is most misleading. The Benedictine rule commanded manual labor, and this command was far from generally dishonored. If in some periods the monks retreated from the fields to the choir-stalls, in other periods the movement was the reverse. Vast areas of Europe were brought under cultivation by the monks. More important than the literal falsehood of this statement, however, is the absence in Duby's book of any sense of what the monks provided to their society. Is it not a kind of production, a kind of toil, to preserve the image of learning and order for a society, to be the men of peace as well as sometimes the peacemakers? Must we all be laborers to have our existence justified? Again, Duby seems to be blind to factors that Dawson immediately saw. Leaving aside the monks' goals as they themselves understood them, and looking at them rather from a purely utilitarian point of view, we note that, taken as a whole, the monks were the counselors of their society, those who often forged social solidarity in the midst of chaos, and those who provided images of more satisfactory patterns of human life.[49]

I will not catalogue all the further errors in Duby's book, which has the temerity to speak of a class struggle in the ninth century; sees nothing in the feasting of the knights but a destruction of the fruits of the eartH; and consistently applies such terms as "sloth" and "idleness" to the lives of the monks, priests, and warriors.[50] It is not at all clear that this relentless use of history for political purposes is better than Dawson's occasionally inept apologetical stance. If Dawson's view of the middle ages could sometimes see more unity than there had been or not sufficiently dwell on the darker side of the story in the manner of say G.G. Coulton, he did not crawl on his belly in the manner of so many of the latter day social and economic historians. I am afraid that the legacy the historian leaves is almost always more fleeting than that of most other forms of knowledge, and there is no point in preserving Dawson's vision of the middle ages word for word. He has, rather, left us an enduring inheritance by way of his definition of and approach to the question of what should come under the historian's eyes. It is our task, in the face of ever-more accumulating data, to try to approach these new materials with his old sympathies.

NOTES

[1]Christopher Dawson, The Historic Reality of Christian Culture: A Way to the Renewal of Human Life (New York 1960), p. 36. I want to thank Mr. John J. Mulloy for calling to my

Glenn W. Olsen

attention this and a number of other passages, some of which are now discussed in his "Is Christian Literature a Contradiction in Terms?" The Dawson Newsletter II, No. 1 (Winter-Spring, 1983) 6-12. The present essay is an extension of my "On The Teaching of Medieval Culture," found on pp. 1-5 of the same Newsletter.

[2]Christopher Dawson, Religion and the Rise of Western Culture (Garden City, New York 1958), ch. 1; and Medieval Essays (Garden City, New York 1959), ch. 1.

[3]The Nature of Culture (Chicago), pp. 131, 137.

[4]Historic Reality, p. 36.

[5]The Crisis of Western Education, With Specific Programs for the Study of Christian Culture by John J. Mulloy (Garden City, New York 1965), pp. 115-116 (pp. 140-42 of the original edition of 1961).

[6]P. 115.

[7](New York 1913).

[8]Crisis of Western Education, p. 116.

[9]P. 47.

[10]Ibid.

[11]Ibid., pp. 47-48.

[12]Ibid., p. 52.

[13]Ibid., p. 54.

[14]Russell Hittinger has kindly given me a copy of a paper, "The Metahistorical Vision of Christopher Dawson," which notes Dawson's preoccupation with the early middle ages, on the one hand, and with contemporary "secularized Christendom," on the other. Dawson's special interest in "the primitive... stages of creativity," Hittinger argues, led him to devote more attention to the early middle ages than to the culmination of medieval culture in the thirteenth century.

[15]Crisis of Western Education, p. 55.

[16]John J. Mulloy has, correctly, warned me of the dangers and limitations of the metaphor of the "vertical," used

throughout this paper. I do not mean by it that every movement of Christian influence in the middle ages was downward from elites, but that many of the most powerful were. As will be made clear below, I also do not mean to suggest a uniformity of views among the elites.

[17](New York 1942), p. 62. Dawson's sweeping claim here is much more appropriate to the high than to the early middle ages.

[18]Ibid., pp. 64-65.

[19]Ibid., p. 65.

[20]Ibid., p. 24.

[21]Religion and the Rise of Western Culture, p. 16. Dawson is citing his earlier Christianity and the New Age (London 1931), p. 96.

[22](New York 1966), p. XXXV.

[23](Garden City, New York 1965), pp. 32-33, uses strong language to lay the destruction of the spiritual unity of Christendom at Luther's door, but then, pp. 34-39, shows how the humanist culture was retained on all sides of the great religious divide.

[24]See the interpretive essay of Martin Larrey, "Towards a reevaluation of the Counter-Reformation," Communio 7 (1980) 209-224.

[25]Glenn W. Olsen, "Lay Spirituality ad majorem Dei gloriam," Communio (1979) 405-412.

[26]In The Modern Dilemma (London 1932), p. 110, Dawson wrote that European civilization had "ceased even nominally to be Christian." The "spiritual capital" of the Christian past had been exhausted, "and civilization is faced with the choice between a return to the spiritual traditions of Christianity or the renunciation of them in favour of complete social materialism."

[27]Glenn W. Olsen, "Bede as Historian: The Evidence from his Observations on the Life of the First Christian Community at Jerusalem," Journal of Ecclesiastical History 33 (1982) 519-530.

[28]Rosalind Hill, "Bede and the Boors," _Famulus Christi: Essays in Commemoration of the Thirteenth Centenary of the Birth of the Venerable Bede_, ed. Gerald Bonner (London 1976), pp. 93-105.

[29]_Progress and Religion_ (London 1929), p. 24.

[30]Pp. 10-11.

[31]_The Dymanics of World History_, ed. John J. Mulloy (New York 1962), p. 65. On p. 52 Dawson speaks of the "spirit of the whole civilization," on p. 58 he writes of "every organism, whether individual or social," and on p. 59 he affirms "the existence of a central life-purpose in every civilization."

[32]_Religion and the Rise of Western Culture_, p. 18. The remainder of this paragraph is inspired by the analysis of Hittinger, above n. 14.

[33]"The Theological Concept of 'Recapitulation' and Its Relation to Culture," _The Dawson Newsletter_ II, No. 1 (Winter-Spring, 1983) 13-14, now published in fuller form in the present volume.

[34]_Religion and the Rise of Western Culture_, p. 12.

[35]Ramón Menéndez Pidal, _The Spaniards in Their History_, tr. Walter Starkie (New York 1966), esp. ch. 5.

[36]_The Intellectual History of Europe_, tr. Jonathan Steinberg (2 vols., Garden City, New York 1968) I, ch. 6. Part of Heer's point, as at p. 131, is that the confusion of religions generated another world of high culture, that of nonconformism to any of the three faiths.

[37]The phrases quoted are from Martin J. Wiener, _English Culture and the Decline of the Industrial Spirit, 1850-1980_ (New York 1981), pp. x and 5. The review by Janet Oppenheim Minihan is found in _The American Historical Review_ 87 (1982) 179.

[38]Tr. L.A. Manyon (London 1961) p. 81.

[39](Secker and Warburg 1981).

[40]The following is heavily dependent on the review by R.B. Dobson in _The Journal of Ecclesiastical History_ 33 (1982) 619.

[41]Quoted in ibid.

[42]Dobson, in ibid.

[43]Ibid.

[44]It is here that the metaphor of the vertical shows its greatest limitations. There is a sense in which "the spirit blows where it wills," so that, in any period, we may find Christian influence in the most unexpected places, defying any simple notion of a descent from upper to lower cultural strata. Nevertheless, in the twelfth century, a ripple of serious Christian living was spreading from especially the monasteries to laymen of all ranks.

[45]An entrance into an immense literature is given by Richard C. Trexler, "The Magi Enter Florence. The Ubraichi of Florence and Venice," Studies in Medieval and Renaissance History, N.S. 1 (1978) 127-218.

[46]See above n. 24. In "Why I am a Catholic," published in The Catholic Times, May 21, 1926, and now partially republished in The Chesterton Review 9 (1983) 110-113, Dawson spoke of "the wonderful flowering of the Baroque culture," and said that the art of the Counter Reformation "led me to the literature of the Counter Reformation, and I came to know St. Teresa and St. John of the Cross, compared to whom even the greatest of non-Catholic religious writers seem pale and unreal." For Dawson's description of the Baroque, see The Dividing of Christendom (New York 1965), chs. XI-XII.

[47]Subtitle: Warriors and Peasants from the Seventh to the Twelfth Century, tr. Howard B. Clarke (Ithaca, New York 1978).

[48]Ibid., p. 53.

[49]A scholarly antidote to Duby's picture is found in Barbara H. Rosenwein, Rhinoceros Bound: Cluny in the Tenth Century (Philadelphia 1982).

[50]Early Growth of the European Economy, pp. 94, 168-69.

CHRISTOPHER DAWSON AND BAROQUE CULTURE:
AN APPROACH TO SEVENTEENTH-CENTURY RELIGIOUS POETRY

R. V. Young

The great virtue of Christopher Dawson as a cultural historian is his ability to consider his subject in the broadest possible terms -- the development of world civilizations and their interactions -- without losing sight of the concrete details of time and place which are the flesh and blood of history. What differentiates Dawson from the other great general historians of century -- Toynbee, say, or Spengler -- is his sensitivity to the nuances and textures of various cultures, his appreciation for the contingent and unexpected. Hence in his critique of Toynbee, Dawson warns, "...there is always a danger that the philosopher will be tempted to simplify the irrational multiplicity and idiosyncracy of the world of history and that the prophet will attempt to anticipate the mystery of divine judgment, like the friends of Job -- that symbol of humanity agonizing in the toils of history."[1]

For Dawson himself the broad vision of the grand sweep of history is not a means of imposing an a priori, synthetic order on the particularity of human events; it is rather a means of understanding just those particular actions of the historical process by seeing them in a larger context. The crucial factor is that in Dawson's work the immediate and the particular are not neglected in the interest of the abstract and general. Doubtless this characteristic is ultimately attributable to Dawson's Christianity -- to his belief that a single historical event, the Incarnation, is of absolute and unique importance.

Dawson's discernment is nowhere better exemplified than in his interest in and appreciation for the baroque culture of the Counter Reformation, "which became," in Dawson's words, "the last great corporate expression of Western religious ideals."[2] Early in his career, when most art historians regarded the Baroque as merely the decadence of the Renaissance, and the term was hardly acknowledged in literary circles, Dawson recognized that baroque culture with its varied elements -- artistic, literary, social, and above all religious -- was a distinct and vital phase in European and Latin American History. "The Baroque culture," he writes, "represents the alliance of two traditions -- the humanist tradition of the Renaissance and the tradition of medieval Catholicism as revived or restored by the Counter-Reformation. These traditions are often regarded as contradictory, but they came together in the Baroque culture, to which each made an important contribution."[3]

From the viewpoint of contemporary secularism the Baroque is merely an historical deadend: a Catholic holdover in cultural backwaters like Spain, Italy, and Austria when Europe as a whole was surging into the Enlightenment and onward to the triumph of modern times. Insofar as "baroque" has been commonly accounted a dyslogistic term, we have a measure of the secularization of the modern world. As Dawson perceived, the Baroque was the last truly Christian culture and we have much to learn from it. Not least among these lessons is a view of the alteration of tone and rhythm that secularization effects in a culture.

England in the seventeenth century provides an attractive territory to the cultural historian interested in exploring the concept "baroque." Students of the arts, especially in literature have been reluctant to apply the term in an English context; after all England was a nati n of the Northern Reformation. Yet in the English poetry of this period, baroque characteristics are quite noticeable; and the names of Shakespeare, Donne, Herbert, Crashaw, Milton, and Marvell almost inevitably are mentioned in any discussion of the literary Baroque. Parallels between, say, Donne and continental poets like Marino or Quevedo remind us that the Reformation in England was a slow, fitful process, winning

its way in England only by intermittent violent out-
bursts against the ingrained social and cultural institutions of the Middle Ages. If it is not too
much of a paradox, we might venture to consider the
hierarchically structured, liturgically formal ecclesiastical establishment in England -- at least
under Archbishop Laud -- as a "Protestant Counter-
Reformation" in the face of the on-going puritan
Reformation. Moreover, as Christopher Dawson's
comments imply, the Baroque, both in its full Catholic embodiment and in various Protestant apparitions
as in England, may be taken as a generally Christian
rearguard action in the face of the growing power of
secularism, born in the wreckage of Christian unity
during the preceding century. An examination of
certain facets of the religious poetry of the period
provides, then, a means of assessing Dawson's ideas
about the religious foundations of baroque culture
in a specific, concrete setting. At the same time,
it provides a means of bringing Dawson's general
historical insights into play for the interpretation
of an especially complex area of literary history.

The complexities of the Baroque extend even to
the definition and derivation of the word. Unlike
"gothic," of which the original, pejorative meaning
is transparent, "baroque" has not yielded up the
precise nature of its insult to the scrutiny of
scholarship. It has been suggested that the origin
of the word is the Portuguese barroco -- a misshapen
pearl. Currently, the most accepted explanation de-
rives it from a term of Scholastic logic, baroco,
the name for the fourth mode of the second figure
among syllogisms; that is, "Every P is M; some S are
not M, hence some S are not P." Benedetto Croce
exemplifies it thus: "Every fool is stubborn; some
people are not stubborn, hence some people are not
fools."[4] Obviously such a syllogism reflects just
that aspect of Scholastic dialectic anathematized by
Renaissance humanists like Erasmus and Vives. Both
of the term's proposed origins suggest that, like
"gothic," it was initially a depreciatory term. It
seems to have been established in this sense in art
history, as the final, decadent phase of the Renaissance, by Jacob Burckhardt in the nineteenth century, and it was only the work of Heinrich Woelfflin, late in the century, that the Baroque was
revalued in more favorable terms. It was also
Woelfflin who first applied the term to litera-

ture.[5] As an art historian, however, Woelfflin defined the change from Renaissance to Baroque in terms of changes in the technique of the visual arts: (1) "The development from the linear to the painterly [malerisch]; i.e. the development of line as the path of vision and guide of the eye, and the gradual depreciation of line...." (2) "The development from plane to recession." (3) "The development from closed to open form." (4) "The development from multiplicity to unity." (5) "The absolute and the relative clarity of the subject."[6] To summarize briefly, the articulation of the individual parts of a baroque painting is less important than the effect of the total composition, while at the same time this total composition lacks the symmetry and visual definition of its Renaissance counterpart. Without explicating Woelfflin's terms further, it is easy to see that their detailed application to literature would be difficult. Literature is more cognitive than the visual arts in the sense that ideas are an element of its actual substance, and it is therefore harder to make clear distinctions about literary techniques than about the techniques of painting, sculpture, and architecture. As a literary concept, "baroque" remains problematic, because efforts to define baroque literature purely in terms of technique and style inevitably end in logical confusion and chronological absurdity. Generally it has proven more satisfactory to follow René Wellek in regarding the Baroque as a period concept in literary history.[7]

Having determined to define the baroque age as the period that comes between the Renaissance and the Enlightenment -- from, roughly, the late sixteenth to the early eighteenth century (and in England, France, and the Netherlands the Enlightenment begins much earlier), we still are left with a blank space that needs filling in. We still want to know what it is that in some sense unites the diverse characters who people the baroque age -- from Cervantes to Milton, from Marino to Pascal, from Santa Teresa de Jesús to John Bunyan. We want to find out the meaning and identity of the era, and it is here that Christopher Dawson can help us.

For Dawson baroque culture is the culture of the Counter Reformation. In the decades following the Council of Trent, the Church set about to regain lost souls and lost territory, and its principal method, in cultural terms, was to recover the theological and devotional treasures of the Middle Ages without repudiating the genuine contributions of Renaissance humanism. One need only consider the Jesuits, who dominated education and missionary work during this period, with their combination of humanist rhetorical and literary studies, Scholastic theology, and Ignatian meditation, which fuses perfectly the mystical devotion of the Middle Ages with the moralist piety of humanism.[8] As Dawson observes, "It was [the] Spanish crusading spirit which was to become the motive force of the Counter Reformation,"[9] and one reason for the predominance of the Spanish contribution to baroque culture is precisely that in Spain the medieval heritage remained most vigorous throughout the Renaissance.[10] The culture of the Baroque, then, is the concrete manifestation of the attempt to curb the forces of nationalism, secularism, and social disunity that emerged with the Reformation and the more extreme elements of Renaissance humanism. There is a very real sense in which the Baroque is Catholicity embattled.

Now it may seem somewhat puzzling to describe the culture of an entire period as "Catholic" at a time when all of Europe manifestly was not -- especially when many of the more notable figures ordinarily regarded as baroque (Milton, Rembrandt, Donne, Bach) were Protestant with varying degrees of intensity.[11] The seeming contradiction, however, can be resolved, again with the help of Christopher Dawson, who reminds us that the real contrary to Catholicism is not Protestantism per se, but another thing, turned loose in the human spirit in the religious havoc wrought by the Reformation. In an intriguing essay entitled "Catholicism and the Bourgeois Mind," first published in 1935, Dawson isolates two distinct personal types -- or perhaps outlooks or approaches to life -- of which one could be called, following Werner Sombart, the "bourgeois" temperament, the other the "erotic" temperament. Of course "erotic" here has nothing to do with sensuality. "Indeed," Dawson writes, "the erotic type par excellence in Sombart's view is the religious mystic, the 'man of desire', like St. Augustine or St. Francis."[12]

R. V. Young

The Baroque has a unique significance inasmuch as it is the last European culture, explicitly organized on Christian principles, to resist the growth and ultimate dominance of the Western world by what Dawson calls the "bourgeois mind."

> It is indeed impossible [he writes] to find a more complete example in history of the opposition of Sombart's two types than in the contrast of the culture of the Counter Reformation lands with that of seventeenth-century Holland and eighteenth-century England and Scotland and North America. The Baroque culture of Spain and Italy and Austria is the complete social embodiment of Sombart's "erotic" type. It is not that it was a society of hovels and peasants and monks and clerics which centered in palaces and monasteries (or even palace-monasteries like the Escorial), and left a comparatively small place for the bourgeois and the merchant. It is not merely that it was an <u>uneconomic</u> culture which spent its capital lavishly, recklessly, splendidly whether to the glory of God or for the adornment of human life. It was rather that the whole spirit of the culture was passionate and ecstatic, and finds its supreme expressions in the art of music and in religious mysticism. We have only to compare Bernini with the brothers Adam or St. Teresa with Hannah More to feel the difference in the spirit and rhythm of the two cultures. The bourgeois culture has the mechanical rhythm of a clock, the Baroque the musical rhythm of a fugue or sonata. [13]

The great Protestant artists of the baroque period were truly Protestant, but they were not truly part of the bourgeois culture which came to flourish in the wake of the Reformation and the disintegration of Christendom. One need only consider Rembrandt -- the extravagant, theatrical Rembrandt -- dying penniless and neglected among Amsterdam's prosperous burghers. Or John Milton:

could anyone have been more disillusioned and disappointed than he in the final outcome of the puritan revolution to which he had sacrificed so much? Part of him was a true bourgeois son of his successful scrivener father, but another part of him, on the eve of the Restoration of Charles II, turned in disgust from his countrymen as they prepared to desert "the good old Cause," "to prostitute religion and liberty to the vain and groundless apprehension, that nothing but kingship can restore trade."[14] In any case, as Chesterton long ago pointed out, the Milton family, from which the poet derived his taste for music and letters, was largely a Catholic family.[15] Protestantism as such added very little to Catholic culture. As Dawson maintains, "It is true that the Reformation...originated as a religious and theological movement, but its historical importance is due less to its religious doctrine than to the social forces it came to represent."[16] The Protestant religious art of the seventeenth century is, then, _religious_ insofar as it retains something of Catholicity. The religious individualism of the early Reformation rapidly turned into economic culture throughout the Western world wherein, for the past two centuries, serious artists have tended to be misfits, eccentrics, bohemians, rebels, and outcasts. Baroque culture was the last culture which could be truly expressed in artistic terms because it was the last culture of a spiritual rather than an economic foundation.

ii

When a Protestant rigorously and consciously rejects every trace of Catholic devotional habit, he will tend to write poems with a minimum of spiritual resonance. This trait is reflected in a famous sonnet by Sir Philip Sidney, who epitomizes the Protestantism of the high Renaissance in England:

LEAVE me ბ Love, which reachest but to dust,
And thou my mind aspire to higher things:
Grow rich in that which never taketh rust:
What ever fades, but fading pleasure brings.

Draw in thy beames, and humble all thy might,
To that sweet yoke, where lasting freedomes be:

Which breakes the clowdes and opens forth the
    light,
That doth both shine and give us sight to see.

O take fast hold, let that light be thy guide,
In this small course which birth drawes out to
    death,
And thinke how evill becommeth him to slide,
Who seeketh heav'n, and comes of heav'nly
    breath.

Then farewell world, thy uttermost I see,
Eternall Love maintaine they life in me.
<u>Splendidis</u> <u>longum</u> <u>valedico</u> <u>nugis</u>.[17]

Sidney is the outstanding representative of the combination of Renaissance humanism and Elizabethan
Protestantism; this poem escapes the label "typical"
only by virtue of its superb craftsmanship and fin-
ish. The balance of Protestantism and humanism,
however, is exceedingly delicate. To be sure, the
aristocratic Sidney is no embodiment of the "bourgeois mind"; but the sonnet, "Leave me o Love," discloses the defectiveness of Sidney's religious orientation which opened the way for the bourgeois as-
cendancy and the attendant secularization.

Apart from the allusion to the Sermon on the
Mount in line three -- "lay up for yourselves treasures in heaven, where neither moth nor rust corrupt" -- and the "sweet yoke" there is no explicitly
Christian reference in the poem, nothing that could
not have come from the <u>Somnium</u> <u>Scipionis</u>. The theme
is high-minded, moral resolution, and the level of
reference is decidedly abstract, with the Deity adduced by way of apostrophe as "Eternal Love." The
poem manifests very little, if any, theological doctrine; indeed, in the stated determination to re-
nounce passion and hold fast to virtue by force of
will, the teaching of Luther and Calvin and their
successors on grace and justification, with its predestinarian version of election, is at least implicitly denied. Even the plea for grace in the last
line is only marginally compatible with the notion
that prevenient grace is itself irresistible. Ironically, the very theology which was to bring the individual closer to his God, by diminishing, when not
simply removing, the intervening ceremonial and sacramental forms of worship, seems only to have made

personal access to God -- at least to Calvin's aloof majestic God -- more difficult. The courtier Sidney, who could write passionately of Astrophel's love for Stella, turns to "Eternal Love" with an air of grim determination rather than ardor, which is exclusively associated with the splendidis nugis of the closing Latin tag. Passion is simply rejected rather than redirected, and thus the way is opened in England for the bourgeois culture with its "mechanical rhythm of a clock."

By way of contrast let us consider the following poem by Lope de Vega, written some thiry years later at the height of the Spanish Baroque:

What causes you to try to be my friend?
What benefit, oh Jesus, comes to you,
That at my doorway covered with the dew
You pass these dark winter nights without end?

Oh! how stiff my heart that would not bend
And open wide! What mad estrangement blew
The chilling frost if my ingratitude
Withered your wounded feet in an icy wind!

How many times the Angel to me cried,
"Lean out the window, Soul, and see the way
That love keeps calling--not to be denied"!

How many times, my Sovereign, with dismay
"Tomorrow I shall open," I replied,
Only to say the same the following day! [18]

There is an obvious parallel between this poem and Sidney's sonnet, "Leave me O Love"; each is a poem of renunication: worldly vanities are to be forsworn for the love of God. But apart from this very general correspondence, all similarity ends. Indeed, it is remarkable that two sonnets on roughly the same theme could be so different.

In Lope's poem Sidney's abstract "Eternal Love" gives way to the figure of the incarnate Christ, imagined as an ardent yet patient lover, courting the soul of the poet as a coy, fickle mistress. In the octave Jesus is imagined with the specificity of two striking details. First, in a figure borrowed from Canticles (5:2), [19] he stands before the poet's door throughout the cold, dark winter night, chilled by the settling dew that gradually soaks him. Obviously there is a symbolic reference to the coldness of a sinner's heart and the darkness of his intellect, but the idea is conveyed through images. This reflection leads the poet to a guilty realization of his own ingratitude, which is not explained but only implied by the second detail: that the ice cold has parched the wounds in the soles of Jesus' feet. This single detail serves to recall the entire sacrifice on Calvary and the debt which each of us owes to our Lord and Savior. There is a deep poignancy in the way the poet's guilt, so overwhelming in the realization of human ingratitude for an infinite benefit conferred at infinite cost, cannot squarely face it and must focus on only one of its painful consequences: the withering of the wounds still open in the pierced feet of the risen Jesus as He awaits a loving response from the sinful soul He woos.

In the sestet the poet reflects upon a repeated scene which further defines the relationship between Jesus and sinful man: the angel -- presumably his guardian angel -- daily calls upon the soul to "lean out the window," and each time the poet promises to do so "tomorrow." As Lope's editor, José Manuel Blecua notes, the poet is echoing a well-known passage from the Confessions of St. Augustine: "For there was nothing for me to answer when you said, 'Arise you sleeper, come away from the dead, and Christ will illuminate you', and everywhere you showed me that you spoke the truth; there was nothing at all that I might respond, convinced by the truth, except some words slow and drowsy, 'Soon, I say, soon, but yet a little longer'. But 'soon, soon' never came, and 'yet a little longer' went on for a long time indeed."[20] In the context of the sonnets of Rimas sacras, it is clear that Lope is thinking principally of the sin of unchastity: there is a constant tension in these poems between carnal love and the love of Christ. Hence the poet ignores the courtship of Jesus because he is enslaved by fleshly desires; implicit in this sonnet is the echo of another famous passage from the Confessions: "But I, a wretched youth, intensely miserable, even at the very outset of my youth had sought from you chastity and said: 'Grant me chastity and continence, but not just yet'. For I feared lest you hear me too soon and heal me too

136

soon of the sickness of concupiscence, which I pre-
ferred to have satisfied than extinguished."[21] As
the allusion to the Canticles indicates, Lope's
alternative to this sin is not the utter suppression
of passion, but rather a passionate response to the
love of Christ, the bridegroom of the soul.

The contrast between Lope's sonnet and Sidney's
is striking and instructive. Sidney was a dedicated
and devout Elizabethan Protestant, a rising leader
in the Leicester-Walsingham faction of Queen Elizabeth's privy council, which favored a foreign policy
of Protestant activism and which, at home, often
sheltered puritan dissenters from the ecclesiastical
discipline of the established church. Sidney's zeal
in opposing the Queen's possible marriage to the
French Catholic Duke of Alencon, younger brother of
Henry III, earned him his sovereign's displeasure.
His apparent fall from royal favor in behalf of
militant Protestantism is probably the ultimate
cause of his substantial literary production, which
was largely composed during his idleness at his
sister's country estate while he was denied courtly
employment. Andrew Weiner's recent study of Sidney
argues that, both as a critic in his Defense of
Poesie and as a poet in the Arcadia, Sidney plays an
important role in developing a specifically "Protestant Poetics."[22] If this is true, then it is
equally true that what is "specifically Protestant"
is only marginally Christian. The sonnet we have
been examining -- which is as close to religious
verse as Sidney comes[23] -- shows little particularly Christian devotion; it could virtually have
been written, as is, by a pious Stoic. Notwithstanding Weiner's assertions, Renaissance humanism
and Christian devotion do not coalesce in Sidney's
poetry. "His concern with man as a rational being,"
writes A. C. Hamilton, "shows why his writings remain profoundly secular despite his strongly religious nature."[24] Once one has accepted Calvin's
aloof, inscrutable God, who chooses some to save,
some to damn, according to His arbitrary, sovereign
will, the realms of reason and religion, of nature
and grace, are necessarily divided by an unbridge-
able chasm.

Ironically then, it is Lope de Vega, a man of
exceedingly irregular life, lapsing into adultery
even after his ordination to the priesthood, whose

poetic vision is firmly grounded in Augustinian moral theology and who embodies in his poetry a genuinely personal relationship with Christ. Often the perpetrator of sins of passion, Lope perceives, nevertheless, that passion itself is not evil, that it is our willingness to participate in Christ's Passion that enables us, finally, to share in His Resurrection. Sidney's acceptance of an essentially Calvinist view of grace and justification in which the role of the human will is null leaves him no means of expressing the presence of God, who can remain only a majestic but distant "Eternal Love." In Lope's sonnet Christ is on earth in a persistent vigil at the sinner's door; it is crucially important, however, that He does not break the door down.

It is this minimum degree of free will left to man, sufficient to respond freely to Christ's grace -- to turn with love in answer to His call -- that makes possible what Christopher Dawson calls the essential characteristic of the Baroque: "that the whole spirit of the culture was passionate and ecstatic."[25] For it is only the freedom to choose to yield to God's will that allows meaning to the surrender. We see the significance of the _willed_ surrender in another of the sonnets of _Rimas sacras_, a poem simply unimaginable coming from a Protestant of Sidney's kind:

> How many times, Lord, have you called me,
> and how many have I with shame responded
> naked as Adam, although clothed
> with the leaves from the tree of sin!
>
> I have followed a thousand times your sacred
>   foot,
> easy to grasp, on a cross fastened,
> and turned away so many other times insolent
> to the very price at which you purchased me.
>
> I covered you with kisses of peace in your
>   despite;
> but if slaves who have fled their master,
> when found, are placed in irons,
>
> today as I return tearfully to see you,
> nail me to you on your cross,
> and you will hold me sure with three nails.[26]

Again the poet contrasts, as vividly and powerfully as possible, the magnitude of Christ's sacrifice on the cross -- the "price" He has expended on our behalf -- with man's reluctance to acknowledge that he has been "purchased at great price." Here the poet confesses his many betrayals of Christ, when "bold" or "insolent" (atrevido) he has turned his back on the "price" -- the cross. He implores that now, instead of being content with offensive "kisses of peace" which are little better than the kiss of Judas, he be united with his Lord once and for all, "nailed to the cross."

The figures of speech in this poem demand careful attention. Lope asks to be put in irons like a runaway slave, but the request is paradoxical because he is willing to be bound, to have his will to betray Christ -- that is, to sin -- curbed. Moreover, in order to be "found" by his pursuing Lord, he must first return of his own volition, since the feet of his master are nailed to the cross; and he must return contritely, "with tears" (con lágrimas) as he beholds the suffering endured by Jesus for him. Since the "fetters" the poet seeks are the nails of the Crucifixion, he is thus asking to share in the Passion of Christ. This is necessarily a voluntary act because our Savior willingly laid down His life for mankind, and the man who would participate in this action must likewise do so willingly. Finally, it is no accident that the final conceit of being "nailed to Christ on the Cross" carries erotic overtones. The poem opens with the poet's admission that he has often responded to his Master's call physically naked, like Adam in innocence, but guiltily "clothed" in leaves of sin. A passionate sinner, the poet sees no hope except in the Passion of his Lord, and he beseeches the sacred bridegroom for the consummation of the cross.

Such use of the images and overtones of secular erotic poetry is a characteristic feature of the devotional poetry of the baroque age.[27] It is the ultimate technique of a poetry which approaches God by means of intimate, personal meditation on specific, concrete details of the life of Jesus, of deity incarnate. It is the literary manifestation of the passion and ecstasy which Dawson regards as definitive marks of baroque culture. The very power of the ecstasy requires that the movement of the human will, however feeble, the turning toward or away from the cross, be not only significant, but finally decisive. The alternative is represented by the sonnet of Sir Philip Sidney, which is humanist in its assertion of neo-Stoic moral resolve, but Protestant only in its hesitation even to name "Eternal Love." When the response of the human will to divine grace is inconsequential, then there is no basis for the meditative dramas depicted by Lope de Vega. Religion retreats into the inner recesses of subjectivity.

iii

The century following the death of Sir Philip Sidney witnesses, however, the greatest flourishing of English devotional poetry, largely among Protestants. Even Richard Crashaw, the outstanding English Catholic poet of the seventeenth century, wrote much of his poetry before he was received by the Church. The simple explanation is that England was not hermetically sealed off from Catholic influences, especially before the Civil War when the court of Charles I was dominated by his French Catholic queen. The important baroque elements in seventeenth-century English literature reflect the pervasiveness and attractiveness of the continental Baroque throughout the period. English devotional poetry, for example, was subject to the influences of Counter-Reformation devotional practices, especially formal meditation.[28] Hence in The Dividing of Christendom, Christopher Dawson singles out a number of seventeenth-century English poets including Milton, Donne, and Crashaw as baroque writers;[29] and we can add Herbert, Vaughan, and Henry King, and in some respects Herrick, Marvell, and Carew.

Apart from Crashaw, John Donne probably furnishes the most obvious example of an English baroque poet. Born of a stubbornly Recusant family -- his brother perished in the Tower of London, where he had been committed for harboring a Jesuit priest -- Donne ultimately became the Anglican Dean of St. Paul's in London; but he never cast off all the marks of his Catholic upbringing. Much of his devotional poetry even shows the influence of St. Ignatius Loyola's Spiritual Exercises, despite the fact that Donne became an important anti-Jesuit polemicist for the English church. The following "holy sonnet" bears many resemblances of imagery and tone to the sonnets by Lope de Vega, examined already:

> Batter my heart, three person'd God; for, you
> As yet but knocke, breathe, shine, and seeke to
>   mend;
> That I may rise, and stand, o'erthrow mee, 'and
>   bend
> Your force, to breake, blowe, burn and make me
>   new.
> I, like an usurpt towne, to'another due,
> Labour to'admit you, but Oh, to no end,
> Reason your viceroy in mee, mee should defend,
> But is captiv'd, and proves weake or untrue,
> Yet dearely'I love you, and would be lov'd faine,
> But am betroth'd unto your enemie,
> Divorce mee,'untie, or breake that knot againe,
> Take mee to you, imprison mee, for I
> Except you'enthrall me, never shall be free,
> Nor ever chast, except you ravish mee.[30]

The poem displays fully the passionate and daringly erotic language of the baroque devotional lyric, and it is part of a set of poems which manifests in its structure the principles of Ignatian meditation. "At the close of the sixteenth century perfectly orthodox Protestant works of devotion made use of contemporary Catholic devotional works, inspired by the Jesuit revival," writes Helen Gardner.[31] Still, given his background, it is curious that Donne should write thus at the very time when he was depreciating the kind of sufferings endured by his own family in the Pseudo-Martyri (1610) and brutally satirizing the founder of the Society of Jesus in Ignatius His Conclave (1611).

What must have been an extreme emotional tension for Donne personally is clearly evinced in the sonnet, "Batter my heart." Critics have long been impressed by its violent, paradoxical conceits and often have recoiled with distaste. Wilbur Sanders maintains that much of this sonnet is "cheaply shocking," and of the final four lines he writes, "The tumbled, passionate utterance suggests real, panic ecstasy, and a horrible absorption in the violation that is about to be undergone.... I make no apology for the vulgarity of my reading," he continues; "the vulgarity is Donne's." Sanders adds that the peculiar qualities of this holy sonnet are the product of "a dangerously uncontrolled sensationalism," and he sees "something hysterically out of control" in many of the Holy Sonnets.[32]

What is, in fact, "out of control," in Donne's devotional verse is its theological basis. The poet beseeches God for the ecstasy, the rapture of surrender, that we have seen as the goal of Lope's Rimas sacras; but genuinely voluntary surrender is impossible to the enslaved will of Protestant theology -- hence the giddy "panic ecstasy" remarked by Sanders, since the poem works at cross purposes with itself. The speaker of Lope de Vega's sonnets is a faithless wife or a slave who has run away from his rightful master. In Donne's sonnet the speaker is not merely captured by Satan, he is "betroth'd" to Satan and hence rightfully belongs to God's "enemie." His release demands from God an act of lawless violence -- a rape, a conceit which implies that the sinner's soul does not yield, does not consent to God's call, but rather must be taken by the force of "irresistible grace." Of course, the very act of writing the poem, of asking -- hence willing -- to be taken against one's will undercuts the poem's presumptive Reformation theology, and this would account for the air of self-conscious performance of which Sanders complains.

It must again be stressed, therefore, that Anglican devotional poetry of the baroque age is not the fruit of a specifically "Protestant poetics"; and it is no coincidence that it was written at a time of extraordinary and increasing conflict within the Church of England between a Calvinist, puritan faction, which sought further reform -- the removal of the last "rags of popery" from the national church -- and an Arminian, hierarchical faction which sought to conserve, even restore, some elements of the Catholic heritage. Whereas in the sonnets of Lope de Vega the tension stretches between the poet's desire to gratify his own pride and lust and his desire to do the will of God -- between, that is, concupiscence and fidelity; in Donne's sonnet the tension runs between the poet's longing and experience and his Reformation theology. The logic of this theology is finally anti-poetic because, in eliminating all contingency from man's destiny, it effectively cancels any sense of drama, which is the heart of literature. One cannot really enter into a dramatic relationship with a God who has already determined each man's fate with no reference whatsoever to his possible responses or actions.

The Anglican devotional poets are capable of writing insofar as they do not pursue the logic of their theology to its conclusion. George Herbert's "To all Angels and Saints" is an apparent exception which handsomely illustrates the rule. In this poem he explains why he will not seek the intercession of the saints, will not, as it were, write a poem to angels and saints. It is a thoroughly Protestant poem, but also a thoroughly parasitic one; if there were no Catholic poems honoring angels and saints, Herbert's poem would be meaningless. It cannot properly be called an embodiment of Protestant poetics so much as a repudiation of Catholic poetry, especially baroque poems which celebrate Our Lady and the other saints. "I would addresse / My vows to thee most gladly, Blessed Maid, / And Mother or my God, in my distresse," the poet says tenderly; "But now, alas," he continues with regret, "I dare not; for our King, / Whom we do all joyntly adore and praise, / Bids no such thing...."[33] This rather jealous Jesus is a far different figure from the patient lover of Lope's sonnets. (For that matter, he is a very different Jesus from Him who, on the cross said to his Mother, "Woman, behold your son"; and to the beloved disciple, "Behold your mother.")[34]

Happily, Herbert is more fequently in a different mood -- a mood quietly but thoroughly baroque. In "Mattens" he recalls the spirit of Lope de Vega's Rimas sacras in which the divine lover patiently and ceaselessly courts the affections of fickle, negligent man:

> My God, what is a heart,
> That thou shouldst it so eye, and wooe,
> Powring upon it all thy art,
> As if that thou hadst nothing els to do?

> Indeed mans whole estate
> Amounts (and richly) to serve thee:
> He did not heav'n and earth create,

Yet studies them, not him by whom they be.[35

The poem concludes with a stanza that is again reminiscent of Lope de Vega. Like the Spanish poet, Herbert beseeches God to grant him the ability to respond fittingly to divine love. Let the fresh light of dawn, when he says his morning prayers, lead him to the divine light:

> Teach me thy love to know;
> That this new light, which now I see,
> May both the work and workman show:
> Then by a sunne-beam I will climb to thee.[36]

Implicit in "Mattens" is Herbert's confidence that the <u>vestigia dei</u> in the creation, the order and beauty of the natural world, can lead man to God if he will but regard the "workman" as well as the "work." This is a recurrent theme in Herbert's collection, <u>The Temple</u>, appearing explicitly in such poems as "Providence" and "The Flower."

The significance of Herbert's confidence in the validity of the contemplation of the creatures can be gauged by the contrast of a poem called "Contemplations" by the New England puritan poet, Anne Bradstreet. This poem ostensibly a meditation on the loveliness and design of universe, in effect rejects the meaningfulness of the realm of creatures in man's spiritual life and affirms the gulf between nature and grace in Calvinist theology. The poet begins by musing on the beauty of an autumn evening. "If so much excellence abide below;" she thinks, / "How excellent is he that dwells on high?" But as her thoughts continue to wander, she recalls that the Garden of Eden was far more lovely than earth now, but Adam, nevertheless, there yielded to temptation and became "a naked thral." She then begins to reflect upon the lack of correspondence between man and the rest of the creation:

> When I behold the heavens as in their prime,
> And then the earth (though old) stil clad in
>   green,
> The stones and trees, insensible of time,
> Nor age nor wrinkle on their front are seen;
> If winter come, and greeness then do fade,
> A Spring returns, and they more youthful made;
> But Man grows old, lies down, remains where

once he's laid.

Still she questions whether to "praise the heavens, the trees, the earth" since they are ultimately all fated to destruction while man "was made for endless immortality." The poem concludes with the thought that the world and all man's worldly works are subject to "Time the fatal wrack of mortal things, / ...But he whose name is grav'd in the white stone / Shall last and shine when all of these are gone."[37] Bradstreet's emphasis on the irrelevance of the natural creatures to man's supernatural end contrasts markedly with Herbert's invoking of a sunbeam, which "may both the work and workman show," to lead him to God.

Finally, there is the markedly sacramental character of Herbert's devotional poetry, so incongrous in the wake of the powerful Calvinist current in the theology of the Church of England to which Herbert himself adhered.[38] In "Love (III)" the relationship between God and man in the eucharistic feast is dramatized in a dialogue between a reluctant guest and a courteous host:

> Love bade me welcome: yet my soul drew back,
>   Guiltie of dust and sinne.
> But quick-ey'd Love, observing me grow slack
>   From my first entrance in,
> Drew nearer to me, sweetly questioning,
>   If I lack'd any thing.
>
> A guest, I answer'd, worthy to be here:
>   Love said, You shall be he.
> I the unkinde, ungratefull? Ah my deare,
>   I cannot look on the.
> Love took my hand, and smiling did reply,
>   Who made the eyes but I?
>
> Truth Lord, but I have marr'd them: let my
>   shame
>   Go where it doth deserve.
> And know you not, sayes Love, who bore the
>   blame?
>   My deare, then I will serve.
> You must sit down, sayes Love, and taste
>   my meat:
>   So I did sit and eat.[39]

145

Certain elements of this poem recall, once more, similar elements in Lope de Vega's sonnets in Rimas sacras. The patient courting of the reluctant sinner who is overwhelmed by the shamefulness of his own conduct is particularly noteworthy in this respect. To be sure, the emphasis on man's worthlessness and Christ's graciousness is characteristic feature of Reformation piety. Still, the importance of the Eucharist as a channel of grace is not; and, although, like his kinsman Sir Philip Sidney, Herbert calls our Lord "Love," his "Love" is a far more lively and concrete figure. Most important, despite the feebleness attributed to speaker of the poem, the verses nonetheless conclude with his action, with a response to proffered grace: "So I did sit and eat." Although Herbert's poetry is not so replete with striking and extravagant conceits as the poetry of Donne, its tone and characteristic themes are in some ways closer to the mood of the continental Baroque. In the case of both poets, however, and of any of their contemporaries who can reasonably be called baroque, an examination of their baroque qualities reveals affinities with the literary culture of the Counter Reformation, whether conscious or unconscious, deliberate or inadvertent.

iv

The Baroque never fully flourished in England, and such shoots as it put forth withered in the fires of the civil war and died in the frost of the interregnum. The fate of the Baroque in England is virtually embodied in the career of Richard Crashaw, the one English poet whose baroque status is disputed by no one. An Anglican clergyman who adhered enthusiastically to the Laudian revival of liturgical ceremony and ecclesiastical art in English churches, with the outbreak of the war he fled to the continent and soon bacame a Catholic and a priest. He died in Italy at the age of thirty-six, shortly after arriving at Loretto to take up his duties as a canon at the shrine of the Holy House of Our Lady. Already under the influence of Italian and Spanish writers--especially Santa Teresa--before his conversion, Crashaw died a youthful exile in the very bosom of the Church. Thus the English Baroque. One poet would seem to cast doubt on this view: the towering figure of John Milton.

While Crahsaw fled to the continent, Milton returned from his continental tour to become one of the intellecutal champions of the puritan rebellion against monarchy and hierarchy. In the 1650s he was an important official in the Cromwellian protectorate. Milton's masterpiece, Paradise Lost, is, nevertheless, a baroque poem in style and vision--a judgment now widely acknowledged among literary scholars. Yet when the matter is considered in moral detail, the character of Milton's epic is not really surprising; for on one important point of theology, of crucial significance, Milton breaks with the vast majority of his puritan contemporaries. He maintains the freedom of the human will to respond decisively to divine grace. This "heresy" from the Calvinist viewpoint is there in Areopagitica and in Milton's theological treatise, De Doctrina Christiana, which remained unpublished for a century and a half after his death. Above all, it is there in Paradise Lost which, as a number of modern commentators have observed, focuses on the deliberate disobedience of Adam and Eve and makes of moral choice the central issue of the Fall.[40] It is for this reason that Paradise Lost, despite the numerous heterodoxies hovering on the periphery--Milton's subordinationism, his mortalism, his materialism, to name but a few--despite these elements which emerge here and there throughout the poem, it is, in its central theme, essentially orthodox and speaks directly to the universal Christian experience. For the epic's main theme is Original Sin, and Milton, like the Council of Trent more than a hundred years before, argues, against the principal thrust of Reformation theology, that fallen man retains sufficient freedom of choice to be resposible for his own eternal destiny, that contingency is an aspect both of the universe as a whole and of the life of the individual.

But Paradise Lost also embodies its own antithesis. The last great epic of the Western world is in some respects an anti-epic, a point skillfully made by Louis L. Martz in remarking the numerous Ovidian echoes which undermine somewhat its Virgilian grandeur.[41] In bidding farewell to Paradise, Milton seems also to bid farewell to Baroque magnificence. After all, the most "heroic" figure in the poem is Satan, and a central theme is precisely the emptiness of his "victory." Adam and Eve lose the earthy Paradise, but they are promised "a paradise within thee, happier far.[42] It is only a little cloud on the horizon, no larger than a man's hand; but we can see here the beginnings of that internalization of religion--its confinement to the individual, subjective psyche--which is so characteristic of what Dawson calls the "bourgeoise mind." In what is probably Milton's last work, his poetical last will and testament, <u>Paradise Regained</u>,[43] the cloud has almost filled the sky; and it is filled with portents of the vanishing of the last vestiges of baroque culture in England and much of Europe.

The most striking feature of <u>Paradise Regained</u> is what is left out of it. Milton's version of the recovery of Paradise represents a subtle but truly momentous deviation from traditional Christian views of Christ's salvific action. It is doubtful whether a reader without preconceptions concerning Milton would ever guess that the action of a poem entitled <u>Paradise Regained</u> comprises not the Passion, Death, and Resurrection of Our Lord, but rather His temptation in the wilderness by Satan.[44] Milton's choice of subject is even more revealing when we consider his early poem, "The Passion," as it stands in <u>Poems of Mr. John Milton</u> (1945). After fifty-six lines of what is universally regarded as some of his worst verse, the poem breaks off with this note: "This subject the author finding to be above the years he had when he wrote it, and nothing satisfied with what was begun left it unfinished."[45] It is curious that, having turned late in life to the subject of Christ's atonement for the sin of Adam, Milton once again eschews the central mystery of the Christian faith. Indeed it is passing strange that he who is widely acknowledged the greatest religious poet of the English language should never have confronted Good Friday and Easter in his poetry.

Milton's "brief epic" is, of course, not brief enough to consider here in detail. We can, however, undertake a few observations regarding the character of the Christ-figure presented in <u>Paradise Regained</u>, which discloses the lineaments of the bourgeois culture which in Milton's day was already assuming its hegemony over the Western world. The Son of God in this poem is a very modern (I might almost say "modernist") conception. According to Barbara Lewalski, the central theme of Paradise Regained is the Son's (and Satan's) discovery of His own true identity, for he "has now emptied himself of all consciousness and awareness of his former condition in heaven."[47] The recovery of Paradise--that is, the effecting of mankind's salvation--consists in Jesus' discovery that he is "Israel's true King, but now in a wholly spiritual sense."[48] The actual mechanism of salvation is, therefore, an internal process in Jesus in which men are called to participate if they, too, would enjoy the "paradise within." Hence Lewalski argues that, for Milton, "the temptation episode is the epitome of Christ's total role, the embodiment of the entire Christian theology of redemption, the turning point of history. As such it is the fitting complement to the epic of the Fall and the proper subject for the Miltonic brief epic."[49]

According to this view, the Crucifixion is almost an afterthought; Our Lord's chief business on earth was to win an argument with Satan. The crucial point in history, if I may be allowed a pun, is no longer the cross, and we are to bring to Christ not our sins but our virtues. This aspect of the poem is even clearer in the interpretation of Irene Samuel, who insists that the theme of Paradise Regained is less a question of an "identity crisis" than of "life style": not "Who am I"? but "how is man to live"? She interprets Milton's Christ in terms even more secularized than Lewalski, and argues away even the last vestige of the miraculous and mysterious from the poem. At the climactic point of Paradise Regained, Satan places the Son on the pinnacle of the temple in Jerusalem and challenges Him either "to stand upright" (this "Will ask thee skill," he insolently remarks) or to cast Himself down that the angels might save Him. "To whom thus Jesus: Also it is written, / Tempt not the Lord they God, he said and stood. / But Satan smitten with amazement fell."[50] There is no miraculous manifestation of the Son's divine nature here, Samuel maintains; Jesus stands by natural human skill, and the Scriptural quotation refers not to himself, as some commentators have maintained, but to God the Father. Milton often differs from standard Renaissance Scriptual interpretation, she continues, "But the direction of his nonconformities was never toward greater mystery, greater miracle, but rather always toward greater rationality, greater availability as a guide in living."[51] If Christ's divine identity is not a central theme of the poem, it is because that identity is finally of minimal importance to "the supremely rational hero of Paradise Regained."[52] In Samuel's view, which is very convincing in its feel for the poem as a whole if not in every detail, "What Milton chiefly does is elaborate the temptations into arguments and the rejections into counter-arguments, so that every man may see in the exemplary answers a complete program for regaining Eden."[53] What is more, this is all accomplished by Christ's purely human nature which seems wholly divorced from whatever of divine nature he enjoyed: "Everything said," Samuel writes, "has established that man as man is wholly adequate to be, say, think, do all that man must to recover Eden, his full human heritage."[54]

One can differ over particular aspects of these readings of Paradise Regained, but it is undeniable that their general view of a rationalistic, secularized Christ is essentially accurate. The Son of God in Milton's poem attains that title as much or more by merit than nature. Paradise is regained by the reasoned arguments of a self-contained, self-controlled rationalist--a Stoic in mood if not in formal philosophy--rather than by the Lamb of God pouring Himself out in passionate sacrifice. As a model--as the focus of an imitatio Christi--he presents firm character, moral idealism, and aloof self-possession as goals for emulation. There is nothing here of the Man of Sorrows, the patient, wounded lover waiting through a winter night outside the door of that inveterate sinner Lope de Vega. It is one of history's great ironies, and we see it crystallizing in Paradise Regained: the severe, predestinarian Calvinism of the puritan revolution, with its contempt for Catholicism's cult of good works and indulgences, is transmogrified into a high-minded Pelagianism, which was, of course, the wave of the future. One need only consider the latitudinarianism of the eighteenth century giving way to the liberal Protestantism of the nineteenth, giving way to....the twentieth century.

Pelagianism may be described as the equivalent of the bourgeois mentality in late classical antiquity; it is a recurrent phenomenon. "For what is the Pharisee," writes Christopher Dawson, "but a spiritual bourgeois, a typically 'closed' nature, a man who applies the principle of calculation and gain not to economics but to religion itself, a hoarder of spiritual merits, who reckons his account with heaven as though God was [sic] his banker? It is against this 'closed', self-sufficient moralist ethic that the fiercest denunciations of the Gospels are directed."[55] Don Wolfe reminds us that Milton was very much a man of the rising middle class, the son of a successful scrivener and money lender.[56] There is an element of the Pharisee in his self-sufficient, rationalist "Son of God," whose preoccupation is principally with his own identity or with establishing his own merit, his "right" to the role of Messiah; and who invites all of us to do likewise. It is not that the poem is devoid of beauty and power; in many ways it is a masterpiece. It is just that the poem falls so short--clearly by design--of what its title seems to promise. "The crucifixion simply is not a theme of major importance in Milton's poem," remarks Irene Samuel, "though it undoubtedly was in Milton's theology and in his faith."[57] We have regrettably little evidence for the latter assertion; the former is a fact which signals a development of importance in English religion and culture.

Dawson's antithesis of bourgeois and baroque culture furnishes a compelling paradigm for the poetry of seventeenth-century England. Of course, it is difficult to identify specific figures as "baroque" or "bourgeois." What we see instead is a tension between these two strains creating a conflict within individual men. Nowhere is it more apparent than in Milton who subverts the baroque grandeur of Paradise Lost with the subjective religiosity of bourgeois individualism, and who undertakes the most sublime of baroque themes in Paraside Regained, only to impose on it the same individualist pattern. In this Milton signalled the coming of our own era in which "we are all," in the words of Christopher Dawson, "more or less bourgeois and our civilization is bourgeois from top to bottom."[58] After the seventeenth century there was no attempt at serious devotional verse in English before the time of Gerard Manley Hopkins. A possible exception is the eighteenth-century poet Christopher Smart, author of

R. V. Young

A <u>Song</u> <u>to</u> <u>David</u>. His fate is not without significance for an understanding of the place accorded
religious devotion in modern Anglo-American culture:
Smart spent two years confined to an insane asylum
and, more significant still, he died in debtors'
prison.

NOTES

[1]"Arnold Toynbee and the Study of History," in <u>Dynamics</u>
<u>of</u> <u>World</u> <u>History</u>, ed. John J. Mulloy (1958--rpr. La Salle, IL:
Sherwood Sugden & Co., 1978), p. 400.

[2]<u>Christianity</u> <u>in</u> <u>East</u> <u>and</u> <u>West</u>, ed. John J. Mulloy
(rev. ed., La Salle, IL: Sherwood Sugden & Co., 1981), pp. 65-
66. See also <u>Progress</u> <u>and</u> <u>Religion</u> (1929--rpr., Garden City,
NY: Doubleday Image, 1960), pp. 146-51; and <u>The</u> <u>Gods</u> <u>of</u>
<u>Revolution</u> (New York: Minerva, 1975), pp. 6-9.

[3]<u>The</u> <u>Dividing</u> <u>of</u> <u>Christendom</u> (New York: Sheed & Ward,
1965), pp. 197-98.

[4]The first etymology is favored by the OED and by the
<u>Oxford</u> <u>Companion</u> <u>to</u> <u>English</u> <u>Literature</u>, ed. Sir Paul Harvey,
rev. Dorothy Eagle (4th ed., Oxford & New York: Oxford Univ.,
1967). A discrepancy among Oxford reference works is created
by the acceptance of the latter etymology in the <u>Oxford</u> Com-
<u>panion</u> <u>to</u> <u>Art</u>, ed. Harold Osborne (Oxford & New York: Oxford
Univ., 1970). Citing Karl Borinski and Benedetto Croce, the
learned René Wellek confidently asserts the latter etymology
in "The Concept of Baroque in Literary Scholarship," in <u>Con-</u>
<u>cepts</u> <u>of</u> <u>Criticism</u>, ed. Stephen G. Nichols, Jr. (New Haven &
London: Yale Univ., 1963), pp. 69-70. Wellek's essay remains
definitive, and I have quoted Croce's example of <u>baroco</u> from
him and generally relied on his account of the <u>history</u> of
"baroque" as a critical concept. I have also found useful in
this regard Wylie Sypher, <u>Four</u> <u>Stages</u> <u>of</u> <u>Renaissance</u> <u>Style</u>:
<u>Transformations</u> <u>in</u> <u>Art</u> <u>and</u> <u>Literature</u>, <u>1400-1700</u> (Garden City,
NY: Doubleday, 1955); Frank Warnke, <u>Versions</u> <u>of</u> <u>Baroque</u>:
<u>European</u> <u>Literature</u> <u>in</u> <u>the</u> <u>Seventeenth</u> <u>Century</u> (New Haven &
London: Yale Univ., 1972); and Harold B. Segel, <u>The</u> <u>Baroque</u>
<u>Poem</u>: <u>A</u> <u>Comparative</u> <u>Survey</u> (New York: Dutton, 1974).

[5]Wellek, pp. 70-73, citing Woelfflin's <u>Renaissance</u> und
<u>Barock</u> (1888). In his 1962 postscript (the essay first appear-
ed in 1946) Wellek mentions earlier isolated occurrences of
the term "baroque" in a literary context.

152

[6]Principles of Art History, trans. M.D. Hottinger, (New York: Dover, 1950), pp. 14-16.

[7]"The Concept of Baroque," pp. 102-14. See also Warnke, pp. 1-20.

[8]Cf. A.H.T. Levi, "Erasmus, the Early Jesuits and the Classics," in R. R. Bolgard, ed., Classical Influences on European Culture, A.D. 1500-1700 (Cambridge: Cambridge Univ., 1976), pp. 223-38.

[9]Christianity in East and West, p. 63.

[10]See R. V. Young, Richard Crashaw and the Spanish Golden Age (New Haven & London: Yale Univ., 1982), pp. 12-16, and the references given there.

[11]Thus Wellek, p. 122, objects to "attempts to...limit baroque to the spirit of the Counter Reformation or to the influence of Spain." Such attempts are "refuted by the existence of a definitely Protestant baroque arising independently of Spanish influence." I would reject only the adverbs "definitely" and "independently" for reasons advanced below in the text.

[12]Dynamics of World History, p. 205.

[13]Ibid., p. 207.

[14]The Ready and Easy Way to Establish a Free Commonwealth (1660) in Milton's Prose Writings, ed. K. M. Burton (London: Dent, 1958), pp. 242-43. In the following clause the bourgeois part of Milton admonishes his fellow citizens "that trade flourishes nowhere more than in the free commonwealths of Italy, Germany, and the Low Countries."

[15]"Protestantism: A Problem Novel," in Chesterton's Stories, Essays, and Poems, ed. Maisie Ward (London: Dent, 1935), p. 228.

[16]Progress and Religion, p. 145.

[17]Certain Sonnets, #32, in The Poems of Sir Philip Sidney, ed. William A. Ringler, Jr. (Oxford: Clarendon Press, 1962), pp. 161-62.

[18]Rimas sacras, XVIII, in Lope de Vega: Obras poéticas, ed. José Manuel Blecua (Barcelona: Editorial Planeta, 1969), I, 324-25: "¿Qué tengo yo, que mi amistad procuras? / '¿Qué

interés se te sigue, Jesús mío, / que a mi puerta cubierto de
rocío / pasas las noches del invierno escuras? // ¡Oh cuánto
fueron mis entrañas duras, / pues no te abrí! ¡Qué extraño
desvarío, / si de mi ingratitud el hielo frío / secó las
llagas de tus plantas puras! // ¡Cuántas veces el Ángel me
decía: / 'Alma, asómate agora a la ventana, / verás con
cuánto amor llamar porfía'! //¡y cuántas, hermosura soberana,
/ 'Mañana le abriremos', / para lo mismo responder mañana!'

[19]Canticum Canticorum, 5:2: "Aperi mihi, soror mea,
amica mea, / Columba mea, immaculata mea, / Quia caput meum
plenum est rore, / Et cicinni mei guttis noctium."

[20]Confessions, 8:5:12: "Non enim erat quod tibi responderem dicenti mihi: Surge qui dormis et exsurge a mortuis, et
illuminabit te Christus et undique ostendenti vera te dicere,
non erat omnino, quid responderem veritate convictus, nisi
tantum verba lenta et somnolenta: Modo, ecce, modo, sine
paululum. Sed modo et modo non habebat modum et sine paululum
in longum ibat." Blecua points out that Lope treats this passage more explicitly in a later poem in Rimas sacras, "Augus-
tino a Dios," p. 522.

[21]Ibid., 8:7:17: "At ego adulescens miser, valde
miser, in exordio ipsius adulescentiae etiam petieram a te
castitatem et dixeram: 'Da mihi castitatem et continentiam,
sed noli modo'. Timebam enim, ne me cito exaudires et cito
sanares a morbo concupiscentiae, quem malebam expleri quam
exstingui." For the conflict between divine and human love in
the Rimas sacras, see sonetos 1-5, 14, 17, 19, 20, 24, 26, 28,
and esp. 29.

[22]Sir Philip Sidney and the Poetics of Protestantism:
A Study of Contexts (Minneapolis: Univ. of Minn., 1978).

[23]Sidney did undertake a metrical translation of the
Psalms, completed by his sister, Mary, Countess of Pembroke,
and a translation of Philip du Plessis de Mornay's Of the
Trewnesse of the Christian Religion, completed (perhaps wholly
rewritten) by Arthur Golding.

[24]Sir Philip Sidney: A Study of his Life and Works
(Cambridge: Cambridge Univ., 1977), p. 6. See also Ringler
"Introduction," Poems of Sidney, p. li.

[25]Dynamics of World History, p. 207.

[26]Rimas sacras, XV, Obras poéticas, p. 323: "¡Cuántas
veces, Señor, me habéis llamado, / y cuántas con vergüenza he

respondido / desnudo como Adán, aunque vestido / de las hojas del arbol del pecado! // Segui mil veces vuestro pie sagrado, / fácil de asir en una cruz asido, / y atrás volví otras tantas atrevido / al mismo precio en que me habéis comprado. // Besos de paz os di para ofenderos; / pero si, fugitivos de su dueño, / hierran, cuando los hallan, los esclavos, // hoy que vuelvo con lágrimas a veros, / clavadme vos a vos en vuestro leño, / y tendréisme seguro con tres clavos."

[27]On poesía a lo divino, or "sacrEd parody," see Bruce W. Wardropper, Historia de la poesía lírica a lo divino en la Cristiandad occidental (Madrid: Revista de Occidente, 1958); and the treatment by Young, Richard Crashaw and the Spanish, chap. II, pp. 20-50.

[28]The classic study remains Louis L. Martz, The Poetry of Meditation (rev. ed., New Haven & London: Yale Univ., 1962). Martz has been challenged by Barbara K. Lewalski, most recently in Protestant Poetics and the Seventeenth Century Religious Lyric (Princeton, NJ: Princeton Univ., 1979). For a brief rebuttal of the latter, see the review-essay by R. V. Young, "Poetry, Devotion and Reformation," Faith & Reason, 6:3 (1980), 238-46.

[29]Dividing of Christendom, p. 201. Dawson also lists as a baroque poet, Edmund Spenser, who is, in my judgment, more usefully regarded as a poet of Renaissance humanism. Similarly, I should dispute his offhand dismissal of Marino and Góngora as "disfigured by meretricious ornament and fantastic verbal conceits." The latter, especially, is among the great poets of the age.

[30]Holy Sonnets, 10, The Divine Poems of John Donne, ed. Helen Gardner (Oxford: Clarendon Press, 1952), p. 11. For the meditative background see Gardner's "Introduction," pp. xl-xli, 1-lv; and Martz, Poetry of Meditation; for the Calvinist elements in this sonnet, see R. V. Young, "Truth with Precision: Crashaw's Revisions of A Letter," Faith & Reason, 4, No. 3 (1978).

[31]Divine Poems, p. lv.

[32]John Donne's Poetry (Cambridge: Cambridge Univ., 1971), pp. 129-30. Cf. John Carey, John Donne: Life, Mind and Art (New York: Oxford Univ. Press, 1981), pp. 37-59, for the relation between Donne's apostasy from Catholicism and the despair in his poetry; and John Stachniewski, "John Donne: The Despair of the 'Holy Sonnets'," ELH, 48 (1981), 677-705.

R. V. Young

[33]The Works of George Herbert, ed. F. E. Hutchinson (Oxford: Clarendon Press, 1941), p. 78, 11. 8-10, 16-18.

[34]Secundem Joannem. 19:26-27: "Cum vidisset ergo Jesus matrem, et discipulum stantem, quem diligebat, dicit matri suae: Mulier ecce filius tuus. Deinde dicit discipulo: Ecce mater tua. Et ex illa hora accepti eam discipulus in sua."

[35]Works, pp. 62-63, 11. 9-16.

[36]Ibid., p. 63, 11. 17-20.

[37]The Complete Works of Anne Bradstreet, ed. Joseph R. McElrath, Jr., & Allan P. Robb (Boston: Twayne, 1981), pp. 167-74.

[38]Both the Reformation theology and the sacramentality in Herbert are pointed out by Joseph H. Summers, George Herbert: His Religion and Art (Cambridge, MA: Harvard Univ., 1954), pp. 49-69.

[39]Works, pp. 188-89.

[40]See especially C. S. Lewis, A Precface to Paradise Lost (Oxford & New York: Oxford Univ., 1942); Joseph H. Summers, The Muses Method: An Introduction to Paradise Lost (Cambridge, MA: Harvard Univ., 1962); and Stanley Fish, Surprised by Sin: The Reader in Paradise Lost (1967--rpr. Berkely: Univ. of Calif., 1971).

[41]Poet of Exile: A Study of Milton's Poetry (New Haven & London: Yale Univ., 1980), pp. 203-18.

[42]Paradise Lost, XII, 587, ed. Alastair Fowler (London: Longoman, 1971). Cf. Martz, Poet of Exile, pp. 185-98.

[43]Samson Agonistes was first published in the same volume with PR in 1671, and the general scholarly consensus is that it was writtin about the same time. The relationship of the two works is dealt with by Balachandra Rajan, "To which Is Added Samson Agonistes'," in B. Rajan, ed., The Prison and the Pinnacle (Toronto & Buffalo: Toronto Univ., 1973), pp. 82-110. Mary Ann Radzinowicz, Toward Samson Agonistes: The Growth of Milton's Mind (Princeton, NJ: Princeton Univ., 198), pp. xi, xvii-xix, 387-407, argues that SA is Milton's final, climactic work. Of course, beginning with an article in PQ, 28 (1940), 145-66, and oft repeated in subsequent years, the late W. R. Parker has maintained that SA was written between 1647 and

1653. He is followed in this view by John Carey, ed., <u>John</u>
<u>Milton</u>: <u>Complete</u> <u>Shorter</u> <u>Poems</u> (London: Longman, 1971).
Although I find the two poems similar in theme and tone, the
data of <u>SA</u> does not really affect my interpretation of <u>PR</u>.

[44]George Williamson, "Plot in <u>Paradise Regained</u>," in
<u>Milton</u> <u>&</u> <u>Others</u> (London: Faber & Faber, 1965), p. 68, distin-
guishes between the action of <u>Paradise Regained</u>, "by which
Christ will earn salvation for man by fulfillment rather than
redemption," and the actual Atonement effected on the cross.
Martz, <u>Poet</u> <u>of</u> <u>Exile</u>, pp. 261-62, maintains that "it is hardly
valid to object that this poem does not present the Christ of
the Gospels. For this is not a rehearsal of the Gospels; it
is rather (as Hopkins would say) a rehearsal of the self,
where the voice of the inner man discovers what a true Son of
God ought to reply to such temptations." Although these observations are perfectly accurate, they do not answer the
question of why Milton would choose so to restrict his treatment of Our Lord's saving work. Moreover, these comments seem
typical of a curious tendency in contemporary criticism to
ignore the radically secular version of Jesus, presented by
Milton--a version of Jesus who is only a perfect teacher and
exemplar, and "Son of God" in the same sense that each of us
can become a son of God.

[45]<u>Complete</u> <u>Shorter</u> <u>Poems</u>, p. 122.

[46]Cf. Young, <u>Richard</u> <u>Crashaw</u> <u>and</u> <u>the</u> <u>Spanish</u>, pp. 25,
for a discussion of Milton's vague treatment of Our Savior's
birth in his Nativity ode.

[47]"Time and History in <u>Paradise Regained</u>," in Rajan,
ed., p. 54. Lewalski gives a complete treatment of the nature
of the Son in the sixth chapter of <u>Milton's Brief Epic</u>: <u>The</u>
<u>Genre</u>, <u>Meaning</u>, and <u>Art</u> <u>of</u> <u>Paradise Regained</u> (Providence:
Brown Univ., 1966), pp. 133-63.

[48]"Time and History," p. 78.

[49]<u>Milton's Brief Epic</u>, p. 321.

[50]<u>Paradise Regained</u>, IV, 560-62, <u>Complete</u> <u>Shorter</u>
<u>Poems</u>, p. 517.

[51]"The Regaining of Paradise," in Rajan, ed., p. 116.

[52]Ibid., p. 120.

[53]Ibid., p. 122.

157

[54]Ibid., p. 124.

[55]Dynamics of World History, p. 206.

[56]Milton in the Puritan Revolution (1941--rpr., New York: Humanities Press, 1963), pp. 322-24.

[57]"The Regaining of Paradise," p. 120n.

[58]Dynamics of World History, p. 200.

CHRISTIANITY, CAPITALISM, MARXISM

John J. Mulloy

As a result of my reading an article by a Professor P. T. Bauer, "Ecclesiastical Economics Is
Envy Exalted," which appeared in the first issue of
a new conservative quarterly, This World, I became
more fully aware that there is a great deal in the
conservative movement, the libertarian conception of
conservatism, which is simply incompatible with
Catholic thought. This attack by Bauer on Pope
Paul's encyclical, Populorum Progressio, intended to
make it appear as simply Marxism in Christian cloth-
ing, made me realize the hostility with which a
certain part of the conservative movement regards
any moral criticism of captialism. It is no doubt a
temptation for conservatives, in revulsion against
the prostitution of Catholic teaching by so-called
Christian Marxists, to adhere strictly to the capitalist system as a defense against the atheism of
Communism and its wholesale violation of human
rights. Nevertheless the Catholic position, as repeatedly expressed in Papal encyclicals -- not only
those of recent Popes, but all the way back to Leo
XIII -- differs sharply from both of these systems;
and the fact that Marxism is so thoroughly atheistic
and materialist in its worldview, should not lead us
blindly to embrace the capitalist ideology as a
means for the defense of Christian principles and
social justice. We must be prepared to make clear
distinctions between Christian principles and the
principles which have been a part of the capitalist
ethic from its very beginning, and which still pre-
vail when this system has not been subject to restraint by outside forces.

John J. Mulloy

In order to clarify my own thinking on this matter, I turned to the various works of Christopher Dawson. I remembered that he had never looked upon the capitalist ideology with favor, for he saw it as the fruit of a revolt against the Christian principles which were accepted as the moral basis for both society and economics when Europe was still professedly Christian. The revolt against Christianity which took place at the time of the European Enlightenment of the 18th century was not restricted simply to the realm of philosophy and religion; it was at the same time a revolt against Christian principles governing the economic order. The right of a man to be his own master in the sphere of religion, leading either to atheism, or to a Deism in which man rather than God decided what the tenets of religion should be, and which therefore did not depend upon a Revelation guarded and explained by the Church, was at the same time the right of the man of property to do whatever he wanted with his capital. He was not to be restrained or restricted in its use by principles derived from the moral order. Economics became a self-governing area of life and could set up its own laws, as with the famous Iron Law of Wages postulated by David Ricardo in the early 19th century. This law claimed that, if you paid the worker above a subsistence wage, you were only preparing for the starvation of future generations of workingmen. For the worker would use this amount over and above subsistence to beget more children, and the resulting surplus of labor on the market, when those children came of working age (which was usually 9 or 10) -- would lead to unemployment and hence starvation for those not able to find work. So, no matter how much you as a Christian or as a humanitarian felt sympathy for the wretched plight of the worker, you must not allow that sympathy to lead you to interfere with the inescapable laws of economics, for you would only bring the worker to a worse condition than the one in which he now existed.

We too easily forget that such economic beliefs were central to the ideology of early capitalism, and we therefore assume that capitalism is a kind of morally neutral system for producing goods, that has no ideology attached to it. In fact, of course, no system of economics or politics, or of any other sphere of human endeavor, can be morally neutral.

It is governed by certain basic ideas and values, since man is a value-bearing animal. And those ideas and values either recognize the supremacy of the moral order, and hence the subordination of economics and politics, or whatever else, to that order, or else they assert their independence of morality and religion. In the latter case, they try to push religious and moral principles off into some corner, where they will apply only to a limited part of man's life, and not to the forum or the market-place or society in general.

Let us first consider Dawson's distinction of the different meanings of the word capitalism:

> The fact is the word Capitalism is commonly used to cover two entirely different things and consequently is responsible for an endless series of misunderstandings and confusions of thought. In the strict sense it means the use of private wealth for the pur-pose of economic production, whether by the individual as in early times, or cooperatively, as in the joint-stock company which is the characteristic form of capitalism in modern times.

> Both these forms of capitalism are accepted by Catholic social theory as lawful and just, and in this sense alone it can be said that the Church approves of capitalism. In the current use of the word, however, Capitalism stands for much more than this. Indeed it stands for so much that it is almost impossible to give an exact definition of it. Broadly speaking it may be described as the economic aspect of that philosophy of liberal individ-ualism which was the religion of the 19th century and which found its poli-tical expression in parliamentary de-mocracy.

> Now this creed -- and the social and economic order which arose from it -- is entirely inconsistent with

Catholic principles and was in fact the
most dangerous enemy and rival that the
Catholic Church had to meet in modern
times. It is a philosophy of separation and irresponsibility which breaks
up the moral organism of society into a
chaos of competitive individualism. It
denies the sovereignty of the moral law
in the economic world, the principle of
authority in politics, and the existence of an objective divine truth in
religion. It makes self-interest the
supreme law in economics, the will of
the majority the sovereign power in the
State, and private opinion the only
arbiter in religious matters.[1]

Moreover, Dawson sees a strong cause-and-effect
sequence between the assertion of the supremacy of
economic factors in society in laissez-faire capitalism and the more thorough economic determinism of
Karl Marx's theory of society. Marxism brought to a
more complete realization the implicit but unorgan-
ized materialism of economic Liberalism. In addition, early capitalism provided the social basis for
the growth of Marxism by the wretchedness and misery
which capitalists inflicted on the working class,
while telling them that unalterable economic laws
prevented them from ever improving their condition.
This was a counsel of despair, and under these circumstances it is understandable that Marx and Engels
found in the condition of the working classes in
England the basis for their theory of social revolution. This was thought to be coming in the near
future, with the overthrow of capitalism by a working class which, as Marx put it in The Communist
Manifesto of 1848, "had nothing to lose but its
chains."

So what the Catholic Church found herself faced
with by the latter part of the 19th century was not
one, but two different enemies to Christian morality
and Christian principles of society. On the one
hand, there was the predominant capitalist system
with its rugged individualism and its atomization of
society into social particles, each seeking to
maximize his own profit at the expense of everyone
else, with the capitalist succeeding at this far
better than the worker because of his greater degree

162

of initiative and enterprise -- as the capitalist ideology gave the reason for the stark contrast between rich and poor. And, on the other hand, there were the doctrines of Marxian socialism, gaining ever-increasing influence, not only among the workers, but also among the bourgeois intellectuals. These teachings replaced the war of individuals against each other in the competitive ideology of capitalism by the war of the classes against each other in the historical determinism of Marxism. Individualism was to be replaced by class solidarity, but the domination of society by economic motives and economic warfare was retained in Marxism, and in fact intensified.

When Leo XIII wrote his famous encyclical, Rerum Novarum, in 1891, he was thus forced to fight a war on two fronts, even as we must still do today. On the one hand, he must correct the errors and speak out against the evils of laissez-faire capitalism and its worship of economic success. And on the other front, he must expose the errors to be found in the more recent ideology of Socialism, which was being presented as the answer to all the ills and injustices of the capitalist system.

By the time that Pius XI wrote his encyclical Quadregesimo Anno in 1931, the 40th anniversary of the publication of Rerum Novarum, Marxism had become established as the reigning theory and practice of government in the largest of the European States -- Soviet Russia -- and was seeking to export its idea of world revolution. At the same time the claims of laissez-faire capitalism to produce economic abundance had suffered a grievous setback through the worldwide economic depression, which began with the collapse of the stock market in the United States in October 1929. The claims of Marxist Communism were thus being given much more attention in capitalist countries than had been true when capitalism was flourishing. Now that it seemed possible that capitalism had received a mortal blow, many thinkers and intellectuals were turning to Communism to provide society and economic life with the kind of principles they needed.

When Dawson wrote the chapters in Religion and the Modern State some three to four years after Quadregesimo Anno, the capitalist economy had still

163

John J. Mulloy

not recovered from the depression. Moreover, National Socialism had taken over Germany in 1933 and
claimed to be a working alternative to Communism,
while Fascism in Italy was trying to organize society on the basis of corporative bodies which
should be completely subordinate to the State.
Dawson's preface to <u>Religion</u> <u>and</u> <u>the</u> <u>Modern</u> <u>State</u> is
dated April 1935, and in it he states that he has
made use of articles from the volume which was
published in periodicals during the last two years,
with six different magazines being listed. So apparently well over half the book was written in 1933
and 1934.

First, let us note Dawson's idea of what the
Catholic attitude should be when confronted with the
two ideologies of laissez-faire capitalism and
Marxian Communism, neither of them in accord with
Christian principles for the social order:

> Actually the Church regards the organ-
> ized materialism of the Socialist State
> as a more formidable enemy than the un-
> organized materialism of Capitalist
> society, since the former is more ex-
> clusive and more intolerant of spirit-
> ual independence. Nevertheless this
> does not mean that she is prepared to
> accept the Capitalist ideal as legiti-
> mate or as morally defensible. Catho-
> licism condemns the Capitalist princi-
> ple of competitive individualism as
> well as the Socialist principle of
> class war. Society is not a mere col-
> lection of irresponsible individuals,
> nor it is a machine for the production
> of wealth; it is a spiritual organism
> in which each individual and every
> class and profession has its own func-
> tion to fulfill and its own rights and
> duties in relation to the whole.[2]

Or again, with a stronger emphasis on the men-
ace of Marxism to Christian society:

> Today the social revolution is no long-
> er merely an ideal, it is a fact that
> rules the lives of millions of men and
> women. Over a considerable part of the

164

globe from the Baltic to the Pacific it
has established a new order, an order
that denies God and the human soul not
in theory but in grim reality.

Now whatever system of government Catholics may favor it must be one that
will protect society from any revolutionary movement that would lead to the
establishment of this anti-Christian
order. For even a dictatorship which
deprives us of our political liberty
would be preferable to an order which
denies those fundamental spiritual
rights without which human life loses
its raison d'être.[3]

This was written almost half a century ago, but
it sounds very much like the distinction being made
today between the totalitarianism which is central
to the Marxist socio-economic order and the authori-
tarian dictatorships which often serve as barriers
against Marxist takeover of a society. And of
course, since the period when Dawson wrote in the
early to mid-thirties, Communism has progressively
advanced to the conquest of China and Eastern Europe, Cuba, and parts of Africa and Southeast Asia,
and is an encroaching threat upon Latin America. Yet
despite the fact of the world having come increasingly under the control of "this anti-Christian
order...that denies God and the human soul not in
theory but in grim reality," we find a considerable
number of Catholic clerics -- not to mention Liberal
Protestant clergymen -- trying to pave the way for
its complete triumph throughout the world. Is it
any wonder that conservatives with a strong sense of
the reality of what Marxist Communism means for the
extinction of human liberty and assault upon Divine
truth, are tempted to fall back upon a wholehearted
defense of capitalism? Nevertheless, as the Popes
have consistently taught, this is not the way to the
establishment of a society which is morally justifi-
able in the eyes of God. We must continue to work
for the Christian reconstruction of the social
order, and not allow the rival systems of Marxism
and laissez-faire capitalism to become substitutes
for that.

John J. Mulloy

As a means to recognizing the dangers inherent in the ideology which gave birth to economic Liberalism, let us see Dawson's account of the origins of modern capitalism:

Rousseau was profoundly hostile to the apologists of luxury, like Mandeville and Voltaire, and to the representatives of economic liberalism such as Turgot and Adam Smith. Here he was on the side not only of conservative critics of the Enlightenment ... but still more of the champions of orthodoxy like the Abbe Prigent and Pere Hyacinthe Gasquet, who maintained the traditional Catholic doctrine with regard to usury and the rights of the poor. As Groethuysen has shown with copious illustrations from eighteenth-century preachers and theologians [i.e., in The Bourgeois, subtitled "Catholicism vs. Capitalism in 18th-Century France"], the Church down to the eve of the Revolution maintained a stiff opposition to the capitalist philosophy and the economic view of life which were already triumphant in Protestant England and Holland. For behind the open battle of the Enlightenment which was being fought out on the ground of philosophy and freedom of thought, there was a deeper and more obscure struggle being waged by the bourgeois spirit, not only against the traditional order, which limited the freedom of commerce and bound industry within the narrow frontiers of the Corporation or Guild, but also against the religious tradition which idealized poverty and condemned the acquisitive and competitive spirit which was inseparable from the new commercial society.[4]

Dawson does not deny that there was an element of humanitarian idealism in this Liberal ideology which had helped to free business from social restraints and advanced the cause of laissez-faire capitalism. But he sees that ideal element, to

166

which he refers several times in the course of his various works, as essentially an inheritance from the Christian culture of the past, from which indeed Liberalism took it over without acknowledging its debt. And these ideals are essentially transitional, for they cannot survive the passing of Christian culture, any more than the flower can survive when cut off from its root. As an illustration of that, in our own time, in latter 20th century America, in a society founded upon the ideals of the Liberal Enlightenment, we see the political acceptance of the killing of the unborn child, the putting to death of the elderly, and the degradation of the human person by means of commercially presented violence, rampant sexuality, and the proliferation of pornography. But central to all of this anti-human movement is the loss of a sense of the transcendent, of the idea of an overarching spiritual order to which man's actions and his social life must conform, if they are not to run blind and plunge mankind into the abyss.

In Religion and the Modern State Dawson notes that it was this element of Liberal idealism which Marx condemned in his analysis of bourgeois culture, because he regarded it as essentially hypocritical, a facade to conceal the reality of exploitation which lay behind it. For Christians on the other hand, Dawson points out, "We may look on the faith of the 19th century in liberal ideals, in freedom and justice and humanity and progress as a redeeming trait in the harsh and unlovely features of bourgeois civilization," even while we "condemn the ruthless subordination of human life to economic ends and the wholesale secularization of culture."[5]

In one of the most striking passages in his writing, Dawson shows how the historical development from the Englightenment to 20th-century capitalist society has meant the triumph of hedonism at the expense of the moral ideals which originally inspired the movement of Liberal thought. It is noteworthy that, in this passage of almost half a century ago Dawson anticipates the ideas of the ecologists and the environmentalists of our own time, and also sees capitalism as becoming essentially a consumer culture -- a theme to which John Paul II has referred in several of his addresses.

167

John J. Mulloy

...today its ideals (i.e., of the Enlightenment) are being swallowed up by
the subversive forces which it has itself liberated. The idealism of the
great Liberal thinkers ended in the
materialism of the acquisitive capitalist society against which the conscience of the modern world is in revolt. What we are suffering from is
the morbid growth of a selfish civilization which has no end beyond itself -- a monstrous cancer that destroys the face of nature and eats into
the heart of humanity. As in the days
of ancient Rome, but on a far larger
scale, men have made themselves the
masters of this world, and find themselves left with nothing but their own
sterile lusts. For this 'leisure civilization' in which the people sit down
to eat and drink and rise up to play is
the dark world which has turned its
face from God and from which God's face
is hidden. It is terrible not only on
account of its emptiness but because
there is a positive power of evil
waiting to fill the void, like the
unclean spirit in the parable that came
out of the waste places into the empty
soul.[6]

After referring to the slavery of lust which
overcame the leisure civilization of the ancient
Roman Empire, Dawson adds:

At the present day we feel this slavery
in its economic rather than in its sensual aspect. Nevertheless the Kingdom
of Mammon and the Kingdom of Belial are
one, and it matters little which of
them is the nominal master, so long as
the world is theirs.

It is the horror of this empty and
sterile world far more than any economic hardship or political injustice
that is driving men to revolutionary
action. Nevertheless the materialism
of the Communist state is but the same

168

thing in another form. It may relieve the tension on the individual by merging his consciousness in that of the mass, but at the same time it shuts out all hope of escape and thus completes his imprisonment.[7]

Now let us take a more extended look at Dawson's conception of Marxism. Before discussing his critique of the Marxist theory, let us first give his description of what Marxist practice was like, in the Soviet Russia of the early to mid-1930s. This was the time of the forced collectivization of agriculture, especially in the Ukraine, which Stalin later told Churchill resulted in ten million deaths among the kulaks, the so-called rich peasants. In Stalinist terms, this meant anyone who owned a farm and did not want to hand it over to the Soviet collective and become a hired hand on the State-run farm. Of this period Dawson writes: "In Russia, however, there is no such contradiction between the State and the Communist party. The State has become nothing more than the instrument of the party, and the power of the party is shown by the Assyrian ruthlessness with which it has in the last few years destroyed the independent life of the Russian peasantry at the cost of an incalculable amount of human suffering."[8]

Then, noting the way in which at this very time of wholesale killing of the peasants by Stalin, the leaders of Liberal thought in the West were promoting the cause of Communism and seeing in it the ideal society of the future, Dawson declares: "...they rally to Communism, because in spite of its cruelties and intolerances, it seems modern and progressive and anti-religious. As Mr. (Malcolm) Muggeridge has pointed out with such biting emphasis in his Winter in Moscow, all those Platonic admirers of Communism from the West find in Russia something that they can understand -- a State run on advanced lines by advanced people; whereas the victims of the Soviet system, the wretched peasants and unprivileged workers and priests, are people of the underworld with whom they have nothing in common and whose sufferings seem distant and unreal."[9]

John J. Mulloy

Thus Dawson concludes that the real issue in Russia "is not an issue between the capitalists and the proletariat, for it is obvious that the real proletarians are the starving peasants of the Ukraine and not the well-fed bureaucrats of Moscow. The vital issue is the subordination of man, body and soul, to the economic machine of the secular State. And the greatest obstacle to the fulfillment of this end is not Capitalism, nor the bourgeois culture, but the Christian faith."[10]

One might note that Dawson is here identifying a phenomenon -- the exploitation of the proletariat by "the new class" of Communist bureaucrats -- which Milovan Djilas, dissident Communist of Yogoslavia, was later to make the subject of an important book on the social realities of Communist practice, which showed the hollowness of the claim of Communism to be creating a classless society.

With regard to the Marxist ideology, Dawson's first criticism of it has as its target the economic determinism on which Marx's theory is founded:

> He [i.e., Marx] condemned the whole humanistic morality and culture as bourgeois, and accepted the machine, not only as the basis for economic activity, but as the explanation of the mystery of life itself. The mechanical processes of economic life are the ultimate realities of history and human life. All other things -- religion, art, philosophy, spiritual life -- stand on a lower plane of reality; they are a dream world of shadows cast on the sleeping mind by the physical processes of the real world of matter and mechanism. Hence Marxism may be seen as the culminating point of the modern tendency to explain that which is specifically human in terms of something else. For the Marxian interpretation of history is in fact nothing but an explaining away of history. It professes to guide us to the heart of the problem, and it merely unveils a void.[11]

CHRISTIANITY, CAPITALISM, MARXISM

But if indeed Marxist theory has at its heart this metaphysical emptiness, why has it had such an attraction for so many people in the West, including especially the intellectuals? For it is the latter, far more than the proletariat, who have been responsible for the rise and spread of Communism, as we see in the case of Marx and Engels, Lenin and Trotsky, and numerous other advocates and disciples of Marx among the intelligentsia of the West. What element in Marxism recommends itself to them, if they are not motivated by a nihilistic rejection of life itself? While not ignoring the influence of nihilism -- the turning against society in a blind impulse of destruction, because social life has lost all ultimate meaning with its loss of its spiritual dimension -- Dawson believes that another reason for the appeal of Communism is that it links together economic determinism with an apocalyptic element of moral denunciation. This latter element is incompatible with the economic interpretation of history. For if all other elements in society are ultimately reducible to economic factors and have no real existence independent of the economic determinism of which they are but the reflection, then this moral indignation against injustice and exploitation has no more validity than the bourgeois ideals of freedom and humanity which the Marxists so bitterly denounce. According to Dawson, Marx himself inserted this moral element into his economic interpretation of history, however much it contradicted it, because his ultimate inspiration was Messianic, and he transposed into secular terms the Jewish Prophetic conception of history. Dawson speaks of the historical environment which had kept alive the strength of apocalyptic expectations in the Jewish communities of Germany and Eastern Europe in the centuries prior to the emancipation of the Jews: "The Messianic hope, the belief in the coming destruction of the Gentile power and the deliverance of Israel were to the Jew not mere echoes of Biblical tradition; they were burnt into the very fibre of his being by centuries of thwarted social impulse in the squalid Ghettos of Germany and Poland. And in the same way the social dualism between the elect and the reprobate, between the people of God and the Gentile world power, was a fact of bitter personal experience of which even the most insensitive was made conscious in the hundred petty annoyances of Ghetto life."[12]

John J. Mulloy

After the emancipation took place, Marx's father became a Christian convert and served as a minor official under the Prussian government, and Karl Marx himself was able to attend German universities and gain an intimate acquaintance with German philosophic thought of that period. Dawson writes of him:

> He had lost his membership of the Jewish community, for he was the son of a Christian convert, but he could not deny his Jewish heredity and his Jewish spirit and become the obedient servant of the Gentile civilization as his father had done. His whole soul revolted against the standards and ideals of the petty bourgeois society in which he had been brought up; yet he had tasted the forbidden fruit of the new knowledge and he could not go back to the Talmud any more than he could return to the Ghetto. The only way of escape that remained open to him was by the revolutionary tradition, which was then at the height of its prestige and popularity. In this he found satisfaction at once for his conscious hostility to bourgeois civilization and for the deeper revolt of his repressed religious instincts.... . For Karl Marx was of the seed of the prophets, in spite of his contempt for anything that savoured of mysticism or religious idealism.[13]

Thus there is in Communism a strong spiritual element which has no basis in the governing principles of Marx's philosophy and in his interpretation of history in purely economic terms. As Dawson has observed:

> This strange paradox of a godless religion and a materialist spirituality has its basis in the internal contradictions of the revolutionary tradition of which Communism is the final product. For that tradition unconsciously drew its dynamic force from religious sources, though it denied and rejected them

172

in its rationalized consciousness. In the same way the Marxian theory of history, for all its materialism, is dependent to a degree that Marx himself never suspected on the antecedent religious view of history which had been formed by the Jewish and Christian traditions.[14]

Consequently, for Western intellectuals who hold to the idea that religion is merely the opiate of the masses, and who believe that a secularist worldview is the only intelligent explanation of reality, the appeal of Marxism comes with peculiar force. For it allows them to appease their spiritual hunger while still denying the fact of its existence, and to reject any transcendent spiritual reality which could satisfy it. Dawson points out how Communism serves to fulfill this religious need:

> Nevertheless it is impossible to deny that Russian Communism does resemble a religion in many respects. Its attitude to the Marxian doctrines is not the attitude of an economist or an historian towards a scientific theory, it is the attitude of a believer toward the gospel of salvation; Lenin is far more than a political hero, he is the canonized saint of Communism with a highly developed cultus of his own; and the Communist ethic is religious in its absoluteness and its unlimited claims to the spiritual allegiance of its followers.

> Thus Communism is not simply a form of political organization; it is an economy, a philosophy, and a creed. And its hostility to Christianity is due not to its political form, but to the philosophy that lies behind it. Communism, in fact, challenges Christianity on its own ground by offering mankind a rival way of salvation. In the words of a Communist poster, 'Jesus promised the people Paradise after death, but Lenin offers them Paradise on earth.'[15]

Dawson makes another criticism of the Marxist philosophy, based on the fact that Marx's economic determinism cannot explain the machine order which is the element required to bring Marx's dialectic of history to its culmination in the classless society. For that order would never have come into existence if economic factors alone were determinative, and there had been no antecedent inventive ideas. Dawson first speaks of the fact that Marx's own motivation for constructing his theory was essentially a Messianic one, not the consequence of economic pressures; and he adds:

> Thus Communism, like every other living power in the world of men, owes its existence to spiritual forces. If it were possible to eliminate these, as the Communist theory demands, and to reduce human life to a purely economic activity, mankind would sink back into barbarism and animality. For the creative element in human nature is spiritual, and it triumphs only by mortifying and conquering the natural conservatism of man's animal instincts. This is true above all of science, for the path of the scientist leads him farther from the animal than the rest of men. He lives not in the concrete reality of sensible experience, like the animal or the savage, but in a rarefied atmosphere of mathematical abstraction in which the ordinary man cannot breathe. If the materialist interpretation of history were true, the scientific intellectualization of nature could no more have arisen than could the metaphysical intuition of reality, and without science there could be no machine order. The true Marxian Communism is not that of a machine order which is the work of the creative scientific spirit, but rather that of the Eskimo, which is the direct product of economic necessity. For the machine is a proof not of the subordination of mind to matter, but of the subordination of matter to mind. [16]

CHRISTIANITY, CAPITALISM, MARXISM

Since Marx was so very much concerned with the dialectic between different classes as providing the dynamics for historical development, and since he especially stresses its dependence on economic structures, I find particularly valuable Dawson's critique of the Marxian view of the origins of the revolutionary movement. Going back to the 18th century, the time when the revolutionary movement in ideas first became widespread, and which, within a relatively short time, led to political and social revolution -- the French Revolution in all of its phases -- Dawson notes certain facts about the classes which promoted and led this twofold revolution in ideas and political structures. In fact, contrary to Marx's analysis:

> In Germany and throughout Eastern Europe, as well as in Italy and Spain, the agents of change were not the new capitalist bourgeoisie but the old professional middle class, the men of letters and the professors, the lawyers and the government officials. Even in France, where economic conditions were more advanced, the capitalists who played a part in the Enlightenment were not the industrial capitalists, but chiefly the 'Farmers General' and the government contractors who represented a tradition as ancient as the publicani of the Roman Empire.
>
> As in Russia so in Europe generally it was the intelligentsia, the class to which Marx himself belonged, and not the capitalists or the proletariat who were the real agents of change and the source of the revolutionary tradition.[17]

Dawson then points out that this class had close relationships with the 18th century State, the so-called enlightened depotisms which represented the tradition of a strong centralized government, along the lines which had first been developed in France in the century of Richelieu and Louis XIV. These traditions were then allied with the movement of Enlightened thought in the 18th century. The power of the absolute monarch was to be used to transform society in accordance with the new ideas, and to make government an effective agent for change.

Thus we find that the situation in Soviet Russia today is not the result of some new and unique development in history which revolutionary economic factors have brought into being. Instead it is the perpetuation of a pattern which was already characteristic of the bureaucratic government of enlightened depotism in the 18th century. The governing class in Marxist states occupies the same position as before; what has changed is the increased power over the working class, and over all of society, which the progress of technology has allowed the government to assume. The development of the new technological order, instead of being a force for the liberation of the workers, as Marx predicted, has become the means for the creation of depotisms more absolute than any ever before known in the history of the world.

Consequently, Marx's conception of class relationships in the dialectic of history is quite different from the actual historical development. As we have seen, rather than industrial capitalism having produced the situation which led to social revolution, the revolutionary ideas were powerful before the industrialization of Europe occurred, and they were promoted by a class having the least connection with industrial development. Moreover, the later economic development of capitalism did not fulfill Marx's expectation of ever increasing misery and poverty for the workers, but developed in the opposite direction -- to a greater participation by the working class in capitalist prosperity. In Western industrialized nations, through the influence of both Christian and humanitarian idealists, the power of government was employed to give greater protection to the workers and to legalize labor unions, by which the workers might move towards equality in bargaining with their employers. Consequently, as Dawson has noted, ours has become a thoroughly bourgeois society. The most important causes for social revolution lie not in the economic condition of the workers, but in the spiritual emptiness which the hedonism of modern industrial society carries with it. What has been the Achilles heel of capitalist or bourgeois society is its moral relativism, and its implicit belief that advances in material well-being are all that is needed in order to make men happy and contented. The mistake of capitalist ideology in this regard is apt to be its undoing, for its basic worldview is so set upon making money and making products that it has no time or energy left for considering the ultimate significance of the society it is creating. It wishes to ignore the basic question of whether a material cornucopia can compensate for a spiritual vacuum in the heart of a society.

So far as Marxism is concerned, it is obvious that the dynamic on which Marx relied for the movement of history has been checkmated by the absolute depotisms created by the Communist governments. Marx's own materialism, instead of providing an ongoing dialectic of social progress, has destroyed the spiritual freedom needed for creative new developments. It would be well, therefore, to look again to the Christian Faith which has not only been the source of Western man's hope for a city set in the Heavens, but has also served as the inspiration for Western culture's transformation of the earthly city, first in Europe, and then, in recent times, throughout the rest of the world as well. It was not the material advances upon which Marx fixed his gaze which were the important factor in the development of world history, but the sense of dynamic spiritual purpose which Christianity has imparted to Western culture.

NOTES

[1]Religion and the Modern State (New York: Sheed & Ward, 1938), pp. 132-133.

[2]Ibid., pp. 133-134.

[3]Ibid., pp. 131-132.

[4]The Gods of Revolution (New York: New York University Press, 1972), p. 37.

[5]Religion and the Modern State, p. 64.

[6]Ibid., p. 143.

[7]Ibid., p. 144.

[8]Ibid., p. 66.

[9]Ibid., p. 67-68.

[10]Ibid., p. 67.

[11]Christianity and the New Age (London: Sheed & Ward, 1931), pp. 20-21.

[12]Religion and the Modern State, p. 87.

[13]Ibid., p. 86.

[14]Ibid., pp. 70-71.

[15]Ibid., p. 58.

[16]Christianity and the New Age, pp. 104-105.

[17]Christianity in East and West (La Salle: Sherwood Sugden & Co., 1981), pp. 85-86.

[18]The Judgment of the Nations (New York: Sheed & Ward, 1942), pp. 23-24.

A FLAW IN THE BISHOPS' PASTORAL

Richard R. Roach, S.J.

Christopher Dawson believed that Christian culture was worth fighting and dying for. In fact, his belief could be stated even more strongly. He believed, as I do, that a Christian may be obliged to take up arms and kill in defense of the culture that makes it possible for him, his wife and family, and for us all, freely to carry out our duties towards God in this life.[1] He never countenanced the evil proposition that it would be better to submit to atheistic or any other anti-Christian tryanny and thereby continue to exist in this world rather than risk killing and being killed in the fight for Christian freedom. This view was not something that he happened to add onto this Catholic faith. Rather, he rightly saw that this faith entailed it.[2] In this darker period after his death, men claiming to be Catholic have called this entailment into question, whereas in truth the denial of this entailment strikes at the very heart of the faith and eventually destroys it. The problem is now before Catholics in the United States and the rest of the world since the publication of a document on war and peace in 1983, which is the copyrighted property of the United States Catholic Conference.

There is a grave flaw in that USCC document entitled "The Challenge of Peace: God's Promise and Our Response." The presence of this flaw is a special embarrassment because the document is regarded as a pastoral letter on the subject from the bishops of the United States. Teaching which has the endorsement of Catholic bishops should not contain such a flaw.

Richard R. Roach, S.J.

The flaw consists in the impression the document gives, to even a fairminded and careful reader, that the Roman Catholic Church, at least after the Second Vatican Council, contenances the false doctrine that Our Lord and Savior Jesus Christ taught absolute or doctrinal pacifism.

Absolute or doctrinal pacifism is the position that condemns all war as immoral. In Christian garb it is the false claim that our Lord and Savior Jesus Christ changed the teaching found in the Old Testament and forbade all killing as part of a "New Law." I believe that from the beginning of the Church this teaching has been associated with heresy; but, be that as it may, the Church has long since settled any doubts about the matter. Our Lord did not forbid His followers to bear arms, nor did He forbid His followers to use force in self-defense. The document gives the impression that these are open questions, and that some may decide that "Jesus" did forbid these things without the Church being able to advise them that their view is wrong.

At the outset we must carefully contrast absolute or doctrinal pacifism, which is incompatible with the Catholic faith, with relative or practical pacifism. The latter can be fully orthodox. McReavy distinguishes absolute from relative pacifism as follows:

> Absolute or doctrinal pacifism condemns all war as immoral; relative or practical pacifism limits its objection to particular wars or forms of war.[3]

The two general varieties of pacifism can and do come in some cases to the same practical conclusions. For example, when it is a question of using what the Second Vatican Council called arma scientifica (scientific weaponry, a term that unfortunately seems to make most people think exclusively of nuclear weaponry or atomic bombs), both kinds of pacifist may refuse to bear arms for reasons of conscience. The fact that certain issues unite representatives of both varieties of pacifism in a refusal to bear arms may lead some to ask why bother with their theoretical differences. I hope to show that their theoretical differences are all important to the faith.

A FLAW IN THE BISHOPS' PASTORAL

The document most clearly seems to teach as truth the false view that Our Lord taught absolute pacifism in, I believe, the following three passages (I will mention a further passage and another general defect later on):

1. On page 8, the third column, and page 9, the first column of the Origins' version[4] we read:

In some cases they are motivated by their understanding of the Gospel and the life and death of Jesus as forbidding all violence.

In the context the "they" refers to Christians, and the rest of the sentence makes them out to be absolute pacifists, because "violence" is not used, as is the custom, to refer to the illicit use of force. (If it were used to signify illicit force, then, of course, we would be right in saying Our Lord forbids it.) Instead, in the context, it refers to "waging war" or "bearing arms," or the like. The next paragraph then treats these Christians, who are historically and doctrinally either separated brethern, or heretics, as if their mistaken views made up a Catholic moral response to the question of war. In a peculiar way, which is neither historically nor doctrinally sound, the document presents what it calls the tradition of non-violence as if it existed side-by-side with a tradition of teaching about the conduct of just and limited warfare. Then, at least in this passage, it seems to insert the false view of a "Christian" absolute pacifism into this tradition of non-violence as if it were acceptable to the Catholic Church. The truth is quite different. A Catholic may be obliged by the sound moral principles which make up the doctrine of just-war to conscientiously object to this particular war or way of conducting war: i.e., relative or practical pacifism. But he certainly must not conscientiously object by invoking false doctrine about what Our Lord taught regarding war. If he did, he could be in the awful position of conscientiously objecting, when that was the right thing to do, but doing so for the wrong reason which could vitiate his act. For example, when Hitler unjustly declared war, Germans, Austrians and Italians had good reasons for refusing to bear arms; but doing so for the wrong reason -- i.e., the false notion that Our Lord forbids us all

181

to bear arms -- would have corruped their refusal.

2.   The second passage is even clearer than the first. It is found on page 12 in the first and second columns of the Origins' version:

> Moved by the example of Jesus' life and by His teaching, some Christians have from the earliest days of the Church committed themselves to a non-violent lifestyle. Some understood the Gospel of Jesus to prohibit all killing.

Those "some," it is implied, did not avail themselves of the truth the Church taught, or they would have corrected their mistaken notion about Our Lord. (This document likes to refer just to "Jesus" as you or I might refer to Reagan or Gandhi, or in the way some middle-class restaurants introduce their waiters. I think this tendency points to another, and even more serious flaw which I will comment on later.) It is true that in the past a man like Tertullian could grow confused and abandon the Church to join an heretical sect that has ceased to exist, and in so doing embrace absolute or doctrinal pacifism. That is no reason to recreate the conditions for engendering like confusion in our day. The Church has long since settled that issue; the Montanists, which is the sect Tertullian joined, have died out. This document should have taught the truth about these matters clearly instead of recreating the kind of confusion that seduced Tertullian.

3.   The third passage is on the same page, third column, and is the most insidious. It insinuates that the Second Vatican Council approved absolute or doctrinal pacifism. In order to make the Council say what it did not say, the USCC document interprets the words of the Council before quoting from the Council document by adding the prepositional phrase, "to all war," thereby falsifying what the Council taught. It goes like this:

> In Paragraph 70 [of Gaudium et Spes] the council fathers called upon governments to enact laws protecting the rights of those who adopted the position of conscientious objection to all war:

((emphasis added in text) After the colon the docu-
ment goes right on to quote <u>Gaudium</u> <u>et</u> <u>Spes</u>, #79.
The reader should note that the quotation does not
contain the prepositional phrase, "to all war.")

I now return to the text of the USCC document
which quotes the Second Vatican Council:

> Moreover, it seems right that laws make
> humane provisions for the case of those
> who for reasons of conscience refuse to
> bear arms, provided, however, that they
> accept some other form of service to
> the human community.

Neither here nor elsewhere does the Second Vatican
Council endorse absolute pacifism, although I believe it is quite correct to assume that the Council
wanted absolute pacifists treated humanely, as well
as those who would refuse to bear arms for reasons
of conscience that the Roman Catholic Church recognizes as founded in God's law. Those in error
should be treated humanely. Nevertheless, I believe
that the Council had primarily in mind those who
refused to bear arms for right reasons. There is a
perfectly sensible and accurate discussion of these
latter along with a discussion of this section of
the Second Vatican Council in a book which I heart-
ily recommend, entitled, <u>The Social Teaching of
Vatican II</u> by Rodger Charles, S.J., with Drostan
MacLaren, O.P.[5] Charles makes clear what the
Second Vatican Council taught in paragraph 79. He
points out that given the nature of contemporary
weaponry (<u>arma scientifica</u>) and the widespread failure to observe proper restraint in the conduct of
war especially during the course of this century,
there are many sound reasons derived from God's law
for refusing to bear arms under a large number of
likely circumstances. This still remains altogether
different from refusing to bear arms because of the
false view that "Jesus" forbade His followers to do
so. Nowhere does the Second Vatican Council explicitly refer to, or endorse, conscientious objection
<u>to all war</u> in the sense of absolute pacifism. Ob-
viously, the USCC document gives the impression that
the Council did. This falsifying little phrase
harms the unity of Christ's household.

In order to prevent that unity from being still more seriously harmed, the bishops in the United States must clarify what they meant when they said:

> As Catholic bishops it is incumbent up-
> on us to stress to our own community
> and to the wider society the signifi-
> cance of this support for a pacifist
> option for individuals in the teaching
> of Vatican II and the reaffirmation
> that the popes have given to non-
> violent witness since the time of the
> Council. [6]

It is the right thing to do if the bishops meant relative or practical pacifism; it is the wrong thing to do if the bishops meant absolute or doctrinal pacifism. The document makes it seem that they include the latter.

Of course I have not yet answered those who would want to know why the theoretical difference between absolute and relative pacifists is significant for the faith. But I had to set out the main lines of the difference before I could attempt to do so, because it involves a subtlety which is not widely attended to. A religious leader could have forbade his followers to engage in war -- i.e., condemned all war as immoral -- and yet not have been an absolute pacifist in the pernicious sense that it makes it an evil doctrine incompatible with the Catholic faith. The judgment that all war is immoral could be a prudential judgment rather than a principled judgment. As a prudential judgment it would be theoretically relative or practical pacifism, and therefore not in principle incompatible with the Catholic faith.

A principled judgment on this matter would go like this: The moral teaching which permitted or required us to defend the lives, property, and rights of the innocent with force, even with deadly force when necessary, is wrong, or has been over-ruled by a higher teaching coming from God. We now obey a rule that forbids all use of force. We must permit the innocent to be violated and even killed if the only way to stop that from happening involves using force, particularly potentially deadly force.

A FLAW IN THE BISHOPS' PASTORAL

A practical judgment on this matter would be quite different and would go something like this: The moral teaching which permitted or required us to defend the lives, property, and rights of the inno- cent with force, even with deadly force if neces- sary, is sound. We assent to the truth of this teaching, but we also recognize that it never obli- ges us to use immoral means, such as intentionally killing some innocent people, when using force to defend other innocent people from being violated or killed. The weapons modern governments use to con- duct war inevitably will lead to direct or inten- tionally killing of the innocent. These weapons are indiscriminate because they are too massive. There- fore, we must refuse to bear arms for such govern- ments because though their cause may be just, their means will inevitably be immoral.

In short, a Catholic relative or practical pacifist would have to abandon his pacifism if he could be shown that both cause and means in the con- duct of the war in which he was asked to bear arms would be just. That is quite different from the situation with an absolute pacifist, who would in- sist that all war, because war involves the use of deadly force, was immoral. He would be appealing to a "higher" morality, and if he attributed that so-called "higher" morality to Our Lord, he would be wrong.

By the way, the point of the example remains the same if the relative or practical pacifist claims that all contemporary governments are without just cause for war.

Fortunately, those who treat "Jesus" as if He were merely a religious leader, who might have in- vented such a "higher" morality, are constrained by the only available records (the New Testament) of His teaching and by the historical record of the Christian faith when making theoretical claims. If they are to make any case at all that "Jesus" taught pacifism, they must find it in the Bible. As a re- sult, either we teach what the Church has consis- tently taught through the ages and knows to be true about Christ's teaching, or we isolate certain New Testament passages and re-interpret His Passion and Death in order to make out a new doctrine to the effect that "Jesus" forbade all killing, as the USCC document allows He may have done. Fine as the distinction is, it is one thing to say that all war is immoral, meaning that no one ever really has a justifying cause or ever really conducts the war in a just way, even if both (having just cause and rightly conducting war) are theoretically possible; and quite another thing to say that "Jesus" forbade all killing. A stark example should make this issue clear.

Let us say that I am an authentic Catholic (one who believes that what the Church actually teaches is true), as I pray that I am by the grace of God. And let us further say that for reasons derived from what the Church actually teaches, I have concluded that in this twentieth century all war is immoral, so I conscientiously object to bearing arms. (I do not hold this view, but I believe an authentic Catholic can.) We further imagine that I am returning from a hunting trip alone and armed. Walking out of the woods to my car I come across a very strong, also armed man attempting to rape a young woman. I would not hesitate to use the gun I am carrying to deter the man from going any further and to hold him until someone could summon the police. If he resisted I would not hesitate to shoot him. If I were forced to shoot, I would not directly intend to kill him, but if he died, I would not judge myself guilty of wrong doing. In other words, my mind would not have been confused by false teaching regarding what Our Lord commanded us about killing. I know He did not forbid all killing. This would not affect my refusal to bear arms for reasons of conscience. That refusal to bear arms, since in the example I am an authentic Catholic, was based on the prudential judgment that governments in our day do not have justifying cause for war or fail to conduct them properly, because they are committed to using indiscriminate weapons, and so forth. So the reader will not be confused, let me say again that I am not a practical pacifist as I have described myself in the example. But I firmly believe that one can be such a practical pacifist and a good Catholic, whereas I firmly believe that no one can be an absolute pacifist and a good Catholic.

If I were, God forbid, an absolute pacifist, I would have refused to use my gun to stop the rapist. (I probably would have refused to go hunting.) In that case, the rapist, being much stronger than I, as well as armed, would have driven me off, knocked me out, or killed me (if I were not lucky enough to have frightened him off for some unknown reason). After I were out of the way, the rape would have continued. I then would be in some measure accountable for the rape. I would have sinned by omission. Herein lies the pernicious character of absolute pacifism. It is a false ideal that can in some circumstances lead one to sin, at least by omission. When force or violence or whatever it is called is the only means to stop a human agent from carrying out an evil deed against another human being, and I am free to use that force, then failure to do so makes me in some measure an accomplice in the evil deed. (Important sense hangs on the word "free" in what I have just said. Certainly I could use force or violence to stop some abortions, thus, perhaps saving a human life. But I am not _free_ to do so in the requisite sense; whereas I am _free_ to stop the rapist.)

Dawson would have been appalled to contemplate a document of some official standing on the topic of war and peace which did not make the preceeding distinction pellucidly clear. Absolute or doctrinal pacifism is an invitation to the kind of sin which Our Lord most vigorously condemned: Pharisaism.[7] Pharisaism has two faces. One face looks to a false rigor of religious observance which enables a man to feel self-righteous. Most even casual readers of the New Testament catch on to this face of Pharisaism. If it is taken as the only face of what Our Lord condemned about Pharisaism, then a false conclusion may easily be drawn to the effect that the Christian faith is antinomian. "Pure" Christians live beyond the law, beyond all law even the moral law. St. Paul apparently had to deal with a form of this heresy as we read in the third chapter of his Epistle to the Romans (3:8).

We must see the other face of Pharisaism if we are to understand exactly what the spiritual evil is that Our Lord condemned. It is this second face which may be found everywhere today, and because it is not widely appreciated, few realize the nature of the evil that surrounds us. Our Lord's account of this face of evil may be found in The Gospel according to St. Matthew, the fifteenth chapter, the third

187

through the ninth verses inclusively, and in the Gospel according to St. Mark, the seventh chapter, the eighth through the thirteenth verses in particular. The point Our Lord makes is that the Pharisees set aside plain, fundamental morality -- the fundamentals of God's law for us -- by appeal to the human traditions which they had set up, and they did this in the spirit of self-righteousness, of being better than others. Absolute or doctrinal pacifists follow this pattern exactly. The absolute pacifist sets aside the plain, fundamental morality, which is God's law for us, and which obliges him to defend the innocent from violent attack with force if necessary, and instead turns to a putative higher morality which merely human traditions have generated, despite some claims to the contrary. Sadly, for the rest of us who believe Our Lord is divine, this putative higher morality of absolute pacifism frequently appeals, as we saw above, to Our Lord's teaching and example. But this appeal is successful only when heresy is at work. The radical meaning of the word "heresy" is to pick and choose. The heretic is one who has taken things out of context and picked them for his own purposes. It is the way merely human traditions are built. In the effort to make Our Lord out as an absolute pacifist, the picking and choosing out of context is two-fold. First the Bible is taken out of the context of the Church. Outside the Church it cannot possibly be rightly understood as the Word of God. Secondly, a couple key verses are taken out of their context in the Holy Scripture and read in a literalist way which denies the rhetorical style which Our Lord used when He first delivered them and which the evangelists were at pains to preserve.

I will not dwell on the heresy of separating the Scriptures from the Church. Those of us who are converts to the Catholic Church, such as Dawson and myself, know well that the idea of revelation makes no sense if the revelation resulted only in a book.[8] A book, or a whole library of books, never means anything specific without an authoritative way of interpreting the written word. In the case of truths like those we who believe find in the Bible, it seems obvious that there must be a living authority, i.e., the Church, to settle precisely what they mean when dispute or doubt or just ordinary questions arise. Without that authority everything the

A FLAW IN THE BISHOPS' PASTORAL

Holy Scriptures teach, including the moral doctrine, would have dissolved in dispute centuries ago. Since I believe in the teaching authority of the Church, I see any effort to separate the Holy Scriptures from the Church as quintessential heresy, and it is simply the case that the Church has long since settled the question that Our Lord did not teach absolute pacifism. Yet, despite the fact that the only true interpretation of Scriptures comes through the Church, even sincere Catholics are troubled by the kind of progaganda that sets up a pacifist reading of Scripture against the authentic teaching. So, a few words about the two most famous passages are in order.

In Our Lord's Sermon on the Mount according to St. Matthew, we read:

> You have heard the commandment, 'An eye for an eye, a tooth for a tooth,' But what I say to you is this: offer no resistance to injury. When a person strikes you on the right cheek, turn and offer him the other. (Matt. 5:38-39)

Our Lord Himself gives the key in an earlier passage to how this comment on the lex talionis, as well as the rest of the Sermon on the Mount, should be understood.

> Do not think that I have come to abolish the law and the prophets. I have come, not to abolish them, but to fulfill them. Of this much I assure you: until heaven and earth pass away, not the smallest letter of the law, not the smallest part of a letter, shall be done away with until it all comes true. That is why whoever breaks the least significant of these commands and teaches others to do so shall be called least in the kingdom of God. Whoever fulfills and teaches these commands shall be great in the kingdom of God. I tell you, unless your holiness surpasses that of the scribes and Pharisees you shall not enter the kingdom of God. (Matt. 5:17-20)

189

Richard R. Roach, S.J.

Contemporary academic jargon would refer to this passage as giving the hermeneutical principle for understanding the entire Sermon. Christ does not abolish the Law and the Prophets, He fulfills them. Therefore, whenever we claim that Our Lord made a change in the Old Law, if our claim has a chance of being true, we must show that the change is the result of fulfilling the law, not a way of abolishing it. Following this principle, the Church would recognize, as is recorded in the Book of Acts, that Our Lord's perfect sacrifice, His Passion, Death, and Resurrection, fulfilled the ceremonial (and dietary) laws of the Old Covenant and thereby abrogated them. But fulfillment of the moral law is different. In this area fulfillment means keeping the law perfectly for all the right reasons and with all the right dispositions, as Our Lord did, and in this sense He fulfilled the moral law. He did not thereby abrogate it. He fulfilled the ceremonial law in the other sense, namely, in the sense that He is our salvation. So, it is now wrong to seek salvation from those observances which have been abrogated by the fact that the salvation they pointed to has in fact been accomplished. In a third sense He fulfilled the juridical precepts of the Old Law by replacing the older organization of the people of God with His Church. The "changing" of the Old Law in the New Testament must be understood in these different senses. So, we are not obliged to circumcision, we may eat pork, we must observe Sunday by attending Mass whenever possible, we must not fornicate, and so forth.

Within the Sermon itself, Our Lord in still another sense "changed" the Old Law. He made it stricter because He forbade divorce and remarriage. Later (Matt. 19:8) Our Lord gives the reason why Moses permitted divorce, namely, "the hardness of your heart" (Douay/Rheims - The New American says, "stubbornness," which is a flat translation indeed.)

In giving this reason Our Lord points to the source of His fulfillment of the Old Law: His new heart which we have come to call the Sacred Heart. It is the love and understanding in His heart which sustains Him through His Passion and Death, wherein by complete self sacrifice He actually fulfilled the Old Law. We are expected to change our hearts to become like His. That is the underlying point of

190

the Sermon on the Mount. As Ezekiel had prophesied, when the new Law came we would be given new hearts of flesh to replace our stony hearts. (Ezekiel 36:26) In the Sermon Our Lord calls us to that change of heart, that repentance, whereby God gives us a new heart if we just let Him. If we understand that this change of heart is what the new law requires of us, and that this new heart is the source of fulfillment of the Old Law and not its abolition, then we can interpret the Sermon on the Mount as the Church has interpreted it for nearly two thousand years.

Let us take first a sexual example because they are always easier to understand from the moral point of view than issues of war and peace. Our Lord provides the example in the Sermon He said:

> You have heard the commandment, 'You shall not commit adultery.' What I say to you is: anyone who looks lustfully at a woman has already committed adultery with her in his thoughts. (Matt. 5:27-28)

Our Lord's rhetoric makes the point very effectively. It is not enough in the New Law to simply fail to commit adultery while indulging in lecherous fantasies. We are all tempted, and Our Lord is not asking us to feel guilty about temptations no matter how persistent they are; for, we are all able to know the difference between temptations and indulging in fantasies of sexual conquest. Our Lord insists that it is not enough to observe the commandment prohobiting adultery simply by not committing that sin in the flesh; we must also purify our hearts from willfully hankering after the sin. Furthermore, He wants to be sure that we do not imagine we have made ourselves righteous if we have succeeded in not committing adultery in the flesh, when we have failed to remove the adulterous intent from our hearts. Anyone who has really tried to remove the adulterous intent from his heart knows how difficult that is, much harder than simply avoiding adultery. In fact it is so hard that the very struggle protects us from self-righteousness. Insofar as we overcome the adulterous intent we know that it is a work of God's grace and not our own achievement. The severity of the struggle removes the temptation to self-righteousness.

For those whose principal weaknesses are not sensual, another example may be better used to make the same point: the absolute prohibition against murder and its extension in the new law to remove murderous intent. Somewhere I remember reading a remark of C. S. Lewis' to a friend asking the friend to pray for him. He (Lewis) was on the way to an academic meeting and was afraid that he would be tempted there to murderous intent. It may sound farfetched to those who do not work in higher education, but I assure them it is not. The story has endeared Lewis to me as a fellow-sufferer. I trust that by the grace of God he overcame temptation well and now prays for those of us who are still struggling.

The point should be clear: the Sermon on the Mount, the whole New Law, is addressed primarily to the heart. Our Lord nowhere abolishes the moral law. God's law obliges us under specific circumstances to use force to defend the innocent. Therefore, Our Lord's reinterpretation of the lex talionis addresses our heart in order to prepare us to face these specific circumstances rightly.

St. Thomas Aquinas said all this very well centuries ago. Following St. Augustine, whose work on the Sermon on the Mount he frequently cites, Thomas noted that the injunction to "turn the other cheek" was just one of a number of injunctions in the Sermon whereby Our Lord sought to block the use of the law to indulge in an evil of the heart.

> In another way they (the Scribes and Pharisees) erred by thinking that certain things which the Old Law commanded to be done for justice' sake, should be done out of a desire for revenge, or out of lust for temporal goods, or out of hatred of one's enemies; and this in respect of three precepts. For they thought that desire for revenge was lawful, on account of the precept concerning punishment by retaliation: whereas this precept was given that justice might be safe-guarded, not that man might seek revenge. [Here Thomas is referring to Matt. 5:38-39 which I quoted above.] Wherefore, in order to

do away with this, Our Lord teaches that man should be prepared in his mind to suffer yet more if necessary.

They thought that movements of covetousness were lawful, on account of those judicial precepts which prescribed restitution of what had been purloined, together with something added thereto, as stated above (Q. 105, A. 2, ad 9); whereas the Law commanded this to be done in order to safeguard justice, not to encourage covetousness. Wherefore, Our Lord teaches that we should not demand our goods from motives of cupidity, and that we should be ready to give yet more if necessary. [Thomas refers to Matt. 5:40-42]

They thought that the movement of hatred was lawful on account of the commandments of the Law about the slaying of one's enemies: whereas the Law ordered this for the fulfillment of justice as stated above (Q. 105, A. 3, ad 4), not to satisfy hatred. Wherefore Our Lord teaches us that we ought to love our enemies, and to be ready to do good to them if necessary. [Thomas refers to Matt. 5:43-44.] For these precepts are to be taken as binding the mind to be prepared to fulfill them, as St. Augustine says (De Serm. Dom. in Monte i. 19).[9]

The form of the solution is clear. Thomas gives quite explicit expression to the solution in his first article on war, which we should note he treats in the context of his treatise on charity. In order to answer the question, whether it is always sinful to wage war, Thomas poses this objection:

Further, whatever is contrary to a Divine precept is a sin. But war is contrary to a Divine precept, for it is written (Matt. v. 39): But I say to you not to resist evil; and (Rom. xii, 19): Not revenging yourselves, my

<u>dearly</u> <u>beloved</u>, <u>but</u> <u>give</u> <u>place</u> <u>unto</u>
<u>wrath</u>. Therefore war is always sinful.

Aquinas then responds to the objection as follows:

> Such like precepts, as Augustine ob-
> serves (<u>De</u> <u>Serm</u>. <u>Dom</u>. <u>in</u> <u>Monte</u> i, 19)
> should always be borne in readiness of
> mind, so that we be ready to obey them,
> and, if necessary, to refrain from re-
> sistance or self-defense. Nevertheless
> it is necessary sometimes for a man to
> act otherwise for the common good, or
> for the good of those with whom he is
> fighting. Hence Augustine says (<u>Ep</u>. <u>ad</u>
> <u>Marcellin</u>. cxxxviii): <u>Those</u> <u>whom</u> <u>we</u>
> <u>have</u> <u>to</u> <u>punish</u> <u>with</u> <u>kindly</u> <u>severity</u>, <u>it</u>
> <u>is</u> <u>necessary</u> <u>to</u> <u>handle</u> <u>in</u> <u>many</u> <u>ways</u>
> <u>against</u> <u>their</u> <u>will</u>. <u>For</u> <u>when</u> <u>we</u> <u>are</u>
> <u>stripping</u> <u>a</u> <u>man</u> <u>of</u> <u>the</u> <u>lawlessness</u> <u>of</u>
> <u>sin</u>, <u>it</u> <u>is</u> <u>good</u> <u>for</u> <u>him</u> <u>to</u> <u>be</u> <u>van-</u>
> <u>quished</u>, <u>since</u> <u>nothing</u> <u>is</u> <u>more</u> <u>hopeless</u>
> <u>than</u> <u>the</u> <u>happiness</u> <u>of</u> <u>sinners</u>, <u>whence</u>
> <u>arises</u> <u>a</u> <u>guilty</u> <u>impunity</u>, <u>and</u> <u>an</u> <u>evil</u>
> <u>will</u>, <u>like</u> <u>an</u> <u>internal</u> <u>enemy</u>.[10]

Aquinas is here teaching Catholic doctrine and interpreting the Sermon accurately. If I am called to
bear arms on behalf of my country, which permits
religious liberty in the sense the Second Vatican
Council used that term, against an enemy force which
would impose atheistic tyranny, then acting under
proper orders, I may kill the enemy combatants in
battle, and the killing does not only not violate
what Our Lord said in the Sermon on the Mount, it is
a good deed because the common good requires it. In
order to preserve the goodness of this act, I must
not act out of hatred or the desire for revenge.

In order to transfer this to a case of self-
defense, a further distinction is needed, that between command and counsel. St. Thomas said:

> Those things which Our Lord prescribed
> about the true love of our enemies, and
> other similar sayings (Matth. v., Luke
> vi), may be referred to the preparation
> of the mind, and then they are neces-
> sary for salvation; for instance, that

> man be prepared to do good to his ene-
> mies, and other similar actions, <u>when
> there is need</u> [emphasis added]. Hence
> these things are placed among the pre-
> cepts. But that anyone should actually
> and promptly behave thus towards an
> enemy when there is <u>no</u> special need
> [emphasis added], is to be referred to
> the particular counsels, as stated
> above [Thomas is referring to the body
> of the article from which this objec-
> tion is taken].[11]

With this distinction in mind, we may analyze "offering no resistance to injury" in the instance of
self-defense as follows: If I am attacked as a
private individual, and I know in this instance that
the common good does not require that I defend myself, and I further know that in this instance my
attacker's good is not served if force is used to
stop the evil of his attack (he will not be made a
better man by my using force to stop his evil), then
I may prefer my attacker's good to my own and risk,
probably endure, suffering the injuries his wicked
attack can bring upon me.

It is difficult to provide a single clear
example of this possibility, but I will offer one
that at least approximates the right balance between
all the factors. Let us say that I, as a priest/
academic, were faced with a student whom I knew and
who in a moment of madness or a fit of passion has
picked up a knife and is trying to rob me. Let us
further stipulate that I know I can disarm him with
a couple well placed blows, but I further know that
these blows will injure him severely. I also think
that I could reason with him successfully, calm him
down, disarm him, and then help him to start to live
a good life. I know of no obligation that prohibits
me from taking this chance. So I risk grave harm by
not resisting injury for the potential good of my
attacker. As a Christian I prefer his good to mine.
I would thereby be following Our Lord's <u>counsel</u> and
I would be going beyond what He commands. What He
commanded in the Sermon on the Mount is that if I
use force to defend myself, which I have a right to
do, then I must not use it with hatred for my attacker or in a spirit of revenging myself upon him.
But he also counsels me to take this kind of chance,

when the Holy Spirit prompts me to, because it is always right to prefer the good of the neighbor to my own good.

Let us say that the story has a very unhappy ending. I get all cut up and nearly die; the student is apprehended and faces severe charges in court. Had I done the better thing? That would depend upon the purity of my heart in the instance and on whether I was obeying the promptings of the Holy Spirit. If my heart were pure and I acted on the promptings of the Holy Spirit, which we need when following the counsels, then I can rest assured that good will come from my sacrifice.

It is easy to change the case very slightly thereby making the case illustrate when taking such a risk would have been wrong and in no way an act of obedience to Our Lord's injunction in the Sermon on the Mount. For example, if I had been obliged to protect another, weaker student from the attack of the student armed with a knife, it would have been quite wrong to forego using the skill I had to deliver a couple of disarming blows. If I had been a husband and father, and by taking the risk were placing the support of my family in jeopardy, it would also be wrong. Or, if I thought the armed student would get away with it and rob again, I would have been wrong to offer no resistance to his evil attack.

If we appreciate the complications in this example, we come to a better understanding why we need a teaching Church and why moral theology seems like such a complex subject. Certainly, we must conclude that Our Lord did not teach absolute pacifism in His Sermon on the Mount. Absolute pacifism teaches us to violate God's law, at least by omission, and to suggest that Our Lord and Savior counselled us to do evil is blasphemy.

The other passage in Scripture which absolute pacifists like to use may also be found in the Gospel according to St. Matthew, the twenty-sixth chapter, the fifty-second verse: The scene after Our Lord's Agony in the Garden of Gethsemani; Judas has just arrived with the crowd who will arrest Jesus. Peter has a sword which he uses for a moment in defense of his Lord. He cuts off the ear of a servant of the high priest. A very ineffective gesture; if it were not tragedy, it would be high comedy.

> Jesus said to him: "Put back your sword where it belongs. Those who use the sword are sooner or later destroyed by it." (Matt. 26:52)

The parallel passage in the Gospel according to St. John gives the servant's name, Malchus, but omits Our Lord's remarks about those who use the sword.

It has long seemed clear to me that in context this remark about those who use the sword most likely refers to those who, following false messiahs, would rebel against Rome. Our Lord had predicted what would happen to Jerusalem because of their rebellion. In fact His predictions were one of the causes of His arrest. It seems natural that He would warn His apostles to stay away from the revolutionary crowd. Judas, His betrayer, is thought to have been one of them, which is another sound reason for suspecting that the remark prohibits unjustified revolution and predicts that those who engage in such activity will be killed by it. This reading is my own, and although I believe it makes good sense, it has not been the standard way of interpreting this remark so as to obviate a false pacifist interpretation.

The standard interpretation, which again St. Thomas exemplifies, consists in distinguishing between using the sword privately and having recourse to it in a public manner for the common good.[12] This is no more or less than the distinction between a properly armed police force and citizens, no matter how apparently justified, taking the law into their own hands as vigilantes or the like. Very rarely indeed is the latter licit, let alone the right thing to do.

Our Lord's case is also unique. As the history of that moment in the Garden of Gethsemani makes clear, Our Lord had the power to subdue those who had come to arrest Him. He submitted to His death as a divine person. Had He been merely human, it is questionable whether what He did would have been right. A mere man should probably have left Jerusalem before matters came to such a pass. Our Lord was not a mere man; He is God and man. The uniqueness of His case consists in the fact of the Incarnation, and the atoning sacrifice which only the God-man could offer.

I believe this truth points to another reason why pacifism leads to heresy. We are expected to imitate Christ in His humanity, not in His divinity. I cannot, nor can anyone else, freely offer myself as the sacrifice that atones for the sins of man. I can only offer myself with Him. My freely going to death could even be evil, if it is not done in the right way and for the right reasons which unite me with His sacrifice. For martyrdom to be a virtue it must be associated with Christ. We sometimes forget these and like truths while those who want to ignore or deny Our Lord's divinity positively avoid them. The avoiders have reason to look for something unique in the Garden of Gethsemani besides Our Lord's divinity. They often claim to find this uniqueness by asserting that Our Lord there taught a new and "higher" morality when He ordered Peter to put back his sword: that is, they claim he taught absolute pacifism. Not only is the doctrine false and one that leads to evil, but it is also a way of avoiding what we should see in that scene, namely, that Jesus is God.

Christopher Dawson's views of Christendom include the conviction that as a culture it rests on the kind of moral theology that undergirds what I have said in interpreting the Sermon on the Mount and Our Lord's arrest in the garden of Gethsemani.[13] Pope John Paul II has begged for the revival of that Christendom in our day. It is no accident that his interpretation of Christ's remarks about the lex talionis in the Sermon on the Mount are in accord with the interpretation I have defended. Pope John Paul II employs the same distinction St. Thomas made centuries before: that between the demands of justice and the exigencies of love. The Holy Father wrote:

> And yet, it would be difficult not to notice that very often programs which start from the idea of justice and which ought to assist its fulfillment among individuals, groups and human

societies, in practice suffer from distortions. Although they continue to appeal to the idea of justice, nevertheless experience shows that other negative forces have gained the upper hand over justice, such as spite, hatred and even cruelty. In such cases, the desire to annihilate the enemy, limit his freedom, or even force him into total dependence, becomes the fundamental motive for action; and this contrasts with the essence of justice, which by its nature tends to establish equality and harmony between the parties in conflict. This kind of abuse of the idea of justice and the practical distortion of it show how far human action can deviate from justice itself, even when it is being undertaken in the name of justice. Not in vain did Christ challenge His listeners, faithful to the doctrine of the Old Testament, for their attitude which was manifested in the words: "An eye for an eye and a tooth for a tooth." This was the form of distortion of justice at that time; and today's forms continue to be modeled on it. It is obvious, in fact, that in the name of an alleged justice (for example, historical justice or class justice) the neighbor is sometimes destroyed, killed, deprived of liberty or stripped of fundamental human rights. The experience of the past and of our own time demonstrates that justice alone is not enough, that it can even lead to the negation and destruction of itself, if that deeper power, which is love, is not allowed to shape human life in its various dimensions. It has been precisely historical experience that, among other things, has led to the formulation of the saying: summum ius, summa iniuria. This statement does not detract from the value of justice and does not minimize the significance of the order that is based upon it; it only indicates, under another aspect, the need

to draw from the powers of the spirit
which condition the very order of justice, powers which are still more
profound.[14]

The Holy Father's remarks, in my judgment, not
only confirm the Thomist interpretation we have
given to the Sermon on the Mount, but they also
capture the true meaning of a sentence from Gaudium
et Spes, #78, which has been used to commend pacifism indiscriminately -- i.e., without the distinction between absolute and relative pacifism. That
sentence, which follows, actually commends only
following Our Lord's counsel when able to do so; it
in no way suggests that Our Lord abolished the use
of force, even deadly force, when the common good
required it.

In the same spirit we cannot but express our admiration for all who forego
the use of violence to vindicate their
rights and resort to those other means
of defense which are available to
weaker parties, provided it can be done
without harm to the rights and duties
of others and of the community. [Em-
phasis added.]

Thoroughly rejecting absolute or doctrinal
pacifism in the name of sound doctrine does not
settle the question of relative or practical pacifism. That question is a real one today and authentic Catholics may resolve it differently. Relative or practical pacifism consists in refusing to
bear arms in specific wars either because the side
that requires me to bear arms has not just cause or
because the authorities are using unjust means in
conducting the war, or both. This is loosely and
popularly referred to as "selective conscientious
objection" and is not recognized in American law.
Of course, American law does not always reflect the
moral law. In truth the only morally right reasons
for refusing to bear arms must be selective, because
the absolute refusal is pernicious.

There are an impressive number of authentic
Catholics who are relative or practical pacifists in
our day. They are so because of the special prob-

lems which those weapons the Church's official documents call <u>arma</u> <u>scientifica</u> (scientific weaponry) bring in their train. Nuclear weapons are not the only kind of scientific weaponry which cause problems. The whole host of chemical, biological, even psychological weapons, must be considered. The common problem they present may be called the problem of discrimination. Is it possible to discriminate between combatants and non-combatants in a way the moral law requires when using such weapons? If it is not, and such weapons necessarily entail a direct or intentional assualt on the innocent, then the absolute prohibition against murder would interdict their use even in a just cause against an unjust aggressor. We may never do evil that good may come. This is the inner heart of the ethic of Christendom. Authentic Catholics who are relative or practical pacifists today widely share the conviction that the scientific weaponry which even the remnants of Christendom might use in their own defense would by their very nature be so indiscriminate that any use of them would violate the absolute prohibition against murder. I recognize the problem, but I do not share their view, at least in this sense. I believe it is possible to design and deploy scientific weaponry which could be used in just, even required defense, without violating the prohibition against murder. I am not confident that the present defense of the United States meets this moral exigency, but I am confident that such a defense is possible. Therefore, I believe we should work toward realizing such a capability, rather than embrace a practical pacifist's position at this time.

In doing so, I would be using what may be considered a loop-hole in the moral law regarding deterrence, but before we look more closely at that, we should attend to a deeper problem that troubles some very conscientious and authentic Catholics who in consequence embrace relative or practical pacifism in our day.

This problem consists in determining how many, if any, innocent men, women, and children may be incidentally killed in the conduct of war, if their deaths, although unintended, were foreseen. We have long recognized that some incidental killing, in principle unforeseen, is licit in war. For example, if in the process of destroying a military target, say an airfield, we incidentally killed a group of civilians who were hiding too near the target, we rightly excused ourselves of blame for their deaths and rightly regarded killing them as an incidental and unintended side-effect of a licit military action. Our exculpation seems also to have depended not only on the fact that we did not intend to kill these innocent people, but also on the fact that we did not foresee that we would kill them. The problem, which I believe it is safe to say that the Church has not adjudicated, is whether we can incidentally kill the innocent in the conduct of war when we foresee that our actions will encompass their deaths, because we can, according to some theories, plausibly maintain that their deaths are unintended and therefore, killing them may not be murder. The minimal definition, or core definition of murder is to intentionally or directly kill the innocent. The problem is: may we use this minimal definition and distinguish between intentionally killing the innocent, which is always forbidden, and a foreseen, but incidental killing of the same, so as to permit ourselves the use, under certain conditions, of weapons we foresee will inevitably kill innocent persons?

I trust this question puts the matter before us clearly. Any reader can see how it bristles with theoretical problems. How do we distinguish between combatants and non-combatants (the innocent in this case)? How do we distinguish properly between what is intended and what is merely foreseen in this case? Is the distinction, once we have successfully made it, decisive for moral judgment about ways of conducting war? That question asks whether, after I have successfully distinguished between intending and merely foreseeing, may I perform an act of war which does not intend to kill the innocent, but which I foresee will? Honest and authentic Catholics dispute these questions today, and the Church has not resolved them. What may we do in the meantime if we believe with Dawson and others that even the remnant of Christendom is worth fighting for? Before these questions are resolved and the authentic teaching voice of the Church has spoken, I belive it is safe to act on what the Holy Father said through Cardinal Casaroli to the United Nations on June 11th of 1982:

A FLAW IN THE BISHOPS' PASTORAL

> In current conditions "deterrence" based on balance, certainly not as an end in itself but as a step on the way toward a progressive disarmament, may still be judged morally acceptable.[15]

I had this official teaching and other expressions like it in mind when I referred to the "loophole" in the moral law regarding deterrence. I believe that in this passage, the Holy Father, teaching officially, is expressing that teaching with studied and deliberate ambiguity. The ambiguity is necessary because the Holy Spirit has not made clear to the Church what is the right answer to the question about incidental killing which I have proposed. The Holy Spirit acting through the Second Vatican Council has reaffirmed that indiscriminate killing is forbidden, but we knew that already. The famous passage in question reads as follows:

> Every act of war directed to the indiscriminate destruction of whole cities or vast areas with their inhabitants is a crime against God and man, which merits firm and unquivocal condemnation. (Gaudium et Spes, #80).

What is significant about this passage is that it does not say what the Council Fathers easily could have said at just this point in the document, if the Holy Spirit had prompted them to do so. They could have said:

> Every act of war which with foresight incidentally encompasses the death of the innocent is a crime against God and man, which merits firm and unequivocal condemnation.

They did not say that because the Church does not know whether or not it is true. Therefore, the Holy Father teaches that we may build and maintain scientific weaponry, which raises the question of incidentally killing the innocent, for purposes of deterring an enemy who is armed with such weapons. He does not say whether that deterrence is merely a bluff -- some have thought that bluffing was the moral outer limit for deterrence with weaponry which would foreseeably kill the innocent incidentally --

203

or whether the deterrence may be mounted with actual intent to use if necessary. Certainly that actual intent would be immoral if the weapons were such, or were deployed in such a way, as to violate what the Council condemned in section #80 of Gaudium et Spes. But not all scientific weaponry necessarily comes under that condemnation; so, if incidental killing of the innocent were licit, then actual intent to use discriminate scientific weaponry, although weaponry which would foreseeably kill the innocent incidentally, would be licit. It seems clear to me that the rethinking of the morality of war, which good Pope John XXIII asked for, must focus on this question of incidental killing.

I strongly suspect that a clue to the right answer may be buried in those passages of the Old Testament which most embarrass contemporary believers: e.g., Deuteronomy 20: 16-18. The question is whether the precedent of a divinely authorized judgment of Doom (the execution of all the inhabitants of a city) on a people trapped in iniquity -- a judgment no human authority could ever licitly pass -- provides authorization for a human judgment, essentially limited by comparison, which would encompass the death of the innocent. For example, the United States would launch weapons proportioned to their military targets in the Soviet Union. ("Proportioned" means that the weapon's force is that needed to destroy the target and not a great deal more. A weapon so proportioned can be used discriminately.) Then, if the target was licitly destroyed, we might reason that it was licit to encompass the deaths of those innocent persons who could not be separated from the target. It is really the question or problem about incidental killing in a slightly different guise, but restated with reference to Biblical precedent. Aquinas was not afraid of the question, e.g., Summa Theologica, I-II, Q.105, A. 3, ad 4, but he does not develop an answer. Nevertheless, even in the brief reference cited, we can see that although Thomas believed a judgment of Doom as commanded in the passage from Deuteronomy under consideration could only be a divine judgment, he also believed that we could see the justice of it.

A FLAW IN THE BISHOPS' PASTORAL

It is not unlike the justice whereby we were all condemned for the sin at the origin of the human race. Then, Our Lord and Savior bore that condemnation in His own body, as well as the judgment passed against our actual sins, throughout His Incarnate Life, Passion, and Death. Finally, in His Resurrection He overcomes that judgment. This is divine justice which we do not adequately understand this side of the grave. God's holiness seems to require Him to condemn even those who are innocent from the limited perspective of merely human justice; then His mercy provides the remedy for their plight, which is also our plight, in the Son. The fact that God judges, condemns and offers mercy in this global way teaches us something about ourselves: namely, the fact that we are interrelated in ways that give rise to what we today like to call "solidarity." Just as there can be solidarity in good causes, and those unworthy of the ideals of the cause may still be counted as part of the movement, so there can be solidarity in evil and those who are not "guilty" may still be caught in the machinations of the corporate evil. If the machinations are such that they will overwhelm other innocent persons not yet ensnared, along with their good institutions or their good solidarity, then it may be possible that in defending against that aggressive corporate evil the defenders may incidentally encompass the deaths of innocent persons.

The parallel is roughly as follows: as God may order the direct killing of those who are innocent in terms of merely human justice, so man may indirectly kill the innocent when he defends himself against a corporate evil which, because it is aggressing against him, he may justly attack with deadly force. If there is any point in this reasoning, it may mean that it might be possible for a government with free institutions which permit teaching the faith (what <u>Dignitatis Humanae</u> calls "religious liberty") to defend itself against atheistic tyranny with acts of war that, although they are not targeted directly on innocent people who are trapped in atheistic tyranny, do in fact foreseeably encompass their deaths indirectly or incidentally. These remarks must be seen as no more than a suggestion of a line of thought that ought to be examined, albeit very carefully indeed.

Richard R. Roach, S.J.

Although, as I have said, I am not a relative pacifist, my position at the moment is ironic. I served as a pilot in the USAF, but I am now a priest; and, as such, I am one of the persons who would come under what the Second Vatican Council said in section 79 of Gaudium et Spes:

> Moreover, it seems right that laws make humane provisions for the case of those who for reasons of conscience refuse to bear arms, provided, however, that they accept some other form of service to the human community.

With my brother priests and all seminarians, I enjoy clerical exemption. That means that humane provision has been made in American law for my clerical refusal to bear arms. A number of things should be noted in this regard. First, I am expected if needed to engage in service which in principle should be just as dangerous as bearing arms: I should be, and I am, willing to serve as a chaplain in combat. Great priests have done so, and have given their lives in that service. They can claim St. Francis of Assisi as a model. Secondly, I am unmarried. I do not have a family that I am obliged to defend. Clerical exemption is rightly connected to a vow of celibacy for the Kingdom. Without it the exemption is much more problematic. A married man has obligations to defend his family. Thirdly, my refusal to bear arms as a priest is not absolute. I can easily construct an imaginary situation in which my obligations to defend someone would take precedence over my clerical obligations. I hope that no such situation will ever arise, but if it did, I would know what to do. So, my clerical state does not make an absolute pacifist out of me.

In summary, the reason for raising a fuss about even giving the impression that Catholics may accept the false teaching of absolute pacifism, when in large matters it may not lead to significantly different action from an acceptable relative pacifism, lies in the fact that absolute pacifism, as all false teaching, can lead one to sin.

A feeling of the presence of this false teaching which leads to sin shows up in other passages thereby strengthening the unfortunate impression the

A FLAW IN THE BISHOPS' PASTORAL

USCC document gives of teaching absolute pacifism. One of these latter comes after a high point in the document, namely, its recognition of the grave evil of abortion (<u>Origins</u>, p. 26, second column ff.). The discussion goes very well until we come up against a sentence at the bottom of page 26 continuing on the top of page 27:

> And we now find ourselves seriously discussing the pros and cons of such questions as infanticide, euthanasia and the involvement of physicians in carrying out the death penalty.

If the bishops' point is that some physicians are denigrating the practice of medicine because, in the name of medicine, they act as executioners rather than as physicians by deliberately destroying human life, then the bishops ought not refer to the death penalty. The morality of carrying out the death penalty would not be the point in question; rather, it would be the issue of physicians disguising the direct killing of human life as a medical treatment.

I trust that the reader remembers the old example used in teaching logic: If you add two apples and an orange, you get three what? If infanticide means directly killing an innocent human life, God's law absolutely forbids it; if euthanasia means directly killing an innocent human life, God's law absolutely forbids it; BUT, God's law does not absolutely forbid the death penalty. Therefore, it is possible that a physician could carry out the death penalty without doing anything wrong. He cannot directly kill an infant or an old and suffering man who is innocent without doing something wrong. But he could carry out the death penalty without doing something wrong. These two apples and an orange add up to moral confusion.

This is the kind of moral confusion that becomes endemic when one cannot distinguish between absolute and relative pacifism. The nature of the evil in question is misapprehended. Killing without qualification is thought to be a moral evil, when it is not. What is absolutely evil is intentionally (directly) killing the <u>innocent</u>. The victims of infanticide are innocent of crime; the victims of euthanasia are innocent of crime; Gary Gilmore was justly executed.

All Christians have to appreciate this distinction otherwise we cannot understand the crucifixion as the Evangelists describe it. What is the distinction between Barabbas and Jesus, and why is it important? Why does the Good Thief admonish the bad thief with the words:

> Have you no fear of God, seeing you are
> under the same sentence? We deserve
> it, after all. We are only paying the
> price for what we've done, but this man
> has done nothing wrong (Luke 23:40-41).

Anyone who cannot appreciate the difference between abortion, infanticide, euthanasia on the one hand, and the death penalty on the other, cannot understand the Bible!

This confusion blinds people to the pattern immanent in all authentic development of moral doctrine. We saw that pattern implicitly while trying to interpret correctly those passages from the Holy Scriptures which absolute pacifists like to adduce in defense of their doctrine. The pattern is essentially one of deepening and interiorizing the moral law. God holds us accountable not only for our acts, but for the spirit in which we do them. That spirit must be one of love of God and neighbor on God's terms at all times; it must be a spirit in which we are disposed to sacrifice our lives, if need be, rather than willfully offend, even in our dispositions, against God's will. We have seen that Our Lord did not abolish the Old Law, so we are expected still to observe its moral norms for justice. But we have also seen that justice is not enough. We know that if we are rightly to resist injury we must do so from motives of love of God and neighbor, and not from motives of revenge. This discretion, sorting out these motives and keeping the right ones intact, is a superhuman work. It is the work of God's grace which we must seek daily in faith through the sacraments, through private prayer and penance, and by good works. In short, we must live the Christian vocation and ask daily both to know God's will for us and the strength to do it.

A FLAW IN THE BISHOPS' PASTORAL

Our Lord Himself is our best example. He knew what He had said in the Sermon on the Mount about not resisting injury and turning the other cheek so the example He gave us near the end of His earthly life is especially significant. Because of the union He has as God with the Holy Spirit and the Father, and because of the grace that flows from that union to His human nature, He as man could discern when the right thing to do, because of His love for the Father and for us, was _not_ to turn the other cheek.

When one of the guards who had brought Jesus before Annas the High Priest slapped Him, Our Lord rightly did not turn the other cheek for another slap, instead He verbally resisted evil by replying: "If I have said anything wrong produce the evidence, but if I spoke the truth why hit me?" (John 18:23) It would not have been good in that case for Our Lord not to have resisted injury and simply to have turned the other cheek, because such an act could have been taken as an admission of guilt. Admitting guilt would have undermined the significance of Our Lord's Passion and Death which in part depends on His innocence.

We must use the same discretion Our Lord used when following His counsels. They are rightly followed only under the guidance of the Holy Spirit. The law, on the other hand, although of itself it cannot save us, must be followed even if we are not in the state of grace. When in a state of mortal sin, we cannot rightly expect guidance from the Holy Spirit to help us to discriminate between goods and determine which is the greater. In that state the Holy Spirit usually seeks only to draw us to repent. Later, once we are within the boundaries of the law, He will guide us in ways to fulfill it.

There is only one seeming exception to this general pattern in the Sermon on the Mount and that it the fact that Our Lord did abolish divorce and remarriage, but it is only a seeming exception to the pattern. Rightly seen it too is only a fulfillment of the law and the prophets. The provision for divorce was an escape clause granted because of the hardness of our hearts. But if we accept His grace, Our Lord overcomes the hardness of our hearts. So we are enabled to live the law as He fulfilled it by restoring it to its pristine form. We should note that the restoration does not excuse any of us from fulfilling any duty we might have under the law. (Once we know about the resurrection there is no duty to raise up children for a brother who dies married, but childless: cf. Matthew 22:23-33, Mark 12:18-27, and Luke 20:27-40). But if what Our Lord said about resisting evil were taken as abrogating, rather than fulfilling the law, and we extended it to include evil done another innocent human being, then we could excuse ourselves from doing our duty to defend the innocent. As we have noted many times now, the counsel so misunderstood could lead us to sin at least by omission.

The pattern in summary is from what is less demanding to what is more demanding without ever contradicting what went before. For example, observance of the sacramental bond which God creates when a marriage takes place between two baptized persons becomes a required means for those so married to love God. His first disciples saw the potential demands of this observance as so great in terms of possible self-sacrifice that they cried out:

> If that is the case between man and wife, it is better not to marry. (Matt. 19:10)

They understood Our Lord's pattern for fulfilling the moral law. It is from the demands of justice to the exigencies of love of God and neighbor on God's terms without ever reneging on the demands of justice, except for not insisting on my rights if sacrificing a right can be the loving and merciful thing to do. This pattern can be applied throughout the history of the Church, and never more startlingly than in our day.

Archbishop Marcel Lefebvre has led the largest quasi-schismatic movement to follow upon the Second Vatican Council precisely because he cannot understand this pattern. He sees the Declaration on Religious Liberty of the Second Vatican Council (Dignitatis Humanae) as contradicting what the Popes taught quite solemnly in the nineteenth century, despite the fact that the document explicitly denies this. He, of course, is not alone in this mistake. Many dissident theologians premise their dissent from, for example, Humanae Vitae, now solemnly reaffirmed in Familiaris Consortio, with Lefebvre's false claim that the Church repudiated Her past when She affirmed religious liberty in the sense it is affirmed in Dignitatis Humanae.

No one familiar with the topic will deny intellectual difficulties in following this development in detail, but the main line is as plain as a pikestaff. The overarching moral imperative of the Second Vatican Council is found in Dignitatis Humanae:

> All men are bound to seek the truth, especially in what concerns God and His Church, and to embrace it and hold on to it as they come to know it.[16]

As I am composing this Pope John Paul II is trying to teach this moral truth to the tyrants who rule the Soviet Union and their puppets ruling Poland. The right to fulfill this obligation is our most fundamental human right after life itself.

I have no doubt but that the present Holy Father, like Christopher Dawson and other defenders of Christendom, would countenance the use of limited force, including lethal force, it would work, to defend and enforce this right. If we appreciate this obligation and the right it implies, then we understand how the Church could seem in one century to condemn religious liberty and in another to defend it. In the nineteenth century a notion of religious liberty was used to create governments that impeded people from fulfilling their obligation "to seek the truth, especially in what concerns God and His Church,..." In these post-Vatican II days of the twentieth century, religious liberty is the legal minimum those oppressed by atheistic tyranny most need in order to fulfill their obligation. The atheism the Church was fighting in the nineteenth century when She attacked what was then called religious liberty is the same enemy She is fighting today when defending religious liberty.

In addition to this part of the development, which shows the continuity in Church teaching, there is also humble admission of the sins we Catholics committed through defending the faith improperly, as well as a better understanding of the role of freedom in the act of faith itself. These parts of the development do not contradict the truths we affirmed in the past either. The core truth has been perfectly constant. In the New Testament it takes such forms as, "Seek first his kingship over you, his way of holiness, and all things will be given you besides" (Matthew 6:33; cf. Luke 12:31). In the thirteenth century St. Thomas taught the same truth as a fundamental principle of the Natural Law.[17] In the late twentieth century the Church teaches the truth through the Second Vatican Council as I recorded it above. I think that is real continuity.

If the Church were to teach what the USCC document gives one the impression She teaches, namely, that absolute pacifism is an acceptable Catholic view, then Archbishop Lefebvre would have a case. If the USCC document were correct in implying that the Second Vatican Council endorsed even the possibility that Our Lord taught absolute pacifism, then Archbishop Lefebvre would seem to be right. Thank God he is not. Were Lefebvre right, the Church Dawson joined would have ended.

I would like to close these observations on the document with an explanation of the reason why I have used scare quotes around the Our Lord's name, "Jesus", on occasion. I think the document is offensive in what it fails to say about Our Lord. The document does not adequately convey the truth of the Incarnation, namely, that Jesus is both true God and true man. A non-believer could affirm virtually everything that the document says about "Jesus." All the document asks of the reader is to regard "Jesus" as a very special man, much in the way some people regard Gandhi. This, of course, is not enough to know Him as He is. But it is the way people today like to regard "Jesus" who want to read the doctrine of absolute pacifism into what has been recorded about Him. Instead of knowing Him in faith as both true God and true man, who by virtue of His divinity and His human innocence was able to offer the perfect atoning sacrifice for our sins, He may be looked on as a special kind of mystical teacher, one who sees beyond ordinary morality to a higher morality which contradicts ordinary morality. The trouble with this higher morality, as I have shown in the case of absolute pacifism, is that it leads to evil, whereas the real Jesus whose name I can use without scare quotes and who is Our Lord and Savior, taught the plain morality of the natural law raised up through His counsels and His perfect sacrifice into something truly higher than anything we human beings could attain of ourselves. Yet it never contradicts what we were expected to attain according to the old law. Higher, yes, in one sense; old, true, and plain in another. The almost constant failure of the USCC document to speak of Him with the titles we Catholics ought always to use invites the unwary to think of Him as an elder Gandhi and not as divine.

In the light of these deficiencies, I think it would be appropriate for the Sacred Congregation for the Faith to issue an instruction concerning what the Church actually teaches regarding pacifism, and for the Catholics in the United States with their bishops to rededicate themselves to the truth of the Incarnation. In this way we could respond to the prophecy Pope John Paul II uttered before the United Nations on June 11th of 1982:

> May I close with one last consideration. The production and the possession of armaments are a consequence of an ethical crisis that is disrupting society in all of its political, social and economic dimensions. Peace, as I have already said several times, is the result of respect for ethical principles. True disarmament, that which will actually guarantee peace among peoples, will come about only with the resolution of this ethical crisis. To the extent that the efforts at arms reduction and then of total disarmament are not matched by parallel ethical renewal, they are doomed in advance to failure.[18]

Authentic Catholics such as the Holy Father, know the one thing that is absolutely necessary if there is to be peace and they further know that without what is absolutely necessary, everything else we might try to do is "doomed in advance to failure." That one thing which is absolutely necessary is a change of heart, i.e., repentance, expressed in prayer and penance; in other words what Our Lady taught us when she appeared to the children of Fatima. Pope John Paul II has endorsed this message strongly. Nevertheless, before the United Nations it would perhaps be unseemly and very likely ineffectual were he to mention what is absolutely necessary for peace. This did not stop him from detailing those steps which we must take if we are to advance the cause of peace and which can be described without explicit reference to faith. His remarks quoted just above continue as follows:

> The attempt must be made to put our world aright and to eliminate the spiritual confusion born from a narrow-minded search for interest or privilege or by the defense of ideological claims; this is a task of first priority if we wish to measure any progress in the struggle for disarmament. Otherwise we are condemned to remain at face-saving activities.

> For the root cause of our insecurity can be found in this profound crisis of humanity. By means of creating consciences sensitive to the absurdity of war, we advance the value of creating the material and spiritual conditions which will restore to everyone that minimum of space that is needed for the freedom of the spirit.

> The great disparity between the rich and the poor living together on this one planet is no longer supportable in a world of rapid universal communications, without giving birth to a justified resentment that can turn to violence. Moreover the spirit has basic and inalienable rights. For it is with justice that these rights are demanded in countries where the space is denied them to live in tranquility according

to their own convictions. I invite all those struggling for peace to commit themselves to the effort to eliminate the true causes of the insecurity of man of which the terrible arms race is only one effect.[19]

Because of its flaws I fear that the USCC document does not contribute to the required ethical renewal and therefore it does not contribute to peace.

NOTES

[1]See The Judgment of Nations (New York: Sheed & Ward, 1942), Part I, Chapter 2, "Democracy and Total War," especially p. 13; see also pp. 185-186.

[2]Ibid., p. 17; see also Part II, Chapter 3, "The Sword of The Spirit," and, The Historic Reality of Christian Culture (New York: Harper & Brothers Publishers, 1960), p. 29.

[3]L. McReavy, "Pacifism," in New Catholic Encyclopedia: Volume X (New York: McGraw-Hill, 1967), p. 855, first column.

[4]May 19, 1983, Vol. 13, No. 1.

[5]Oxford: Plater Publications, and San Francisco: Ignatius Press, 1982, pp. 215-223.

[6]Origins, op. cit., p. 12, column 3.

[7]For Dawson's view of Pharisaism see Dynamics of World History, edited by John J. Mulloy (La Salle: Sherwood Sugden & Company Publishers, 1978), p. 206.

[8]See Dynamics of World History, pp. 284-285; see also, The Judgment of Nations, pp. 142-143.

[9]Saint Thomas Aquinas, Summa Theologica, I-II, Q. 108, A. 3, ad 2; translated by the Fathers of the Dominican Province (New York: Benziger Brothers, 1947).

[10]Ibid., II-II, Q. 40, A. 1, ad 2.

[11]Ibid., I-II, Q. 108, A. 4, ad 4.

Richard R. Roach, S.J.

[12]Cf., _Summa Theologica_, II-II, Q. 40, A. 1, _ad_ 1; cf. also, A. 2.

[13]See _The Crisis of Western Education_ (New York: Sheed & Ward, 1961), Chapter 12, "The Theological Foundations of Christian Culture."

[14]Pope John Paul II, _Dives in Misericordia_, section 12.

[15]Address to the United Nations, June 11, 1982, _L 'Osservatore Romano_ (English edition), June 21, 1982, p. 4, second column, section 8 of the document.

[16]_Dignitatis Humane_, #1, Flannery, pp. 799-800.

[17]See _Summa Theologica_, I-II, Q. 94, A. 2 c.

[18]_L'Osservatore Romano_, op. cit., section 12 of the document.

[19]Ibid.

CHRISTOPHER DAWSON:
RECOLLECTIONS FROM AMERICA

Chauncey Stillman

When I learned in 1958 from Dean Douglas Horton that the Harvard Divinity School had invited Christopher Dawson as the first incumbent of the Charles Chauncey Stillman Chair, and that he had accepted, I was greatly pleased, having been familiar with Dawson's work for some years. His pre-eminence in the English intellectual world was unquestioned; so I knew that the Catholic Chair would start with a renowned scholar. The appointment was complete news to me who had never sought to be consulted, after the establishment of the gift in conversations with President Pusey.

My first meeting with the Dawsons and with the Hortons was at a dinner that the Hortons gave at their Cambridge house that Autumn. There was just the five of us, and a congenial atmosphere prevailed under their cordial hospitality. Mrs. Horton was Mildred McAffee, former President of Smith College, who had commanded the WACs during World War II. After that dinner I continued to see the Dawsons fairly often. It was at a subsequent visit to Cambridge that I attended a lecture of Dawson's with A. Graham Carey. It was more a seminar than a lecture because we sat around a long table. Dawson was already frail, with feeble speaking voice that could not have carried in a lecture hall.

I had the Dawsons to dinner with the Graham Careys from Cambridge, and Mrs. Joseph R. Hamlen, at the Somerset Club. Christopher was lacking in small talk, but his silence was, somehow, not intimidating. Valery Dawson was always merry, and could keep the ball rolling conversationally. She subsequently told me lightly: "People start off afraid of me, because they think I, too, must be a highbrow -- but I'm not. I just like music and laughter." The Dawsons came to visit us at Wethersfield House, Amenia, New York, the following June. An intense heat spell had just come to an end, and Wethersfield was cool and silvery in atmosphere: "like England," they rejoiced. Our guests gasped with relief after the discomfort of Cambridge. I did not tell them that Wethersfield too, indeed the whole Northeast, had suffered from the same heat wave.

My guest-book records that the Dawsons stayed at Wethersfield on four occasions -- each time a week -- in June 1959, 1960, 1961, and finally in the summer of 1962. On at least two of the visits, their fellow guest was Father John LaFarge, S.J., with whom Christopher got on famously. They would have long conversations in the house or on seats in different parts of the garden where they would take leisurely strolls. Their discourse was far beyond the intellectual depth of the rest of us; so life went on pleasantly around them with general conversation at meals. The Dawsons enjoyed motoring: I remember a daylong drive in the rainy Catskills, also taking them to dine with Mrs. Lydig Hoyt, who was entertaining the C.P. Snows at "The Point," Staatsburg, and also to tea with Mrs. Lytle Hull at Staatsburg -- a bit tense because a hurricane threatened.

Life in Cambridge, Massachusetts, had proved difficult to the point of hardship to the Dawsons. They had been given an apartment atop three flights of stairs, without elevator -- daunting to elderly people. They had always been accustomed to living in the country and taking long walks, whereas in Cambridge there was no provision for walking except in the cemetery, which they soon discovered. Valery Dawson had never done any housework, but at Cambridge she had to cope without domestic help. No wonder Wethersfield provided a welcome respite.

One of the things that most pleased Christopher at Wethersfield House was the library. Though not large or particularly scholarly, it contained the eleventh edition of the Encyclopaedia Britannica, the thirteen-volume <u>Oxford English Dictionary</u>, and <u>A Catholic Commentary on Sacred Scripture</u> (published by Nelson), which he consulted happily. He gave me a copy of Archbishop David Mathew's <u>Catholicism in England</u>, in which he is mentioned among the twentieth-century highlights.

After Dean Horton's retirement, Christopher told me wistfully that Douglas Horton, a Congregational minister, had a sound theological and historical education, so that they could converse easily. Other members of the Harvard Divinity School faculty had, he deplored, hazy or erroneous notions of such concepts as "atonement" and "redemption," so that discussion was slowed down by the need to define terms.

Dawson was completely without "side," that is, without any desire to show off, or to shine. He usually seemed to be wool-gathering, looking into space, inattentive to the talk around him. His manner was laconic; his remarks without emphasis. One day Valery remarked, "Christopher has written twenty books," His only comment was a soft, "twenty-one." Of course, beyond this, he had written innumerable articles, reviews and lectures.

I recall a few instances of his unobtrusive sense of humour. I offered Valery a cocktail one evening, from which she recoiled in a flutter: "No, no, no, no, no. I never have -- I couldn't possibly." Christopher, who was enjoying a martini, drawled in exaggerated languor: "Oh come on, Valery, do have a cocktail; it will pep you up." The comedy lay in the contrast between his languor and her vivacity. Another instance: I had told him how, at table with an eight-year-old daughter and her classmates, I had tried to enter the conversation by saying brightly, "I hear you girls are studying dinosaurs." Unfortunately, I pronounced the first syllable "dinn" instead of "die." Later my daughter reproved me privately: "It's very embarrassing to have a daddy who calls a '<u>dienosaur</u>' a '<u>dinnosaur</u>.'" The story struck Christopher as funny, and he commented: "I would have said '<u>dinnosaur</u>' myself."

On one occasion, a self-important ornithologist came to call. Impressed by Christopher, he launched into a series of reminiscences such as "The Royal

Ornithological Society gave a dinner in my honour
with the Duke of Omnium in the chair. The Duke introduced me as the most brilliant lecturer he had
ever heard." Christopher stared into space apparently unheeding, but when the man left, Christopher
remarked expressionlessly, "Odd that a bird fancier
should set such store on Dukes."

We delighted in the following instance of a
great mind's lack of observation. At junctions on
the tortuous four-mile approach to our entrance
drive from the State highway there are placed four
narrow direction signs, pointed like an arrow at one
end, reading "Wethersfield Farm." Christopher asked
me, "Why is it named 'Wethersfield'?" I replied:
"After the Connecticut colony my father's family
founded; besides, I like the name 'Wethersfield' for
a farm." He exclaimed, "But there are so many of
them!" An instance of his accurate power of observation, however, albeit of a different kind, is
this: The landscaping was being extended in the
gardens. Christopher pointed to a spot and said, "A
tree is needed there for punctuation," I said
"That's just what Mrs. Poehler (the landscape archi-
tect) says. A beech tree has been ordered for that
very spot." We think of that tree, now grown tall,
as "the Dawson tree."

The Dawsons also visited the late Archbishop
(later Cardinal) Wright in Pittsburgh. In Boston,
Cardinal Cushing and Valery were a great combination. He had the inspiration of having an honorary
degree conferred upon her. Both Dawsons were im-
mensely gratified. Our guest-book holds a snapshot
of Valery in academic robes and Christopher smiling
jubilantly, and her humorous inscription reading
"June 18-25, Dr. Valery Dawson, LL.D., the loqua-
cious, dynamic and dashing, but briefless barrister
of Cambridge, Massachusetts." We also have jolly
memories of Valery at the swimming pool, applauding
Harry Fitzgibbon's fancy diving. And at the piano
with my daughters, singing Madame Butterfly and La
Boheme. Christopher enjoyed listening, silent but
smiling.

I told Christopher that I had heard Hilaire
Belloc in a lecture at Fordham in 1936 state: "I
have examined the claims of all the English Catholic
[he said Cahthlic] recusant families, and not one of

them is continuous. At some point they all submitted to persecution and professed Protestantism." Dawson sounded more distressed than indignant in reply: "Did he really say that? There are more than twenty well-known recusant families who suffered for the Faith." He took a pencil and pad and listed some twenty to thirty names such as "Stonor, Tempest, Vaus, Mostyn," and so on. I have the list in some book.

Dawson's knowledge was the most encylopaedic I have ever encountered. Apparently, he could read a page at a glance and retain the contents forever. Repeatedly I tried to catch him out without success. I pointed to an Arabian horse, saying, "It's named Bashi Bazouk. Do you know what that means?" He instantly replied, "A Turkish irregular soldier." On a wall outside the Somerset Club is a plaque mentioning the painter, John Singleton Copley. When questioned about Copley, Dawson gave me a concise biography of both the painter and his son. He also remarked that the name Somerset was taken from a British man-of-war in the Battle of Boston, which he knew all about.

It was thanks to the Dawsons that I came to know Frank Sheed, his publisher and friend. Years later, remarking to Mr. Sheed on Dawson's phenomenal memory, he agreed, but added, "I am the only person that ever caught him out. He had forgotten the names of the only two men, father and son, who had occupied the throne of Peter. I supplied them for Christopher."

I and my daughters felt badly when, because of Christopher's health, the Dawsons returned to England earlier than planned. They had stayed with us at least four times at Wethersfield, and also in New York City on another occasion on their way out west. At least three times, on my subsequent visits to England, I would go to see them at Budleigh Salterton in Devonshire. I recall my daughter, Elizabeth's going from London to Budleigh by train on her own to lunch with them. After a time, Christopher, although still frail and weak, put on a bit of weight and had better colour. He would be sitting in a wheelchair, smoking cigarettes incessantly. The last time I called, his son, Philip, met me at the door saying that his father was dying. I tried to drive away, but Philip said, "You must come in; my father wants to see you." Christopher opened his eyes and smiled warmly, pressing my hand silently. The next day, in London, I heard that he died that night.

*   *   *

One day, while talking of how childhood association stamped one's concept of home, I observed that I could feel permanently contented only against a background of green slopes pasturing cattle. Christopher sympathised, but amended that he would substitute flocks of sheep for herds of cattle. When, eventually, I visited Philip Dawson in the Yorkshire dales, I remembered the remark. Philip took me to visit his father's boyhood home, and his parents' graves, in that pastoral region.

INDEX OF NAMES

223

Francowitz, Mathias, 50

Gabriel, 75
Gandhi, 182, 212-213
Gardner, Helen, 141, 155
Gasquet, P. H., 166
Gibbon, Edward, 7-8, 25
Gilmore, Gary, 208
Gilson, Étienne, 18
Golding, Arthur, 154
Góngora, 155
Gregory VII, Pope, 33
Gregory of Nyssa, St.,
    61, 94
Gregory of Tours, 15, 29,
    52
Groethuysen, 166

Hamilton, A. C., 137
Hamlen, Mrs. Joseph, 217
Harnack, Adolf von, 25-26
Heer, Friedrich, 112
Hegel, 4, 33, 59
Henoch, 66
Henry III, 137
Herbert, George, 128, 140,
    143-146, 156
Herrick, 140
Hill, Rosalind, 123
Hitchcock, James, 49
Hittinger, Russell, ix, xi,
    122, 124
Honorius III, Pope, 33
Hopkins, G. M., 151, 157
Horton, Douglas, 217, 219
Hoyt, Mrs. Lydig, 218
Huizinga, Johan, 117
Hull, Mrs. Lytle, 218
Hume, David, 7-8
Husserl, Edmund, 46-48, 56

Ignatius, St., 106, 118, 140
Irenaeus, St., 4-6, 61, 93

Jacob, 68, 89
Jaspers, 59
Jeremiah, 73

Jesus, 62, 64, 65, 135-
    136, 139, 143, 148-
    149, 157, 173, 180-
    186, 196-197, 208-
    209, 212-213
Jezebel, 79
Joachim of Fiora, 11
Job, 127
John XXIII, Pope, 204
John, St., 197
John of the Cross, St.,
    125
John Paul II, Pope, 167,
    198, 211, 213-214
John the Baptist, St.,
    45, 74
Jonas of Orléans, 116
Joshua, 77, 94
Judas, 139, 196-197

King, Henry, 140
Knox, Msgr. Ronald, 53
Korah, 70
Kroeber, Alfred, 99

LaFarge, S.J., John, 218
Larrey, Martin, 118, 123
Laud, Archbishop, 127
Lefebvre, Archbishop M.,
    210-212
Lenin, 171, 173
Leo XIII, Pope, 159, 163
Levi, A. H. T., 152
Lewalski, Barbara, 148-149,
    155, 157
Lewis, C. S., 156, 192
Louis XIV, 175
Lubac, Fr. Henri de, 63
Luther, 28, 123, 134

MacIntyre, Alasdair, 37
MacLaren, O.P., Drostan,
    183
Malchus, 197
Mandeville, 166
Marino, 128, 130, 155
Maritian, Jacques, 56
Mark, St., 188
Martin of Braga, 116
Martz, Louis L., 146, 155,

225

NOTES ON THE AUTHORS

PETER J. CATALDO is the editor of this volume. He received his B.A. in Philosophy at St. Anselm College in 1978. He received his M.A. in Philosophy at St. Louis University in 1981. Mr. Cataldo is currently a Ph.D. candidate in Philosophy at St. Louis University, where he has taught philosophy.

RUSSELL HITTINGER received his B.S. in History, summa cum laude, at the University of Notre Dame in 1975. He received his M.A. in Philosophy at St. Louis University in 1981. He is currently a Ph.D. candidate in Philosophy at St. Louis University, where he teaches Ethics and Philosophy of Human Nature. Mr. Hittinger is the co-founder of The Society for Christian Culture.

PAUL QUAY is a priest of the Society of Jesus. Born in Chicago in 1924, he served for three years during World War II in the U.S. Army Signal Corps, in the Southwest Pacific. He received a Ph.D. in Theoretical Physics from M.I.T., Licentiates in Philosophy and Theology from West Baden College, and an A.B. in Classics from Loyola University of Chicago. Following a post-doctoral year at Case.I.T., he spent two and a half years in France and Germany studying contemporary philosophy and Ignatian Spirituality. He taught at St. Louis University (1967-1981), where he held a joint appointment as Associate Professor in both Physics and Theology Departments, and at Loyola University of Chicago, where he is now Research Professor of Philosophy. Efforts to give the Spiritual Exercises of St. Ignatius in the original manner focused his interest on the topic of this paper as well as on his other research interests: the theological presuppositions of the discernment of the spirits and moral theology as a subdivision of spirituality rather than a separate discipline. He has published some 45 articles in learned journals in these areas as well as in physicsl and philosophy of science; and also, several on "brain-death" legislation.

GLENN W. OLSEN received his B.A. from North Park College in 1960, and his M.A. and Ph.D. from the University of Wisconsin in 1962 and 1965. He has been a Fulbright Fellow in Italy and the recipient of an American Council of Learned Societies Grant. His publications, in ancient and medieval Church

227

history, intellectual history, and canon law, have appeared in STUDIA GRATIANA, TRADITION, COMMUNIO, the SCOTTISH JOURNAL OF THEOLOGY, THE CATHOLIC HISTORICAL REVIEW, the JOURNAL OF ECCLESIASTICAL HISTORY, and elsewhere. He has taught at Seattle University, Fordham University, and at present is a Professor of History in the University of Utah.

R. V. YOUNG holds the M. Phil. and Ph.D. from Yale and is currently Associate Professor of English at North Carolina State University. He is the author of RICHARD CRASHAW AND THE SPANISH GOLDEN AGE (Yale, 1982) and a number of articles on seventeenth-century poetry in scholarly journals. In addition he has published on moral and religious issues in such periodicals as ENVIRONMENTAL ETHICS, FIDELITY, THE HUMAN LIFE REVIEW, and NATIONAL REVIEW. Dr. Young is an editor of the JOHN DONNE JOURNAL and associate editor (book reviews) of FAITH & REASON.

JOHN J. MULLOY is the editor of Christopher Dawson's DYNAMICS OF WORLD HISTORY (Sheed & Ward, 1957: reprint with new foreword in Sherwood Sugden, 1978), and CHRISTIANITY IN EAST AND WEST (Sherwood Sugden, 1981). He contributed an appendix to Dawson's THE CRISIS OF WESTERN EDUCATION (Sheed & Ward, 1961), containing "Specific Programs for the Study of Christian Culture." He is the co-founder of the The Society for Christian Culture, and the Editor of THE DAWSON NEWSLETTER. He has contributed numerous columns and articles on Dawson's thought, and on Christian writers from John Henry Newman onward to THE WANDERER, the NEW OXFORD REVIEW, and FIDELITY magazine.

RICHARD RUSSELL ROACH was born on October 12, 1934, in Seattle, Washington to Ruth Hall and Russell A. Roach. He was educated in the public schools of Seattle and Bremerton, finishing with a B.A. from the University of Washington in Drama in 1955. Because he had been assisted in college by a partial scholarship from the United States Air Force, upon graduation he entered the U.S.A.F. as a second lieutenant. He became a pilot and was assigned to fly all-weather interceptors in northern Maine. He left active duty in 1958 in order to enter the novitiate of the Oregon Province of the Society of Jesus, then located at Sheridan, Oregon. After the usual course of Jesuit studies, including a period of teaching high school at the Jesuit High School in Portland, Oregon, he was ordained a priest in 1969.

He completed doctoral studies at Yale University and is presently an associate professor of moral theology at Marquette University. He has authored numerous articles in scholarly journals, including COMMUNIO and THE JOURNAL OF MEDICINE AND PHILOSOPHY. He has also contributed chapters to several books, including "Moral Theology and the Mission of the Church," in PRINCIPLES OF CATHOLIC MORAL LIFE, ed. by William E. May (Franciscan Herald Press, 1980).

CHAUNCEY D. STILLMAN was born in New York City in 1907. He received his A.B. from Harvard in 1930, and his M.A. (Architecture) from Columbia in 1935. He served active duty in the United States Naval Reserve from 1942 to 1945, and he was Commodore of the New York Yacht Club from 1964 to 1967. He has been Privy Chamberlain to His Holiness since 1963 (Gentiluomo di S.S.). Mr. Stillman is a widower with two living daughters and five grandchildren; he resides in Axmenia, N.Y.